Messiah Yeshua, Divine Redeemer

Christology from a Messianic Jewish Perspective

Other Books by Dr. Arnold G. Fruchtenbaum

The Sabbath

Jesus Was a Jew

A Passover Haggadah for Jewish Believers

Israelology: The Missing Link in Systematic Theology

Ha-Mashiach: The Messiah of the Hebrew Scriptures

An Historical and Geographical Study Guide of Israel: With a Supplement on Jordan

The Historical and Geographical Maps of Israel and Surrounding Territories

God's Will & Man's Will: Predestination, Election, and Free Will

The Footsteps of the Messiah: A Study of the Sequence of Prophetic Events

The Remnant of Israel: The History, Theology, and Philosophy of the Messianic Jewish Community

Faith Alone: The Condition of our Salvation (An Exposition of the Book of Galatians and Other Relevant Topics)

Ariel's Bible Commentary Series:

The Messianic Jewish Epistles (Hebrews, James, I & II Peter, Jude)

Judges and Ruth

The Book of Genesis

Biblical Lovemaking: A Study of the Song of Solomon

Ariel's Come and See Series:

The Word of God: Its Nature and Content

What We Know About God: Theology Proper

MESSIAH YESHUA, DIVINE REDEEMER

CHRISTOLOGY FROM A MESSIANIC JEWISH PERSPECTIVE

ARNOLD G. FRUCHTENBAUM
TH.M., PH.D.

Messiah Yeshua, Divine Redeemer: Christology from a Messianic Jewish Perspective
Arnold G. Fruchtenbaum, Th.M., Ph.D.

ISBN 978-1-935174-57-8

Library of Congress Control Number:
2015940601

REL101000 RELIGION / Messianic Judaism

All Scripture quotations, unless otherwise noted, are from the *1901 American Standard Version* (Oak Harbor, WA: Logos Research Systems, Inc., 1994). However, the archaic language has been changed with one exception: The archaic *ye* has been retained in order to distinguish the second person plural from the singular *you*. The words "Jesus" and "Christ" have been replaced with *Yeshua* and Messiah.

Editor: Christiane Jurik, M.A.
Proofreaders: Pauline Ilsen, Joni Bohannon
Printed in the United States of America
Cover illustration by Jesse and Josh Gonzales (*http://www.vipgraphics.net)*

Published by Ariel Ministries
P.O. Box 792507
San Antonio, TX 78279-2507
www.ariel.org

This volume is dedicated to

Denise Velarde

Who has faithfully served as my secretary when Ariel Ministries returned to San Antonio after twenty-one years in Tustin, California. She is commended for a smooth transition from California to Texas.

Contents

CHAPTER XVII

CHAPTER XVIII

CHAPTER XIX

Introduction

What is Come and See?

Come and See is a multi-volume collection of Messianic Bible studies transcribed from Dr. Arnold Fruchtenbaum's original radio broadcasts. For the book series, the manuscripts made from these transcripts were expanded, and text was added. Each study is a solid foundation upon which you can stand—a whiteboard from which you can teach or a podium from which you can preach the uncompromised truth to your congregation. This extensive collection is replete with expert knowledge of Hebrew, Greek, the *Talmud*, the history of the Jews, the geography of *Eretz Yisrael*, the land of Israel, a scholar's command of the Word—and the illumination of the *Ruach HaKodesh* (the Holy Spirit). *Come and See* will edify you in your personal devotion or small group Bible study regardless of which topic you choose.

What Will You Discover in This Volume?

Volume three of *Come and See* examines what we know about God the Son. In systematic theology, this topic is called Christology, or the doctrine of the Son. This is a major section of systematic theology and is a further study in the *Come and See* series we have been developing for you.

Systematic theology is, of course, a logical development of what the Bible teaches about various subjects. The first main division is Bibliology, which is the study of the Scriptures. We addressed the topic in volume one of *Come and See, The Word of God*. This is a logical beginning, since what we know about theology comes from the Scriptures themselves.

The second main division is Theology Proper, which is the doctrine of God. We addressed this topic in volume two of this series, *What We Know About God*. The study developed our understanding of God the Father and emphasized the deity, the theism, and the trinitarianism of God.

In the study you hold in your hands today, we are focusing on the third main division of systematic theology, which is Christology, also called the doctrine of the Son or the doctrine of the Messiah.

Questions and Study Suggestions for the Course

At the end of each chapter, you will find questions and study suggestions. The goal in integrating questions into this course is to bring application that is relevant to the subject.

Get a Certificate of Completion!

In an effort to help reinforce your learning, we are also providing an exam for each volume of *Come and See*. As you complete each study, please visit us at www.ariel.org to take the final exam. Select *Come and See* from the menu options for details. The questions you will find online quiz your knowledge, while the questions at the end of each chapter are supposed to help you apply what you learned to your life. Upon successful completion of each exam, you will receive a certificate of completion.

Our desire is to provide a way for you to track through each study and monitor your progress. We would encourage you to study in small groups before taking the exams as a way to help prepare one another and stay accountable through each of the volumes.

The ultimate goal of this collection is for disciples of *Yeshua* (Jesus) to grow in their faith and to live out their calling to make disciples. We hope you enjoy the *Come and See Series*!

Chapter I

The Doctrine of the Messiah

This book is devoted to the doctrine of the Messiah. Theologians call this doctrine Christology. The term comes from two Greek words: *Christos* and *Logos*. *Christos*—which means "anointed"—is transliterated into English as "Christ;" it is the Greek equivalent of the Hebrew word *Mashiach*, or "Messiah." *Logos* means "word" or "doctrine." So Christology is "the word of the Messiah" or "the doctrine of the Messiah."

The question might arise as to why it is important to examine the person of *Yeshua*. The answer lies in His claims. *I am the way, and the truth, and the life: no one comes unto the Father, but by me*, He said in John 14:6 and thus claimed that the eternal destiny of every human being would depend upon how they viewed Him. If His claims are true, the decision one makes about Him will determine whether he spends eternity in heaven or in hell.

However, what can we really know about the Son of God? After all, nothing compares to Him. He is the One who was in the beginning **with** God and **was** God. He is the Mighty God, yet He was made flesh, born of a virgin, and dwelt among us. He is the One who came to serve and brought the sword. He is the Eternal Father, yet He died an utterly humiliating death. Could there be a greater dichotomy?

The life and impact of *Yeshua Ha-Mashiach*, God's only Son, forces us to stretch our minds beyond the human realm and into a sphere that encompasses the finite and the infinite. Many theologians have tried to define that which the Apostle Paul called the *unsearchable riches of Messiah* (Eph. 3:8). Christology deals with the person of the Messiah and purposes to include all aspects pertaining to His life and work, and above all else, the redemption He accomplished. Christology also looks at His eternal state, His power and glory, and the future He holds in His hand.[1]

A. Biblical Christology

There are four key factors which we must always keep in mind in order to develop a true biblical Christology, a true doctrine of the Son. Failing to keep all four of these factors in mind has created various heresies during the course of church history.

- ✡ The first factor is a **true and proper deity**. The deity of the Son must be emphasized and understood in all of the aspects that that term demands.
- ✡ A second factor is a **true and proper humanity**. Not only must *Yeshua* be viewed as truly God; He is also truly man.
- ✡ The third factor is **the unity of deity and humanity in one person**. For a true Christology, there must be a proper concept of this unity. The Messiah must always be viewed as only one person, who is both God and man, and the unity of the deity and humanity of His person must be properly understood.
- ✡ The fourth factor is **the two distinct natures in one person**. In order to develop a biblical Christology, one must properly understand the distinction between the divine nature and the human nature in the one person of *Yeshua*.

Many in church history have failed to keep these four essential factors in mind and have developed various heresies, which we will now look at.

[1] Question 1 on page 8.

B. Heresies in Christology

Who can truly fathom how *Yeshua* can be both one hundred percent God and one hundred percent man? This mystery is called the hypostatic union. "Hypostatic" is a term derived from the Greek word *hypostasis*, meaning "foundation, substance, or subsistence." The union of Messiah's humanity and divinity is seen in one *hypostasis*, or individual existence. Each of the nine false views presented in this section either overemphasizes or underemphasizes the Messiah's deity or humanity.

1. Ebionism—Denies the Deity

The heresy of Ebionism, which can be traced back to the second century, denied the deity of *Yeshua*. The followers of this doctrine claimed that Messiah was a man who was the son of both Joseph and Miriam (Mary). At His baptism, He was declared to be the Messiah and empowered by the Holy Spirit. While Ebionism had a view of His humanity, it failed on the part of His deity.

2. Gnosticism—Denies the Humanity

Gnosticism denied the humanity of *Yeshua*. It is commonly assumed that the teaching first appeared in the second century and that over time, several types of this heresy developed. Docetism, the first type, claimed that Messiah only appeared to have a human body and that He was not really incarnate. Another variation of Gnosticism claimed that Messiah did have a real body, but it was not a material body. Yet another type of Gnosticism went so far as to say that *Yeshua* and Messiah were distinct entities. *Yeshua* was the son of Miriam and Joseph, while the Messiah was a divine spirit who descended upon *Yeshua* at the baptism. At his crucifixion, the Messiah left the man *Yeshua* to suffer on his own.

All forms of Gnosticism have the common problem of not wanting to accept Messiah's true and full humanity.

3. Monarchianism—Denies the Humanity

Monarchianism also denied the humanity of *Yeshua*. It was first proposed in the second century by Paul of Samosata, the bishop of Antioch. There were three different forms of the doctrine. Dynamic Monarchianism taught that Messiah was the Son of God by adoption. Being fully man, He was tested by God. After successfully passing the test, He was adopted as the Son. Upon His baptism, humanity became deity.

The second form of the heresy is called Modalistic Monarchianism. It claimed that Messiah was only a mode or manifestation of God. The followers of this doctrine denied the Trinity and taught that there was only one God, but that He revealed Himself in three different modes, with Messiah being only one of those modes or manifestations of God.

The third form of this heresy is called Modified Monarchianism. According to this view, the Father, the Son, and the Holy Spirit are just different names for the one God.

4. Arianism—Acknowledges Only Partial Deity

Arianism held to a partial deity. It is commonly attributed to Arius (c. 250–336), a presbyter in Alexandria, Egypt. According to this heresy, Messiah was created by God before anything else. Although He pre-existed all things, He Himself was not eternal. His divine nature was similar to but not the same as that of God. This view was condemned early in church history by the Council of Nicea in 325.

5. Apollinarianism—Denies the Humanity

Apollinarianism also denied the humanity of *Yeshua*. It received its name from Apollinaris of Laodicea (died in 390), who claimed that Messiah did not have two separate natures. He had a human body and a human soul but instead of a human spirit, He had the divine *logos*. This view was also condemned by an early church council at Constantinople in 381.

6. Nestorianism—Assumes Two Persons

Nestorianism was a philosophy propagated by the patriarch of Constantinople, Nestorius (c. 386-450). He and his followers conveyed the belief in two separate persons, thus denying even the possibility of the hypostatic union. In this view, the Messiah was the *prosopon*, a term derived from Greek theater which originally meant "face" or "mask." Instead of trying to act out certain emotions on stage, the actors wore masks (*prosopa*) that displayed to the audience the mood of the person portrayed. *Prosopon* is most often translated as "person." Messiah was the *prosopon* of the union of two natures: humanity had the form of God bestowed on it. Deity took upon itself the form of a servant. This resulted in the appearance of the Messiah. His two natures were separable; hence there were two persons. This view was condemned by the Council of Ephesus in 431.

7. Eutychianism—Mingled into One Nature

Eutychianism was derived from the ideas of Eutyches of Constantinople (c. 380–456). He believed in only one nature and claimed that *Yeshua* was neither truly God nor truly man, but that His two natures were mingled to produce a third new nature that was partially God and partially man. This was condemned by the Council of Chalcedon in 451.

8. Monophysitism—Fused into One Nature

Like Eutychianism, Monophysitism propagated the idea of the one nature which was a fusion of the divine and the human. It claimed that after the incarnation, there was only one nature in Messiah.

9. Monothelitism—Propagates One Will

Monothelitism developed over the course of several centuries but was formally introduced in Armenia and Syria in 629. It claimed that Messiah did not have a separate human and divine will. Hence, there was also only one nature in Him. This view was condemned by the Third Council of Constantinople in 681.

Many of these heresies are no longer in existence. Some of them, though, are being propounded today by various cults.[2]

---

[2] Question 2 on page 8.

C. Questions and Study Suggestions

Question 1: The Swiss theologian Karl Barth once was asked to name the most profound truth he had learned from his studies of theology. His answer was surprisingly simplistic: "Jesus loves me, this I know, for the Bible tells me so." Read Deuteronomy 29:29. How does this verse support Barth's statement? How do you personally deal with the fact that "the finite cannot grasp the infinite," as some medieval theologians put it?

Question 2: Read John 8:58 and 10:30, followed by John 1:14. Let's assume you meet a person who did not grow up in a country influenced by Judeo-Christian values and teachings. How would you explain to such a person who *Yeshua* was?

Chapter II

The Messiah in the Hebrew Scriptures

The Hebrew Scriptures (Old Testament) have traditionally been divided into three main divisions: the Law, the Prophets, and the Writings. All three divisions contain Messianic prophecies. In this chapter, we will look at the progressive revelation of the Messianic prophecies in the Hebrew Scriptures, specifically those that were fulfilled at the First Coming of the Messiah. Theologically, this is known as Messianic Christology. It is important to remember that the revelation was progressive. For instance, from what was revealed in the five books of the Law, one could not know that Messiah was to die. The Law mainly presents Messiah as a king and a redeemer. The Prophet Isaiah (c. 700 B.C.) is the one who reveals to us that Messiah would die. Messianic Christology is important because it shows that these Messianic prophecies were perfectly fulfilled in the life of *Yeshua* and cannot be fulfilled in any other way.[3]

---

[3] This chapter is based in large parts on the author's previously published work, *Ha-Mashiach: The Messiah of the Hebrew Scriptures* (Ariel Ministries, TX, 2014). However, the text has been edited heavily to adapt it to the format and purpose of this book.

A. The Law

The section in the *Tanakh* (Hebrew Scriptures) called "The Law" encompasses the five books of Moses. In Hebrew, this section is called the *Torah*. There are five main passages to consider.

1. Genesis 3:15

> *and I will put enmity between you and the woman, and between your seed and her seed: he shall bruise your head, and you shall bruise his heel.*

Genesis 3:15 predicted that the Messiah is going to be reckoned after *her seed,* the seed of the woman. This is highly unusual, since genealogies in Scripture were always reckoned after the man, and not after the woman. This is why in all the genealogies of Scripture, be they Old or New Testament genealogies, virtually only the male line is given. A woman's name might be mentioned, but usually only in passing and only in conjunction with her husband, never as a separate entity.

In Genesis 3:15, we are told that in the case of the Messiah, things are going to be different in that His lineage would be reckoned after the seed of the woman and not after the seed of a man. This is the first hint of the virgin birth which was clarified by Isaiah 7:14. The reason why it will be necessary for the Messiah to be reckoned after the seed of the woman is because He would not have a human father. All the rest of mankind receives its humanity from both father and mother. *Yeshua* was the exception to the rule in that His entire humanity came only from the mother. Furthermore, His genealogy cannot be traced through a male line. So where the Messiah is to be reckoned after the seed of the woman, it predicts clearly that He would be born of a virgin.

The prophecy goes on to say that the seed of the woman would *bruise your head,* meaning He would crush the head of the serpent. The serpent is Satan (Rev. 12:9). Thus, the picture is that Satan's attack against the Messiah would cause Him only a slight wound: Satan *shall bruise* the Messiah's *heel.* The Messiah, on the other hand, will *bruise* Satan's *head.* In Hebrew, the word for "bruise" is *shuph,* which can be translated as "to bruise" or "to crush." Gibeah of the Benjamites

While Satan's attack on Messiah would be comparable to a slight wound, the Messiah's attack on Satan would prove to be a crushing blow to the head.

The point of this first Messianic prophecy is that the Messiah was to come from humanity. He would be human. He would be born of a woman, and only from a woman, without the fertilization by the male sperm.

In the light of New Testament revelation, it is easy for us to recognize this as the first Messianic promise; but how was this promise understood by Adam and Eve? How was it understood by their progeny? We do have some early echoes of it in the book of Genesis. The first example is what Eve says of Cain in Genesis 4:1. The ASV translates this verse as: *And the man knew Eve his wife; and she conceived, and bore Cain, and said, I have gotten a man with the help of Jehovah*. However, in the Hebrew text, Eve literally says, "I have gotten a man: Jehovah." We see this same Hebrew phraseology translated this way elsewhere, as in Genesis 4:2 and in Genesis 6:10. What Genesis 4:1 shows is how Eve understood the promise of Genesis 3:15. She understood that it included the entrance of a divine person into human history by birth, born of a woman, a child. She believed that Cain, her firstborn son, was the fulfillment of the promise of Genesis 3:15; therefore she said, "I have gotten a man: Jehovah."

Eve's theology was correct. It is her application of the promise that was wrong. Cain proved not to be the one she thought he was.

Another early echo of the promise of Genesis 3:15 is found in Genesis 5:28-29:

> [28] *And Lamech lived a hundred eighty and two years, and begat a son:* [29] *and he called his name Noah, saying, This same shall comfort us in our work and in the toil of our hands, which comes because of the ground which Jehovah has cursed.*

Lamech names his son Noah, which means "rest." He was convinced that it would be Noah who would give rest to his people. It is clear from this that Lamech understood that Noah would play a significant role in divine history, but he misunderstood that role, thinking that his son Noah was going to be the promised Messiah. The name he gave his son shows that he thought Noah would be the Messiah. Indeed, Noah did play a major role in divine history, but not the Messianic role.

Finally, Genesis 6:1-4 tells the story of fallen angels intermarrying with human women:

[1] *And it came to pass, when men began to multiply on the face of the ground, and daughters were born unto them,* [2] *that the sons of God saw the daughters of men that they were fair; and they took them wives of all that they chose.* [3] *And Jehovah said, My spirit shall not strive with man for ever, for that he also is flesh: yet shall his days be a hundred and twenty years.* [4] *The Nephilim were in the earth in those days, and also after that, when the sons of God came unto the daughters of men, and they bore children to them: the same were the mighty men that were of old, the men of renown.*

When Satan caused his fallen angels to intermarry with human women, he attempted to thwart the promise of Genesis 3:15. He was trying to find a way to keep that promise from ever being fulfilled. His goal was to corrupt the seed of the woman, and he almost succeeded. The result of the intermarriage described in the verses above was a grotesque, superhuman race, the *Nephilim*. If the seed of the woman was corrupted, the promised Messiah could not come. To eliminate this threat to His Messianic program God brought the judgment of the Flood upon the earth. So this passage shows how Satan understood the promise of Genesis 3:15.

2. The Seed of Abraham — Genesis 22:18

Equally important to the topic of Messianic Christology is the seed of Abraham. The word "seed" in the Hebrew Bible is usually singular. Sometimes it is used as a collective, not an absolute singular. An example of this is Genesis 26:4a which states that the seed of Abraham will be as numerous as the sand of the sea and as the stars of heaven: *And I will multiply your seed as the stars of heaven, and will give unto your seed all these lands.* Obviously, in that context, God is speaking of many descendants of Abraham. However, the term "seed" is still in the singular. In the collective singular, "seed" simply means "many," and in this verse, it refers to the people of Israel.

But sometimes the word "seed" is also used in the absolute sense, addressing only one person. So the phrase "seed of Abraham" is used in the absolute individual sense as well. One example of this usage is Genesis 22:18 which reads, *And in your seed* (singular) *shall all the nations of the earth be blessed. Because you have obeyed my voice.* This is a reference to the Messiah, and it is what Paul teaches in Galatians 3:16: *Now to Abraham were the promises spoken, and to his seed. He says not, And to seeds, as of many; but as of one, And to your seed, which is Messiah.*

The point of the term "the seed of Abraham" in reference to the Messiah is this: While the seed of the woman passage in Genesis 3:15 emphasizes that Messiah would be born into humanity, the seed of Abraham limited the seed of the woman to being a descendant of Abraham. Therefore, the seed of the woman was to be limited to only one branch of humanity, and that was the Jewish branch: the seed of Abraham.

3. Genesis 49:10

The sceptre shall not depart from Judah, Nor the ruler's staff from between his feet, Until Shiloh come: And unto him shall the obedience of the peoples be.

The point of this prophecy is that the tribe of Judah cannot lose its pre-eminence, or its identity, until the Messiah comes, and when He does come, He will have the obedience of the Gentiles.

Like ours, most translations of this passage read: *Until Shiloh come*. Because the word *Shiloh* is capitalized, some people take it to be a proper name and call Messiah by the name "Shiloh." However, the word should be taken as a possessive pronoun, meaning "whose it is." Literally, Genesis 49:10 reads, "until He comes whose it is." This fits very well with another similar prophecy found in Ezekiel 21:25-27, where we do have the translation of the same word as *Until He comes whose right it is.*

The main point of this prophecy then is to limit the "seed of the woman" even further. First, as the seed of the woman, Messiah would have to be human. Second, as the seed of Abraham, He would have to be a Jew. But now third, with this prophecy, He must also be of the seed of Judah. It limits the seed to a specific tribe among the family of Abraham, ruling out eleven other tribes.

Another term to pay attention to in this prophecy is *sceptre*. It emphasizes the kingship of the Messiah. The verse promises that Messiah will be a king, and the kingship of Israel would be from the tribe of Judah. Because He has to come before Judah's singular identity was lost, we can also pinpoint the time frame of His arrival, for after A.D. 70, it was no longer possible to trace tribal descent in Israel. In an attempt to subdue a revolt in the land, the Romans attacked Jerusalem and burned the Temple. In the Temple was the registry. After the building was destroyed and the documents were burned to ashes, it became impossible to prove from which tribe one descended. Therefore, Messiah had to have come sometime before the year A.D. 70.

4. The Predictions of Balaam

Balaam pronounced four oracles which contained important information about the Messiah and are therefore important for the topic of Messianic Christology. The first oracle is found in Numbers 23:7-10 where Balaam points out that Israel will be a nation that will not be recognized as such. She will be dwelling alone and *not be reckoned among the nations*. This first oracle also points out the increase of Israel numerically. Then it emphasizes that Israel's final blessing is what Balaam would have desired for himself.

The second oracle of Balaam is found in Numbers 23:18-24. In these verses, the prophet mentions the future sinlessness of Israel. At that time, God will be in the midst of Israel as a king.

Balaam's third oracle is found in Numbers 24:3-9 where the prophet describes the future condition of Israel and her king.

Balaam's fourth oracle is found in Numbers 24:15-24. The verse of interest for this study is verse 17: *I see him, but not now; I behold him, but not nigh: There shall come forth a star out of Jacob, And a sceptre shall rise out of Israel, And shall smite through the corners of Moab, And break down all the sons of tumult.* In this verse, Balaam prophesies that *a star* shall arise *out of Jacob*, and this star is the Messianic star. It is coupled with a scepter, and so the star represents a king.

The point of the four oracles of Balaam is to show that the Messiah is going to be a king. This brings us to the fifth and final Messianic prophecy within the framework of the Law of Moses.

5. Deuteronomy 18:15-19

> [15] *Jehovah your God will raise up unto you a prophet from the midst of you, of your brethren, like unto me; unto him ye shall hearken;* [16] *according to all that you desired of Jehovah your God in Horeb in the day of the assembly, saying, Let me not hear again the voice of Jehovah my God, neither let me see this great fire any more, that I die not.* [17] *And Jehovah said unto me, They have well said that which they have spoken.* [18] *I will raise them up a prophet from among their brethren, like unto you; and I will put my words in his*

mouth, and he shall speak unto them all that I shall command him. 19 And it shall come to pass, that whosoever will not hearken unto my words which he shall speak in my name, I will require it of him.

The point of the prophecies in Deuteronomy 18:15-19 is that the Messiah is going to be a prophet *like unto* Moses. He will be like Moses in five areas:

1. He will be a prophet, as Moses was a prophet (Num. 12:6-8).
2. He will be a redeemer, as Moses was a redeemer (Ex. 3:10).
3. He will be a mediator, as Moses was a mediator (Ex. 19:16-25).
4. He will be an intercessor, as Moses was an intercessor (Ex. 32:7-14, 30-35).
5. He will be a leader, as Moses was a leader (Ex. 3:10).

So within the framework of the Law, we have discovered that Messiah will be:

- ✡ a human being
- ✡ a Jew
- ✡ of the tribe of Judah
- ✡ a king
- ✡ a prophet[4]

B. The Prophets

The second section of the *Tanakh* called "The Prophets" contains 17 passages which are relevant to the topic of Messianic Christology. Each one in its unique way provides information about who the Messiah is and how, when, and where He would be born.

1. Isaiah 7:14

Therefore the Lord himself will give you a sign: behold, a virgin shall conceive, and bear a son, and shall call his name Immanuel.

[4] Study Suggestion 1 on page 56.

The entire context of this verse is, of course, Isaiah 7:1-17, and though we won't be able to discuss this passage in detail within the framework of Christology, we will summarize the important points.

Isaiah 7:1-2 serves as historical background to the prophecy of 7:14, which is the threat to the House of David:

> [1] *And it came to pass in the days of Ahaz the son of Jotham, the son of Uzziah, king of Judah, that Rezin the king of Syria, and Pekah the son of Remaliah, king of Israel, went up to Jerusalem to war against it, but could not prevail against it.* [2] *And it was told the house of David, saying, Syria is confederate with Ephraim. And his heart trembled, and the heart of his people, as the trees of the forest tremble with the wind.*

The two kingdoms of Israel and Syria built an alliance against the kingdom of Judah, and their purpose was not only to do away with King Ahaz, who was ruling at that time, but also to bring down the whole dynasty of David. If they did succeed, it would render the previous prophecy of I Chronicles 17 null and void.

So in Isaiah 7:3-9, God sends a message to Ahaz:

> [3] *Then said Jehovah unto Isaiah, Go forth now to meet Ahaz, you, and Shear-jashub your son, at the end of the conduit of the upper pool, in the highway of the fuller's field;* [4] *and say unto him, Take heed, and be quiet; fear not, neither let your heart be faint, because of these two tails of smoking firebrands, for the fierce anger of Rezin and Syria, and of the son of Remaliah.* [5] *Because Syria, Ephraim, and the son of Remaliah, have purposed evil against you, saying,* [6] *Let us go up against Judah, and vex it, and let us make a breach therein for us, and set up a king in the midst of it, even the son of Tabeel;* [7] *thus says the Lord Jehovah, It shall not stand, neither shall it come to pass.* [8] *For the head of Syria is Damascus, and the head of Damascus is Rezin; and within threescore and five years shall Ephraim be broken in pieces, so that is shall not be a people:* [9] *and the head of Ephraim is Samaria, and the head of Samaria is Remaliah's son. If ye will not believe, surely ye shall not be established.*

In verse 3, God commands Isaiah to meet Ahaz. He also tells him to take his son Shear-jashub, whose name means "a remnant will return," with him.

Then in verses 4-6, God spells out the plot against the House of David. After encouraging Ahaz to take comfort in His promise (v. 4a), God commands him not to be afraid. He defines the objects of Ahaz's fear as the kings of Israel and Syria

(v. 4b). Then, God summarizes their conspiracy, which is to do away with the House of David and to set up a brand new dynasty under Tabeel. Ahaz is not to be afraid of these things because this conspiracy is doomed to failure (vv. 5-6).

In verses 7-9, God goes on to pronounce a judgment on this confederacy. He prophesies that this conspiracy will not succeed (v. 7). He then pronounces a judgment upon the conspirators, promising that both are going to be off the scene within a very short period of time (vv. 8-9a). Finally, God warns Ahaz personally (v. 9b): "If you do not believe, you will not be established." The House of David is guaranteed its role upon the throne, but this is not a guarantee to Ahaz personally. So if Ahaz wants to be established, he must believe. If not, then there is no guarantee for him personally.

Then, in verses 10-12, God offers to give Ahaz a sign that He will deliver him:

> [10] *And Jehovah spoke again unto Ahaz, saying,* [11] *Ask you a sign of Jehovah*
> *your God; ask it either in the depth, or in the height above.* [12] *But Ahaz said, I*
> *will not ask, neither will I tempt Jehovah.*

In the Hebrew text, the word "you" in verse 11 is in the singular. So Ahaz is being personally addressed. He is offered a sign, and he can ask anything he wants, be it in heaven, on the earth, or below the earth. Whatever sign he requests, God will provide it for him. Whatever it takes for him to believe, God will perform it.

The word "sign" does not always require the miraculous. But for something to be a sign, it always requires something very unusual. In this context, it demands a miracle, because the purpose of it is to produce faith in Ahaz. But the king rejects the offer, giving a fake spiritual answer (v. 12). In reality, it is false spirituality, since God Himself offered the sign. The king, not really wanting to trust the God of Israel, refused it. So now, God Himself is going to provide a sign:

> [13] *And he said, Hear ye now, O house of David: Is it a small thing for you to*
> *weary men, that ye will weary my God also?* [14] *Therefore the Lord himself will*
> *give you a sign: behold, a virgin shall conceive, and bear a son, and shall call*
> *his name Immanuel.*

The sign God promises does not pertain to Ahaz personally, but to the *house of David*. Every time the word "you" is used in verses 13 and 14 in the Hebrew text, it is in the plural, meaning "you-all" or "ye." God is no longer addressing King Ahaz personally. Now He is addressing the whole House of David, and it is the entire House of David that is being threatened with removal by the conspirators.

These verses are very important and need to be analyzed in more detail. The sign is being introduced with the word "behold." The Hebrew term may refer to something either in the past, the present, or the future. But a simple rule of Hebrew grammar is that whenever "behold" is used with an active participle, it always refers to something yet future. The verb phrase *shall conceive* is an active participle. The conception itself, therefore, is future. God is not referring to a pregnant woman standing right there in the crowd, as those who want to discredit this important prophecy claim. Rather, Hebrew grammar requires that not only the birth was in the future, but also the conception itself.

Then God says that is *a virgin* who shall conceive. The Hebrew word here is *almah*, and it has the definite article, making it "the virgin." The fact that the definite article is used means it must refer to a specific, definite woman who is somehow known in one of two ways. Either she is a woman referred to in the immediate context or she is a woman generally already known. In the immediate context, no woman has been mentioned. So the word *almah* cannot refer to any woman of that time. Rather, according to the principle of previous reference, it must refer to a woman or a concept already known by the general population. Of course, that generally known concept would be Genesis 3:15, where it mentions the "seed of the woman." When we refer to "the Madonna" today, people in general know what we mean, because there is a general knowledge to what the term refers. It is a reference to a specific woman. By the same token, in the days of Isaiah, the "seed of the woman" was generally well known by the Jewish population to refer to the woman of Genesis 3:15. That is why the definite article is used in Isaiah 7:14.

The word *almah* should be distinguished from two other Hebrew words. One is *na'arah*, which is usually translated as "damsel." It could refer to a virgin, as in I Kings 1:2, or to a non-virgin, as in Ruth 2:6.

A second key word is *betulah*, which usually means a virgin of any age; but it does not always mean "virgin." In a passage like Joel 1:8, for example, it is used of a young widow, a young woman who had been married but had lost her husband. Obviously, she was not a virgin. Furthermore, since the word *betulah* does not clearly mean "a virgin," it sometimes receives an explanatory statement. For example, Genesis 24:16 refers to a girl as *betulah*, but then an explanation is added that she was *a virgin* [betulah], *neither had any man known her.* The same phenomenon is found in Judges 21:12a, where it says, *And they found among the inhabitants of Jabesh-gilead four hundred young virgins* [betulahs], *that had not known man by lying with him.* It should also be noted that wherever *betulah* does mean "virgin," it could refer to a virgin of any age.

The reason why Isaiah does not use *na'arah* or *betulah* to describe the woman in verse 14 of chapter 7 is because he wants to specify that this message is clearly speaking of a virgin and specifically a young virgin. *Almah* is the only Hebrew word that fits the bill. It means "virgin," but not a virgin of any age. It means specifically a young virgin of marriageable age.

The word *almah* is used in six other passages in the Old Testament:

- ✡ Genesis 24:43
- ✡ Exodus 2:8
- ✡ Psalm 68:25
- ✡ Proverbs 30:18-19
- ✡ Song of Solomon 1:3; 6:8

In none of these passages is *almah* used of a married woman. Furthermore, in about 250 B.C., when Jewish scholars translated the Hebrew Scriptures into Greek (the Septuagint), they translated *almah* in Isaiah 7:14 as *parthenos*, a Greek word which does clearly mean "virgin." So Jewish scholars who lived well before the time of *Yeshua* understood the word *almah* to mean "virgin" and used the Greek equivalent, *parthenos,* to emphasize it.

So what happens if this woman gives birth to a child? The very fact that *almah* refers to an unmarried woman leaves us with only two options. Either the child will be illegitimate or it will be born of a virgin. In light of the fact that the Isaiah passage speaks of something God is going to do, it shows that this could not be an illegitimate child, because that would create moral problems concerning God. Therefore it must refer to a virgin giving birth to a child. Furthermore, a young woman giving birth to an illegitimate child would not be a sign. To this day, illegitimate children are still being born. However, if a virgin gave birth to a child, then it would be a true sign.

The prophecy of Isaiah 7:14 ends with the child's name, *Immanuel*, which literally means "With us, God." When the parents name a child, it always shows the thinking of the parents. But when God names a child in Scripture, it shows the actual character of that child, and the character of this child is: "With us, God."

Several conclusions can be drawn from the Isaiah 7:14 prophecy:

- ✡ This was to be a sign to the House of David, not just to Ahaz personally.
- ✡ In the seven usages of the word *almah*, it is never used of a married woman.
- ✡ The very context of the sign requires this to be a miracle. So it cannot refer to an illegitimate child, but it has to refer to the child of a virgin birth.
- ✡ The very flow of the context demands a virgin birth because chapters 7-12 are one unit. In chapter 7, Immanuel is to be born. In chapter nine, Immanuel is born. In chapter 11, Immanuel is reigning and ruling.
- ✡ The first sign of verses 13-14, then, is to the House of David, emphasizing that it will not disappear until the birth of a virgin-born son.

Isaiah 7:15-17 contains a second sign, this time to Ahaz personally because the word "you" is once again in the singular:

> [15] *Butter and honey shall he eat, when he knows to refuse the evil, and choose the good.* [16] *For before the child shall know to refuse the evil, and choose the good, the land whose two kings you abhor shall be forsaken.* [17] *Jehovah will bring upon you, and upon your people, and upon your father's house, days that have not come, from the day that Ephraim departed from Judah-even the king of Assyria.*

In verse 16, again a child is mentioned. The Hebrew word here is *ha-na'ar*, which means "the lad." Just as was the case with *almah*, the definite article which accompanies the word raises the question: Was there another lad mentioned somewhere in the context? The answer is "yes." Verse 3 speaks about Isaiah's own son, Shear-jashub. The point of this sign to Ahaz is that before Isaiah's own son is old enough to make moral choices, the two kings of the conspiracy will be off the scene. They will be dead and gone.

Verses 14-17 of Isaiah 7 mention two signs then: one is to the House of David—the sign of a virgin-born son—and one is to King Ahaz personally. It involves Isaiah's son and predicts that before Shear-jashub is old enough to make moral choices, the threat to the House of David will no longer be there.

The key point of Isaiah 7:14 is that Messiah will be born of a virgin.

2. Isaiah 9:6-7

> [6] *For unto us a child is born, unto us a son is given; and the government shall be upon his shoulder: and his name shall be called Wonderful, Counsellor, Mighty God, Everlasting Father, Prince of Peace.* [7] *Of the increase of his government and of peace there shall be no end, upon the throne of David, and upon his kingdom, to establish it, and to uphold it with justice and with righteousness from henceforth even for ever. The zeal of Jehovah of hosts will perform this.*

The first part of verse 6 tells us Immanuel has two origins, a human and a divine. *For unto us a child is born*—this is the human origin. The verse emphasizes natural birth. Yet, this *son is given*, He is a unique gift of God, so He also has a divine origin. He is the Son of Psalm 2:7: *I will tell of the decree: Jehovah said unto me, You are my son; This day have I begotten you.*[5]

a. The Messiah's Names

In the second part of verse 6, His divine origin is emphasized. This can be seen in the four names found there. Each name has two parts to it, and the first three of these are clearly used of God alone.

(1) Wonderful Counselor (Pele-Yoeitz)

In some translations, a comma is placed between *Wonderful* and *Counsellor*, making the two words two separate names. But the word "wonderful" is in the construct state and should be taken together with *Counsellor.* There are some words in Hebrew which are used only of God and never of men. One example of these is *pele*, rendered here in English as "wonderful." In English, "wonderful" may be freely used of many things, but in Hebrew it is typically reserved for that which is divine. It can also be found in Isaiah 25:1: *I will praise your name; for you have done wonderful* [pele] *things.* In Isaiah 28:29, it also clearly refers to God: *This also comes forth from Jehovah of hosts, who is wonderful* [pele] *in counsel.*

---

[5] A more detailed explanation of this Messianic title of *Yeshua* is given on page 39 and in chapter 5.

(2) Mighty God (El-Gibbor)

Obviously, this name is never used of a mere man. It is also found in the very next chapter in Isaiah 10:21: *A remnant shall return, even the remnant of Jacob, unto the mighty God.*

(3) Eternal Father (Avi-Ad)

In the Hebrew Bible, the word *Avi-Ad* occurs only in Isaiah 9:6. However, the name is really the word "father" (in Hebrew *av*) in the construct state (*avi*), with "perpetuity or advancing time," or *ad*. In combination, this becomes "the Father of Eternity." There are other references in which "father" appears similarly, albeit not in this exact bound-form with *ad*, or "eternity." One example of this is Isaiah 63:16b, *you, O Jehovah, are our Father; our Redeemer from everlasting is your name.* In the Hebrew text, "father," or *av*, is in the construct state again, which makes it *avi*. This time, *avi* is combined with the first person plural pronoun "us" (*nu*), making this the "father of us," or *Avi-Nu*. So the word "father," used in Isaiah 9:6 as a proper name for the child who will be born is clearly used of God in Isaiah 63:16b.

(4) Prince of Peace (Sar-Shalom)

This is the only one of the four names which can be used of man and God. Isaiah 26:3 says, *The steadfast of mind you will keep in perfect peace.* The object and subject of the sentence is God Himself. Again in Isaiah 26:12, the work of peace is attributed to God: *Lord, you will establish peace for us.* As stated above, the fourth name, *Prince of Peace*, is sometimes used of man in the Hebrew text. If we limit our attention to the book of Isaiah, however, then the work of peace is the work of God only.

b. The Messiah's Office

Verse 7a adds the information that the government will be upon the shoulder of the Messiah. He will reign as king, and here, we learn five things about His reign:

1. As to the course of His reign, it has *no end*.
2. The basis of it is the Davidic Covenant.
3. The effects of it are that *peace* is established and upheld.
4. The means is by *justice* and *righteousness*.
5. Its extent is going to be *for ever*.

Verse 7b contains a pledge and a guarantee: *The zeal of Jehovah of Hosts will perform this.* The zeal of God will make sure that these prophecies will indeed come to their fulfillment.

Summarizing the elements of this passage that are relevant to the topic of Messianic Christology, we can note that the Messiah is going to be a king and the God-Man.

3. Isaiah 11:1

And there shall come forth a shoot out of the stock of Jesse, and a branch out of his roots shall bear fruit.

This verse emphasizes Messiah's lowly origins. Three things can be pointed out. First, it says, *there shall come forth a shoot.* A shoot is a twig. The picture is that from what appeared to be nothing but a dead stump, suddenly a shoot or twig begins to grow, producing new life.

Second, the verse refers to *the stock of Jesse*. This word "stock" refers to the stump of a felled tree. Of course, Jesse, a humble shepherd, was David's father. However, when one thinks of David, a mighty and royal house comes to mind. The point of referring to Messiah here as *the stock of Jesse* rather than as "the seed of David" is to indicate the time frame of Messiah's arrival: Only when the royal House of David has sunk back to the insignificant level that it was during Jesse's day would the Messiah appear.

Third, the verse mentions *a branch out of his roots shall bear fruit.* The word "branch" refers to a fresh, green shoot which grows out of a felled tree's roots. This means it grows very low to the ground. But the fact that Messiah will be born "very low to the ground" does not mean that He will remain within the lowliness of His origin. Rather, the verse promises that He will "produce fruit."

In summary, we can note that the Messiah will only come when the Davidic dynasty has lost its power and glory.

4. Isaiah 40:3-5

[3] The voice of one that cries, Prepare ye in the wilderness the way of Jehovah; make level in the desert a highway for our God. [4] Every valley shall be exalted, and every mountain and hill shall be made low; and the uneven shall be made level, and the rough places a plain: [5] and the glory of Jehovah shall

be revealed, and all flesh shall see it together; for the mouth of Jehovah has spoken it.

This passage points out that the First Coming of Messiah will be preceded by a forerunner. All four Gospels testify that this verse was fulfilled by John the Baptizer (Mt. 3:3; Mk. 1:3; Lk. 3:4; Jn. 1:23).

5. Isaiah 42:1-4

[1] Behold, my servant, whom I uphold; my chosen, in whom my soul delights: I have put my Spirit upon him; he will bring forth justice to the Gentiles. [2] He will not cry, nor lift up his voice, nor cause it to be heard in the street. [3] A bruised reed will he not break, and a dimly burning wick will he not quench: he will bring forth justice in truth. [4] He will not fail nor be discouraged, till he have set justice in the earth; and the isles shall wait for his law.

This Messianic passage makes four points, and each point is made by a specific verse. The first point is found in verse 1, where Messiah's status is emphasized. He will be a *servant* whom God will *uphold*. He is God's *chosen* one, in whom God's soul is going to *delight*. He will be anointed with the *Spirit*, and that anointing will cause Him to bring *justice to the Gentiles*.

The second point is found in verse 2, where Messiah's manner of ministry is described. He *will not cry*; He will not *lift up his voice*; He will not shout *in the street*. The point here concerning His manner is that Messiah would not be characterized by street-preaching. Not that there is anything wrong with street-preaching. It is what the disciples practiced. However, *Yeshua* was not going to be a street-preacher.

The third point is found in verse 3, where Messiah's way is emphasized. The fact that He will not break *a bruised reed* means that He will not crush the oppressed. The verse goes on to say that He will not quench *a dimly burning wick*. In other words, He will not discourage people. Lastly, He *will bring forth justice* and truth.

The fourth point is made in verse 4, where the Messiah's success is noted. The verse makes it clear that He will not fail. He will not be discouraged. He will bring forth justice to the earth. Distant lands will wait for His law. This prophecy seems to be contradicted by the following Messianic passage in Isaiah 49.

6. Isaiah 49:1-13

> [1] *Listen, O isles, unto me; and hearken, ye peoples, from far: Jehovah has called me from the womb; from the bowels of my mother has he made mention of my name:* [2] *and he has made my mouth like a sharp sword; in the shadow of his hand has he hid me: and he has made me a polished shaft; in his quiver has he kept me close:* [3] *and he said unto me, You are my servant; Israel, in whom I will be glorified.* [4] *But I said, I have labored in vain, I have spent my strength for nought and vanity; yet surely the justice due to me is with Jehovah, and my recompense with my God.* [5] *And now says Jehovah that formed me from the womb to be his servant, to bring Jacob again to him, and that Israel be gathered unto him (for I am honorable in the eyes of Jehovah, and my God is become my strength);* [6] *yea, he says, It is too light a thing that you should be my servant to raise up the tribes of Jacob, and to restore the preserved of Israel: I will also give you for a light to the Gentiles, that you may be my salvation unto the end of the earth.* [7] *Thus says Jehovah, the Redeemer of Israel, and his Holy One, to him whom man despises, to him whom the nation abhors, to a servant of rulers: Kings shall see and arise; princes, and they shall worship; because of Jehovah that is faithful, even the Holy One of Israel, who has chosen you.* [8] *Thus says Jehovah, In an acceptable time have I answered you, and in a day of salvation have I helped you; and I will preserve you, and give you for a covenant of the people, to raise up the land, to make them inherit the desolate heritages:* [9] *saying to them that are bound, Go forth; to them that are in darkness, Show yourselves. They shall feed in the ways, and on all bare heights shall be their pasture.* [10] *They shall not hunger nor thirst; neither shall the heat nor sun smite them: for he that has mercy on them will lead them, even by springs of water will he guide them.* [11] *And I will make all my mountains a way, and my highways shall be exalted.* [12] *Lo, these shall come from far; and, lo, these from the north and from the west; and these from the land of Sinim.* [13] *Sing, O heavens; and be joyful, O earth; and break forth into singing, O mountains: for Jehovah has comforted his people, and will have compassion upon his afflicted.*

For the sake of clarity, this passage will be divided into four segments, beginning with Isaiah 49:1-4. These verses speak about someone who is declared to be God's *servant* (v. 3), the Messiah. We read about His call (v. 1) and the special position He holds in relation to God the Father (v. 2). He is His Servant, and He is called *Israel* (v. 3) for this Servant is the ideal Israelite. However, He is discouraged (v. 4a). It appears that, in light of Israel's rejection of His Messiahship, His ministry is a failure. What starts as a complaint ends in an expression of faith (v. 4b). The Servant trusts that the justice due to Him from God the Father will indeed come to Him.

God's answer to the Servant's sentiments is found in verses 5-6. In verse 5, God reminds His Servant of His original commission, which was to regather the people of Israel and restore them into their land. But in verse 6, He points out that Messiah has also a new commission. It does not replace the first commission, but adds to it. His new commission is to become *a light to the Gentiles*. The reason why God allowed Israel to reject the Messiah is so that for a period of time, Messiah could be this light to the Gentiles. It would have been too simple a thing for the Messiah to only restore Israel.

In verse 7, the rejection and exaltation of the Servant is summarized. This Servant may be rejected by men, but He is going to be exalted by God.

Verses 8-13 describe how the Messiah will restore Israel. It is this Servant who will bring the Jewish people back to the land (v. 8). God intends to remove all obstacles to Israel's return; and this He will do (vv. 9-11). The regathering is going to be worldwide (v. 12). The good news of this prophecy leads Isaiah to conclude this section with a hymn of praise (v. 13).

7. Isaiah 50:4-9

> [4] *The Lord Jehovah has given me the tongue of them that are taught, that I may know how to sustain with words him that is weary: he wakens morning by morning, he wakens mine ear to hear as they that are taught.* [5] *The Lord Jehovah has opened mine ear, and I was not rebellious, neither turned away backward.* [6] *I gave my back to the smiters, and my cheeks to them that plucked off the hair; I hid not my face from shame and spitting.* [7] *For the Lord Jehovah will help me; therefore have I not been confounded: therefore have I set my face like a flint, and I know that I shall not be put to shame.* [8] *He is near that justifies me; who will content with me? let us stand up together: who is mine adversary? let him come near to me.* [9] *Behold, the Lord Jehovah will help me; who is he that shall condemn me? behold, all they shall wax old as a garment, the moth shall eat them up.*

This passage, too, can be divided into three sections, beginning with verse 4 and a description of the discipling of the Servant. As the Messiah was growing up, God the Father would awaken Him in the wee hours of the morning to take Him aside and train Him for the mission to which He has indeed been called.

Verses 5-6 describe how the Servant is despised. He did not react to His mistreatment, but simply took it in the manner in which He was trained (v. 5). And so even when He realized that part of His mission included suffering and death, He did not turn His face away from it. Obediently, He gave His back *to the smiters* and His cheeks *to them that plucked off the hair* (v. 6).

Verses 7-9 tell how the Servant was aided by the Lord Jehovah. Despite all this suffering, the Servant will not be disgraced (v. 7). In fact, He will be vindicated (v. 8), so that no one can declare Him guilty (v. 9).

In summary, this passage points out that Messiah will be personally trained by God the Father; and during His life, He will undergo suffering, mistreatment, and shame.

8. Isaiah 52:13–53:12

Because the next major Messianic prophecy from the Prophets is rather long, we will not be able to detail everything in this very rich passage. However, a short summary will be given. The passage can be divided into five main divisions. Each division contains three verses and is titled by the first sentence or phrase of that particular paragraph.

a. Behold, My Servant Shall Prosper—52:13-15

> 13 *Behold, my servant shall deal wisely, he shall be exalted and lifted up, and shall be very high.* 14 *Like as many were astonished at you (his visage was so marred more than any man, and his form more than the sons of men),* 15 *so shall he sprinkle many nations; kings shall shut their mouths at him: for that which had not been told them shall they see; and that which they had not heard shall they understand.*

From His ascension onward, the Servant will *be exalted* (v. 13). His suffering, though, precedes the victory, and so we learn once again of His humiliation and terrible mistreatment (v. 14). In fact, He will be so disfigured that He will no longer resemble a man. This will be a natural byproduct of being beaten with a Roman scourge. The victory, though, is His, and He will eventually conquer all (v. 15).

b. Who Has Believed Our Message?—53:1-3

> [1] *Who has believed our message? and to whom has the arm of Jehovah been revealed?* [2] *For he grew up before him as a tender plant, and as a root out of a dry ground: he has no form nor comeliness; and when we see him, there is no beauty that we should desire him.* [3] *He was despised, and rejected of men; a man of sorrows, and acquainted with grief: and as one from whom men hide their face he was despised; and we esteemed him not.*

Israel will respond with unbelief and rejection of the Messiah at His First Coming (v. 1). Building upon what was stated in Isaiah 11:1, we are reminded that the Servant of God is fully human (v. 2). Again we read that He will be growing up low to the ground *as a tender plant*, and nothing unique about His upbringing would make Him stand out. Rather than being one who would attract others to Him, as far as His outward, physical features are concerned, men would tend to be repelled by Him (v. 3). This clearly implies that *Yeshua* was not as handsome as some artists have rendered Him.

c. Surely He Has Borne Our Griefs and Carried Our Sorrows—53:4-6

> [4] *Surely he has borne our griefs, and carried our sorrows; yet we did esteem him stricken, smitten of God, and afflicted.* [5] *But he was wounded for our transgressions, he was bruised for our iniquities; the chastisement of our peace was upon him; and with his stripes we are healed.* [6] *All we like sheep have gone astray; we have turned every one to his own way; and Jehovah has laid on him the iniquity of us all.*

When this Servant of God suffered, He did so for others and not because of His own sin (v. 4). Not only did He suffer for others, He also died for others as their substitute (v. 5). But Israel did not recognize her Messiah. Like sheep that had *gone astray*, they had *turned every one to his own way*, so God laid upon the Messiah *the iniquity* of them all (v. 6). This reemphasizes that both His suffering and death were clearly substitutionary.

d. He Was Oppressed and Afflicted, yet He Opened Not His Mouth—53:7-9

> [7] *He was oppressed, yet when he was afflicted he opened not his mouth; as a lamb that is led to the slaughter, and as a sheep that before its shearers is dumb, so he opened not his mouth.* [8] *By oppression and judgment he was taken away; and as for his generation, who among them considered that he was cut off out of the land of the living for the transgression of my people to*

whom the stroke was due? [9] *And they made his grave with the wicked, and with a rich man in his death; although he had done no violence, neither was any deceit in his mouth.*

As the Servant suffered, He did it in silence and without complaint (v. 7). He endured an unjust trial and death for the sake of His people (v. 8). Isaiah puts it rather graphically: *as for his generation, who among them considered that he was cut off out of the land of the living for the transgression of my people to whom the stroke was due?* That is a clear statement of substitutionary death. Finally, the Servant was buried (v. 9). Here, the point is made that while He had died a criminal's death and was assigned a criminal's grave, divine justice ruled, and He was buried in a rich man's tomb.

e. Yet It Pleased Jehovah to Bruise Him, He Had Put Him to Grief—53:10-12

[10] *Yet it pleased Jehovah to bruise him; he has put him to grief: when you shall make his soul an offering for sin, he shall see his seed, he shall prolong his days, and the pleasure of Jehovah shall prosper in his hand.* [11] *He shall see of the travail of his soul, and shall be satisfied: by the knowledge of himself shall my righteous servant justify many; and he shall bear their iniquities.* [12] *Therefore will I divide him a portion with the great, and he shall divide the spoil with the strong; because he poured out his soul unto death, and was numbered with the transgressors: yet he bore the sin of many, and made intercession for the transgressors.*

Messiah's death would become *an offering for sin* (v. 10). The news is good: By His substitutionary death, He would be able to justify the many who believe on Him (v. 11). Ultimately, the Servant is going to be rewarded because He was willing *to pour out his soul* (v. 12).

9. Isaiah 61:1-3

[1] *The Spirit of the Lord Jehovah is upon me; because Jehovah has anointed me to preach good tidings unto the meek; he has sent me to bind up the broken-hearted, to proclaim liberty to the captives, and the opening of the prison to them that are bound;* [2] *to proclaim the year of Jehovah's favor, and the day of vengeance of our God; to comfort all that mourn;* [3] *to appoint unto them that mourn in Zion, to give unto them a garland for ashes, the oil of joy for mourning, the garment of praise for the spirit of heaviness; that*

they may be called trees of righteousness, the planting of Jehovah, that he may be glorified.

These verses talk about the two different comings of the Messiah. The First Coming is described in verses 1-2a. The Messiah is going to be anointed with the Holy Spirit, and His task will be to accomplish several things:

- ✡ To preach the *good tidings* of the gospel to man
- ✡ To *proclaim liberty to the captives*
- ✡ To open *the prison* of *them that are bound*
- ✡ To proclaim the acceptable *year of Jehovah's favor*

At His First Coming, Messiah will bring redemption and freedom from sin, from Satan, and from the world.

The Second Coming is dealt with in verses 2b-3. When He comes again, He will proclaim *the day of vengeance* and *comfort all that mourn*. The symbols used in verse 3 point to the kingdom He will appoint unto Zion.

10. Jeremiah 23:5-6

> [5] *Behold, the days come, says Jehovah, that I will raise unto David a righteous Branch, and he shall reign as king and deal wisely, and shall execute justice and righteousness in the land.* [6] *In his days Judah shall be saved, and Israel shall dwell safely; and this is his name whereby he shall be called: Jehovah our righteousness.*

These verses deal primarily with the Second Coming of Messiah, but there is an aspect of them which relates to His First Coming, too. Verse 5 tells of a man who will be a son of David. He will rule and reign as king. The kingship of Messiah is yet to come, but this verse clearly speaks of Messiah as a descendant of David and thus stresses His humanity. In verse 6, however, this man is given a name which is applicable to God alone: *Jehovah*—or YHVH—*our righteousness.* Throughout the Hebrew Scriptures, the divine name YHVH is given to God alone, yet here the man of verse 5 is clearly given the name of God in verse 6. This again presents us with the clear concept of Messiah as the God-Man.

11. Micah 5:2

But you, Beth-lehem Ephrathah, which are little to be among the thousands of Judah, out of you shall one come forth unto me that is to be ruler in Israel; whose goings forth are from of old, from everlasting.

It has already been shown that a great many Scriptures point to the divine as well as the human nature of the Messiah. This has been clear from as early as Genesis chapters three and four, and it continues through to the prophecy of Micah. Micah was a contemporary of Isaiah, prophesying at the same time, but in a different part of Judah. In Isaiah 7:14, we read that Messiah was to be born of a virgin; here in Micah 5:2, we read where that birth is to take place. Messiah is not to be born in Jerusalem, as might have been expected, but in Bethlehem. This was perhaps hinted at in Isaiah 11:1, but is now stated clearly. This is Bethlehem Ephrathah, as distinguished from another Bethlehem in Galilee. This Bethlehem is the Bethlehem of David and of Judah, and it is situated south of Jerusalem.

The One to be born is said to *come forth unto me*; in other words, He is being born in order to fulfill a particular mission, a specific purpose of God. As regards His human origin, He is to be born in Bethlehem, but regarding His divine origin, His *goings forth are from of old, from everlasting.* The NASB translates this phrase as *from long ago, From the days of eternity*, and these are the strongest Hebrew words ever used for eternity past. They are used of God the Father in Psalm 90:2. What is true of God the Father is also said to be true of this One who is to be born in Bethlehem.

Again we have a passage which shows that Messiah is to be human—being born at a specific point in time and at a specific place—yet having existed since all eternity past. Hence, He is divine.

12. Zechariah 9:9-10

9 Rejoice greatly, O daughter of Zion; shout, O daughter of Jerusalem: behold, your king comes unto you; he is just, and having salvation; lowly, and riding upon an ass, even upon a colt the foal of an ass. 10 And I will cut off the chariot from Ephraim, and the horse from Jerusalem; and the battle bow shall be cut off; and he shall speak peace unto the nations: and his dominion shall be from sea to sea, and from the River to the ends of the earth.

These verses blend the two comings of the Messiah into one picture. Verse 9 relates to the First Coming, while verse 10 relates to the Second Coming. This is not clear from the text itself, but can be established from other passages of Scripture. The background to these verses is the invasion of the Middle East by a foreign king prophesied in verses 9:1-8. These verses were fulfilled by Alexander the Great. But in verse 9, in contrast to this invading Gentile king, we find reference to a future Jewish king. Israel is told to rejoice because her king is coming not against her, but to her. Jerusalem is to rejoice because, unlike Alexander, this king is characterized by righteousness, a point also made by Jeremiah 23:5-6. In contrast, Alexander the Great died in a drunken stupor. Israel's king will offer salvation, while Alexander came with conquest, destruction, and death. And finally, the future king will be lowly and humble, while Alexander came with pomp and power. "Lowly" here has the sense of being brought low through oppression. Messiah was indeed oppressed.

Furthermore, in contrast to Alexander the Great on his white steed, this king is to come riding on a donkey. Specifically, He is to ride on the foal of a donkey—a creature not yet broken, one which has never been ridden before.

Verse 10, in which all weapons of war are going to be removed from the land, deals with the events of the Second Coming of the Messiah.

13. Zechariah 11:1-17

This Messianic prophecy is so long that for the purpose of this book, it will have to be summarized. The passage has three main divisions.

a. Verses 1-3

Verses 1-3 describe a judgment upon Israel and a devastation of the land which was fulfilled in the year A.D. 70 and 135:

> *[1] Open your doors, O Lebanon, that the fire may devour your cedars. [2] Wail, O fir-tree, for the cedar is fallen, because the goodly ones are destroyed: wail, O ye oaks of Bashan, for the strong forest is come down. [3] A voice of the wailing of the shepherds! for their glory is destroyed: a voice of the roaring of young lions! for the pride of the Jordan is laid waste.*

b. Verses 4-14

Verses 4-14 deal with the theme of the rejection of the true Shepherd, and this provides the first reason for the devastation of the land described in verses 1-3:

> [4] *Thus said Jehovah my God: Feed the flock of slaughter;* [5] *whose possessors*
> *slay them, and hold themselves not guilty; and they that sell them say,*
> *Blessed be Jehovah, for I am rich; and their own shepherds pity them not.*
> [6] *For I will no more pity the inhabitants of the land, says Jehovah; but, lo, I*
> *will deliver the men every one into his neighbor's hand, and into the hand of*
> *his king; and they shall smite the land, and out of their hand I will not deliver*
> *them.* [7] *So I fed the flock of slaughter, verily the poor of the flock. And I took*
> *unto me two staves; the one I called Beauty, and the other I called Bands;*
> *and I fed the flock.* [8] *And I cut off the three shepherds in one month; for my*
> *soul was weary of them, and their soul also loathed me.* [9] *Then said I, I will*
> *not feed you: that which dies, let it die; and that which is to be cut off, let it*
> *be cut off; and let them that are left eat every one the flesh of another.*
> [10] *And I took my staff Beauty, and cut it asunder, that I might break my*
> *covenant which I had made with all the peoples.* [11] *And it was broken in that*
> *day; and thus the poor of the flock that gave heed unto me knew that it was*
> *the word of Jehovah.* [12] *And I said unto them, If ye think good, give me my*
> *hire; and if not, forbear. So they weighed for my hire thirty pieces of silver.*
> [13] *And Jehovah said unto me, Cast it unto the potter, the goodly price that I*
> *was prized at by them. And I took the thirty pieces of silver, and cast them*
> *unto the potter, in the house of Jehovah.* [14] *Then I cut asunder mine other*
> *staff, even Bands, that I might break the brotherhood between Judah and*
> *Israel.*

In verses 4–6, Zechariah is given a commission: He is given a role to act out as a message to the people. The part he is to play, a shepherd feeding his flock, is symbolic of Messiah at His First Coming. The flock (v. 4) is symbolic of Israel. The sheep are being destroyed by their owners, symbolic of Rome, and even *their own shepherds*, symbolic of the Jewish leaders who have no pity on them. The flock, the people of Israel, has been abandoned by man (v. 5); but they have also been abandoned by God (v. 6). God states that He will cause each and every man to fall *into the hand of his king.* At first this seems a little confusing since, at the time of the Roman occupation, Israel had no king. However, we read in the Gospels that when *Yeshua*, the true Shepherd, stood at His trial, Pontius Pilate declared to the people, "Here is your king." But the Pharisees rejected *Yeshua* and cried out, "We have no king but Caesar" (Jn. 19:15). Hence, since they rejected Messiah as king, it was to that king, Caesar, that God handed them over for judgment. In the war with the Romans in A.D. 70, a total of 1,100,000 Jews were killed and 97,000 were taken into slavery.

In verses 7–11, Zechariah carries out his commission. He feeds the flock doomed to slaughter (v. 7), especially *the poor of the flock*, or, according to some translations, the afflicted. "The poor and the needy" is a common phrase in the Prophets and is always a reference to the righteous remnant of Israel.[6] While Messiah came to minister to the whole of Israel, there was a special emphasis in His ministry towards the believing remnant within Israel.

Zechariah employs two staffs in this work. One is given the name *Beauty* and the other is given the name *Bands*. The staff called Beauty was for the protection of the flock; the staff called Bands was to keep the flock together and preserve its unity.

In verse 8, Zechariah faces the opposition of three other shepherds. In the context of the ministry of *Yeshua*, these three shepherds are symbolic of the Pharisees, the Sadducees, and the scribes, the main elements of Jewish leadership during the period of the First Coming. One of the results of *Yeshua's* ministry was the destruction of these three groups. The reason for their destruction is the mutual antagonism described in verse 8.

Although verse 7 described the faithful shepherding of the flock, verse 9 mentions an abrupt cessation in the feeding of the flock. In the ministry of *Yeshua*, this part of the prophecy was fulfilled by the events of Matthew 12, a chapter which describes the pivotal point in His ministry: the rejection of His Messiahship on the grounds of demon possession. The accusation of demon possession constituted the "unpardonable sin," and from that moment on, the judgment of A.D. 70 during which the Temple was destroyed was inevitable. When Israel committed the unpardonable sin, the Messiah stopped feeding the flock as a whole and dealt only with individuals within the nation.

In verse 10, with the cessation of feeding, Zechariah takes the staff named Beauty and breaks it. This symbolizes God's removal of Israel's protection and the inevitability of the A.D. 70 judgment. Note that *peoples* is in the plural, meaning

---

[6] During the course of history, Israel as a whole was rebellious and unrighteous many times. But there has always remained within Israel a small group of righteous, believing people, termed "the Remnant of Israel."

"Gentile nations;" Israel is now vulnerable to Gentile attacks, and in A.D. 70, the attack of the Romans was to be devastating indeed.

In verse 11, the afflicted of the flock, that is, the believing remnant, see the breaking of the staff Beauty as the word of God and understand the significance of it. During the ministry of the Messiah, the Jewish believers did indeed understand that judgment was coming, that it was from the hand of the Lord, and that it was inevitable. In A.D. 66, when the Romans besieged Jerusalem, the believers within the city realized that the time of judgment had arrived and that they were not to join the fight but should leave the city. Later in that year, the siege was temporarily lifted, and the entire Messianic Jewish community from Jerusalem and the whole Land of Israel (some one hundred thousand people) left Israel and found refuge in Pella, east of the Jordan River.

Verses 12–14 describe the value placed upon the work of the good shepherd. In verse 12, the good shepherd approaches the leadership of Israel and asks for his wages to be paid according to what they think he is worth. He is paid *thirty pieces of silver*. While today that may sound like a reasonable amount, it was, in fact, a display of contempt. Under the Mosaic Law, thirty pieces of silver was the value of a dead slave (Ex. 21:32); therefore, being paid thirty pieces of silver was more insulting than being paid nothing at all. The leadership of Israel had judged that the work of the good shepherd was of no more value than that of a dead slave.

The words of verse 13 are extremely important here. It is Zechariah who has been paid the thirty pieces of silver, but who is actually being insulted? The NASB translates this verse as: *Then the LORD said to me, "Throw it to the potter, that magnificent price at which I was valued by them."* This is said in sarcasm; thirty pieces of silver was not a *magnificent price*, as we have just seen. It is the LORD who is the Good Shepherd, thus it is the LORD whose work is so despised as to be valued at only thirty pieces of silver. It becomes very clear that Zechariah is merely an actor playing out a prophetic role, something the prophets often were commanded to do by God, and that this role is to be fulfilled by Jehovah Himself when He becomes a man, as revealed in previous prophecies.

Zechariah is then told to take the thirty pieces of silver and throw them away by throwing them into the potter's area of the Temple Compound. These words found their fulfillment when Judas Iscariot was paid thirty pieces of silver by the Jewish leaders to betray *Yeshua*. Afterwards, Judas did what Zechariah did and threw the coins into the potter's section of the Temple Compound. All of this is described in Matthew 26:14-16 and 27:3-10. It should be noted that the thirty pieces of silver were paid to Judas by the chief priests, who would have taken the money from the Temple treasury. This money was intended for the specific purpose of purchasing sacrifices. Although they did not realize it, that is exactly what the priests did. They purchased a sacrifice; the Messiah was to be the final sacrifice for sin.

The response to the contempt of verse 13 is in verse 14. Zechariah takes the second staff, called *Bands*, and breaks it. This again is a prophetic act, this time signifying that the flock is to be scattered and the unity of Israel destroyed. During the war against the Romans from A.D. 66-70, various factions developed amongst the Zealots. They began fighting amongst themselves, destroying each other's food stocks and killing each other. Ultimately, it was the civil strife within Jerusalem which caused it to easily fall to Rome. The destruction of unity therefore led to the scattering of the flock; the great dispersion of Jewry did indeed begin in A.D. 70.

c. Verses 15-17

Verses 15-17 provide the second reason for the devastation of verses 1-3 which was their acceptance of the foolish shepherd in contrast to the Good Shepherd:

> [15] *And Jehovah said unto me, Take unto you yet again the instruments of a foolish shepherd.* [16] *For, lo, I will raise up a shepherd in the land, who will not visit those that are cut off, neither will seek those that are scattered, nor heal that which is broken, nor feed that which is sound; but he will eat the flesh of the fat sheep, and will tear their hoofs in pieces.* [17] *Woe to the worthless shepherd that leaves the flock! the sword shall be upon his arm, and upon his right eye: his arm shall be clean dried up, and his right eye shall be utterly darkened.*

In verse 15, Zechariah is again given the commission to play the role of a shepherd, only this time, he has to play the role of a foolish shepherd.

In verse 16, he is given the reason and the purpose for doing this. A foolish shepherd will arise and be accepted by the majority of the Jewish people. Although some take this to refer to the Antichrist, this author takes it to refer to the first false messiah after *Yeshua*, whose name was Simon bar Kochba (also spelled Shimon bar Kokhba). The nation did accept him as their messiah, a historical event that brought Israel to further ruin.

In verse 17, God proclaims judgment upon the foolish shepherd. His *arm*, which was to be used to protect the flock, in keeping with the staff named

Beauty, is going to be dried up; *his right eye*, which was supposed to keep a look-out to make sure the flock does not scatter, in response to the staff named Bands, will be dried up as well.

This particular prophecy makes several points:

- The Messiah is going to be accepted by a minority of the Jewish people.
- He is going to be rejected by the leadership of Israel.
- He is going to be sold out for the price of thirty pieces of silver.
- These pieces of silver will end up in the house of the potter.

14. Zechariah 12:10

And I will pour upon the house of David, and upon the inhabitants of Jerusalem, the spirit of grace and of supplication; and they shall look unto me whom they have pierced; and they shall mourn for him, as one mourns for his only son, and shall be in bitterness for him, as one that is in bitterness for his first-born.

The main point of this verse in the area of Messianic Christology is that the Messiah is going to be *pierced*.

15. Zechariah 13:7

Awake, O sword, against my shepherd, and against the man that is my fellow, says Jehovah of hosts: smite the shepherd, and the sheep shall be scattered; and I will turn my hand upon the little ones.

This verse also points out that Messiah is both God and man. The shepherd of 13:7 is the Good Shepherd of 11:4–14. The humanity of Messiah is obvious. In this verse, He is called *the man*. The words which follow are never adequately translated into English, and so the divinity of Messiah is not made obvious. What is translated as *my fellow* is "my equal" in the Hebrew. The verse should really read, "and against the man, my equal." Of course, in order to be equal with God, Messiah must actually be God. This may not be obvious in English translations, but is very clear in the original Hebrew.

This verse also emphasizes the violent nature of Messiah's death and again states that His death will be the cause of the dispersion of Israel.

The verse, then, simply summarizes Zechariah 11 and the story of the Good Shepherd, but there are two main points from the perspective of Messianic Christology:

- ✡ The Messiah is going to be the God-Man.
- ✡ The Messiah is going to die a violent death.

16. Malachi 3:1

The last of the Messianic Christology passages from the Prophets is Malachi 3:1:

> *Behold, I send my messenger, and he shall prepare the way before me: and the Lord, whom ye seek, will suddenly come to his temple; and the messenger of the covenant, whom ye desire, behold, he comes, says Jehovah of hosts.*

Like the Isaiah forty passage, this verse speaks of the fact that the Messiah will be preceded by a forerunner. Of course, this forerunner was John the Baptist (Mt. 11:10; Mk. 1:2; Lk. 7:27).[7]

C. The Writings

The third section of the *Tanakh* is called "The Writings," and it encompasses eleven books, such as the Psalms and Proverbs. We will look at seven passages that pertain to our topic of Messianic Christology.

By way of introduction, a note about the Psalms is in order. The book of Psalms could be summarized in a single sentence: "The Psalms are the poetic versions of the messages of the Law and the Prophets." The book is often regarded as purely devotional reading. While it is certainly very useful as such, it would be wrong to limit it to only that. The whole book of Psalms is full of profound doctrine and deep spiritual truths couched in poetic terms.

---

[7] Study Suggestion 2 on page 56.

1. Psalm 2:7-12

> *[7] I will tell of the decree: Jehovah said unto me, You are my son; This day have I begotten you. [8] Ask of me, and I will give you the nations for your inheritance, And the uttermost parts of the earth for your possession. [9] You shall break them with a rod of iron; You shall dash them in pieces like a potter's vessel. [10] Now therefore be wise, O ye kings: Be instructed, ye judges of the earth. [11] Serve Jehovah with fear, And rejoice with trembling. [12] Kiss the son, lest he be angry, and ye perish in the way, For his wrath will soon be kindled. Blessed are all they that take refuge in him.*

The section of this Psalm that is relevant to Messianic Christology encompasses verses 7–12. It should be stated that these verses cannot possibly be applied to David. While David was a great king, God never gave him authority over all *the nations* (v. 8), nor did he ever rule *the uttermost parts of the earth*. These verses speak of Messiah who, as the psalmist would have heard from the prophets, will rule over the entire world.

One of the titles given to Messiah is "Son of God." This is applied to Messiah twice in Psalm 2, in verses 7 and 12. This Messiah, who is to be king in Jerusalem and over the whole world, is also, uniquely, the Son of God.

In summary, this Psalm makes three points:

1. Messiah is going to be the Son of God.
2. Messiah will be king in Jerusalem.
3. Messiah is going to rule over the Gentiles.

2. Psalm 16:1-11

> *[1] Preserve me, O God; for in you do I take refuge. [2] O my soul, you have said unto Jehovah, You are my Lord: I have no good beyond you. [3] As for the saints that are in the earth, They are the excellent in whom is all my delight. [4] Their sorrows shall be multiplied that give gifts for another god: Their drink-offerings of blood will I not offer, Nor take their names upon my lips. [5] Jehovah is the portion of mine inheritance and of my cup: You maintain my lot. [6] The lines are fallen unto me in pleasant places; Yea, I have a goodly heritage. [7] I will bless Jehovah, who has given me counsel; Yea, my heart instructs me in the night seasons. [8] I have set Jehovah always before me: Because he is at my right hand, I shall not be moved. [9] Therefore my heart is*

glad, and my glory rejoices; My flesh also shall dwell in safety. [10] *For you will not leave my soul to Sheol; Neither will you suffer your holy one to see corruption.* [11] *You will show me the path of life: In your presence is fulness of joy; In your right hand there are pleasures for evermore.*

Messiah's refuge is going to be God the Father (v. 1). His delight will be in the saints (v. 3). God the Father is Messiah's total trust in life (vv. 5-9). God the Father will resurrect the Messiah back to life (vv. 10-11). Though all these points are important, the emphasis of this passage is the fact that Messiah is going to die. Then He is going to be raised from the dead, which is a vital piece of information in the realm of Messianic Christology.

3. Psalm 22:1-31

The thirty-one verses of this psalm can be divided into two sections, with the first section encompassing verses 1-21. This passage can be broken up into six sub-sections. First, verses 1-2 record Messiah's cry for help: [1] *My God, my God, why have you forsaken me? Why are you so far from helping me, and from the words of my groaning?* [2] *O my God, I cry in the daytime, but you answer not; And in the night season, and am not silent.*

Second, verses 3-5 emphasize God's past deliverance of this person: [3] *But you are holy, O you that inhabits the praises of Israel.* [4] *Our fathers trusted in you: They trusted, and you did deliver them.* [5] *They cried unto you, and were delivered: They trusted in you, and were not put to shame.*

Third, verses 6-8 point out that the Messiah is going to be despised:

[6] *But I am a worm, and no man; A reproach of men, and despised of the people.* [7] *All they that see me laugh me to scorn: They shoot out the lip, they shake the head, saying,* [8] *Commit yourself unto Jehovah; Let him deliver him: Let him rescue him, seeing he delights in him.*

Notice three things here: He is going to be reproached by the people (v. 6). He is going to be scorned (v. 7). He is going to be taunted (v. 8).

Fourth, verses 9-11 note that God is the Messiah's total trust since His birth:

[9] *But you are he that took me out of the womb; You did make me trust when I was upon my mother's breasts.* [10] *I was cast upon you from the womb; You are my God since my mother bore me.* [11] *Be not far from me; for trouble is near; For there is none to help.*

Fifth, verses 12-18 give a description of His agony:

> *12 Many bulls have compassed me; Strong bulls of Bashan have beset me round. 13 They gape upon me with their mouth, As a ravening and a roaring lion. 14 I am poured out like water, And all my bones are out of joint: My heart is like wax; It is melted within me. 15 My strength is dried up like a potsherd; And my tongue cleaves to my jaws; And you have brought me into the dust of death. 16 For dogs have compassed me: A company of evil-doers have enclosed me; They pierced my hands and my feet. 17 I may count all my bones; They look and stare upon me. 18 They part my garments among them, And upon my vesture do they cast lots.*

We learn that He is going to be surrounded and stared at (vv. 12-13). Furthermore, He will suffer physical agony (vv. 14-17a). He will be *poured out like water*, which means extreme perspiration. His bones will be *out of joint*. His heart will be like *melted wax*, which means He will have a ruptured heart. His strength will be gone. His tongue will cleave to the roof of His mouth, emphasizing extreme dryness as a result of thirst. His hands and feet will be pierced. His bones will protrude under His skin, as well as be out of joint. In other words, His physical agony will be tremendous. Finally, we learn that His clothing will be divided among His tormentors (v. 17b).

Sixth, verses 19-21 contain Messiah's prayer for help:

> *19 But be not you far off, O Jehovah: O you my succor, haste you to help me. 20 Deliver my soul from the sword, My darling from the power of the dog. 21 Save me from the lion's mouth; Yea, from the horns of the wild-oxen you have answered me.*

The second main division of Psalm 22 encompasses verses 22-31 where the exaltation of the Messiah is described. This section can also be subdivided into six units.

First, verse 22 notes that Messiah will declare His deliverance in the assembly of God's people: *I will declare your name unto my brethren: In the midst of the assembly will I praise you.* Here again, one can detect a hint of the resurrection. We just read in verses 1-22 about His death. To be able to tell people of His deliverance requires that He be resurrected.

Second, in verse 23, there is a call to Israel to be in awe of God because of what He has done on Messiah's behalf and for what Messiah has done on their behalf: *Ye that fear Jehovah, praise him; All ye the seed of Jacob, glorify him; And stand in awe of him, all ye the seed of Israel.*

Third, verse 24 gives the reason for the praise: *For he has not despised nor abhorred the affliction of the afflicted; Neither has he hid his face from him; But when he cried unto him, he heard.* The reason why Israel should stand in awe of God is that He has delivered the afflicted One.

Fourth, in verse 25, we see that the Messiah will now fulfill all of His vows: *Of you comes my praise in the great assembly: I will pay my vows before them that fear him.*

Fifth, in verses 26-29, it says that God will bear rule over all the earth:

> 26 *The meek shall eat and be satisfied; They shall praise Jehovah that seek after him: Let your heart live for ever.* 27 *All the ends of the earth shall remember and turn unto Jehovah; And all the kindreds of the nations shall worship before you.* 28 *For the kingdom is Jehovah's; And he is the ruler over the nations.* 29 *All the fat ones of the earth shall eat and worship: All they that go down to the dust shall bow before him, Even he that cannot keep his soul alive.*

Sixth, verses 30-31 indicate that God's works are going to be declared to following generations: 30 *A seed shall serve him; It shall be told of the Lord unto the next generation.* 31 *They shall come and shall declare his righteousness Unto a people that shall be born, that he has done it.*

To summarize the key points, we can note that Messiah is going to suffer a very agonizing death. During the course of His death, His garments are going to be divided among His tormentors. His bones will be *out of joint*. He will cry for help, saying, "My God! My God! Why have you forsaken me?" But He will be resurrected from the dead.

4. Psalm 110:1-7

> 1 *Jehovah says unto my Lord, Sit you at my right hand, Until I make your enemies your footstool.* 2 *Jehovah will send forth the rod of your strength out of Zion: Rule you in the midst of your enemies.* 3 *Your people offer themselves willingly In the day of your power, in holy array: Out of the womb of the morning you have the dew of your youth.* 4 *Jehovah has sworn, and will not repent: You are a priest for ever After the order of Melchizedek.* 5 *The Lord at your right hand Will strike through kings in the day of his wrath.* 6 *He will*

judge among the nations, He will fill the places with dead bodies; He will strike through the head in many countries. [7] He will drink of the brook in the way: Therefore will he lift up the head.

Within the seven short verses of Psalm 110, all four periods of the Messianic program are included: the First Coming, the interval (or church age), the Second Coming, and the Messianic Kingdom. The psalm divides into three sections or stanzas, a stanza usually being referred to as a "strophe" in Hebrew poetry.

a. Strophe One—110:1-2

We should note first of all that the psalmist here is David. David was king over all of Israel. He established a Jewish empire by subjugating the surrounding nations and collecting tribute from them. David had no human lord; there was no authority over him except Jehovah Himself. Yet, in verse 1 of this psalm, David speaks of two lords, *The LORD* [Jehovah] *says to my Lord*. (NASB) David is speaking of two personalities here—*Jehovah* and *my Lord*. Considering the fact that David had no human "overlord," who could *my Lord* be? The only way to understand this verse is to see Jehovah as God the Father and "David's Lord" as Messiah. It is Messiah, therefore, who is invited to sit at God's right hand. What we have here is a prophecy which was fulfilled at *Yeshua's* ascension from earth to heaven after His resurrection, when He had completed His redemptive work and sat down at His Father's right hand.

Implicit within this prophecy is the concept of the God-Man. We know from I Kings 2:19 that anyone who sits at a king's right hand must be equal with the king. When one king made a visit of state to another king, he would sit at his host's right hand. Since Messiah is invited to sit at God's right hand, it follows that Messiah must be equal with God.

As to His humanity, Messiah is to be a descendant of David, and as to His deity, He can sit at the right hand of God. He is to sit there for some period of time, until *I make your enemies your footstool.* This statement presupposes the First Coming and its rejection. The First Coming is to be in hostile circumstances. In verse 2, the enemies of verse 1 are said to be in Zion itself. Because the First Coming is rejected, Messiah is invited to sit at the right hand of God for a period of time, until His enemies subject themselves to Him.

b. Strophe Two—110:3-4

Here we find the change of heart looked for in the enemies of Messiah. When Messiah comes a second time, in the day of His power, His people will be willing volunteers.

Then, in verse 4, a new and very important statement is made concerning Messiah: He will be a priest after *the order of Melchizedek*. According to Genesis 14, a priest in this order could be both a priest and a king. This was before the time of Moses, since under the Mosaic Law this would no longer be possible. The Law of Moses demanded that all priests had to be of the tribe of Levi and that kings had to be of the tribe of Judah. In order for this prophecy to be fulfilled, therefore, it is clear that it will be necessary for the Law of Moses and the Levitical order to be removed. Verse 4 also states that Messiah's priesthood and kingship will be eternal.

c. Strophe Three—110:5-7

These verses deal with the Second Coming of the Messiah. He will be the all-conquering King (v. 5). He will destroy the wicked (v. 6). He will have the ultimate and final triumph (v. 7).

The main point this psalm makes concerning the Messiah is that He is going to be both King and Priest, because He will be a priest after the order of Melchizedek. Again, it points out His First Coming, His rejection, His ascension, and His present session at the right hand of God the Father.

5. Proverbs 30:4

> *Who has ascended up into heaven, and descended? Who has gathered the wind in his fists? Who has bound the waters in his garment? Who has established all the ends of the earth? What is his name, and what is his son's name, if you know?*

A series of six questions is asked. The first four require obvious answers, all involving the work of creation and who is able to do this work. The obvious answer to these first four questions is "God." The fifth question is, *What is his name*? The answer is *YHVH*. In Hebrew, these four letters comprise His name. Then comes the sixth—the trick—question. *What is his son's name*? At that point in history when Agur wrote this passage, it was not yet revealed what the name of the Messiah was going to be. Later, Isaiah gives us a number of names and says that He will be called Immanuel. The book of Daniel calls Him the Anointed One, *Mashiach*, Messiah. It is only in the revelation of the New Testament where the answer to this question is to be found. His personal name is *Yeshua*. However, the point of Proverbs 30:4 is that God does have a Son whose name had not yet been revealed.

6. Daniel 9:24-27

More than any other book of the Hebrew Scriptures, the writings of the Prophet Daniel confront us with evidence of the time of Messiah's coming—evidence that many people would rather not see. However, it is there and cannot be ignored. That Daniel was indeed a prophet is well substantiated. *Yeshua* Himself referred to him as *Daniel the prophet* (Mt. 24:15). Daniel accurately prophesied the rise of the Medo-Persian, Greek, and Roman empires, even at a time when the Babylonian Empire, which preceded them all, was at its height. He accurately predicted the fortunes, conflicts, wars, and conspiracies of the two kingdoms of Syria and Egypt between the fracturing of the Greek Empire and the conquest by Rome. He prophesied the role of the Maccabees during this period. It is Daniel's detailed accuracy in his prophecies that has caused many critics to try to give a late date to his book, although no evidence has been discovered that would negate its composition at the time that it claims to have been written. At the very latest, the book was completed around 530 B.C.

The key prophecies which are of interest in our present study are contained in verses 24-27 of Daniel 9:

> [24] *Seventy weeks are decreed upon your people and upon your holy city, to finish transgression, and to make an end of sins, and to make reconciliation for iniquity, and to bring in everlasting righteousness, and to seal up vision and prophecy, and to anoint the most holy.* [25] *Know therefore and discern, that from the going forth of the commandment to restore and to build Jerusalem unto the anointed one, the prince, shall be seven weeks, and threescore and two weeks: it shall be built again, with street and moat, even in troublous times.* [26] *And after the threescore and two weeks shall the anointed one be cut off, and shall have nothing: and the people of the prince that shall come shall destroy the city and the sanctuary; and the end thereof shall be with a flood, and even unto the end shall be war; desolations are determined.* [27] *And he shall make a firm covenant with many for one week: and in the midst of the week he shall cause the sacrifice and the oblation to*

cease; and upon the wing of abominations shall come one that makes desolate; and even unto the full end, and that determined, shall wrath be poured out upon the desolate.

It will be wise to survey the entire chapter in order to see what engendered the prophecy of when Messiah would come.

a. The Background—9:1-2

The date for Daniel's prophecy is *the first year of Darius*, which means that it occurred in the year 539 B.C., about sixty-six or sixty-seven years after the Jews initially went into exile to Babylonia. Daniel was studying the Scriptures, and from these Scriptures he came to understand that the number of years for the completion of *the desolations of Jerusalem* was almost over, since the duration was to be seventy years. It is obvious that he was reading Jeremiah 25 and 29.

Reckoning the seventy years from the year 605 B.C., when the first of three deportations went into exile, would bring the end of the seventy years to 536 B.C. Daniel realized that the captivity had only about three years to go. The city and Temple were not destroyed until 586 B.C., and if the seventy years began then, it would mean the seventy years would not end until 515 B.C. But Daniel's calculation began with 605 B.C., the first deportation—not 597 B.C., the second deportation, nor 586 B.C., the destruction and final deportation.

Daniel not only expected the captivity to end after seventy years (Jer. 29:10), he also expected the termination of *the desolations of Jerusalem*; he acts as if the Messianic Kingdom would immediately follow the Babylonian Captivity. As the Word of God was to be established on the basis of prayer, he prayed, and realizing that the prerequisite for the establishment of the kingdom was the confession of national sin (Lev. 26:40), he confessed the sins of Israel.

b. Daniel's Prayer—9:3-19

In his prayer, Daniel acknowledged Israel's sin and guilt which had been incurred by disobedience to the Law of Moses and by disobedience to the prophets who came after Moses. He then pleaded for mercy. Daniel made his plea on the basis of righteousness—not Israel's, but God's righteousness. He also pleaded for mercy on the basis of God's grace, for Israel did not merit mercy; but the grace of God was, and is, able to extend it anyway.

c. The Arrival of Gabriel—9:20-23

While Daniel was presenting his supplications, he was interrupted; he apparently had intended to say more when Gabriel arrived. The interruption came "about the time of the evening offering." This refers to the daily, regular evening sacrifice that was offered while the Temple stood. Although it had not been practiced for nearly seven decades, Daniel showed his longing for the return from captivity and for the rebuilding of the Temple by remembering the sacrifice.

Gabriel told Daniel that the purpose of his visit was: first, to correct Daniel's misunderstanding concerning when the Messianic Kingdom would be set up; and second, to present God's revelation which contained a timetable for Messiah's First Coming.

d. The Decree of the Seventy Sevens—9:24a

Gabriel's prophecy to Daniel began with the words, *Seventy weeks are decreed upon your people and upon your holy city.* Many English versions, like the one we are using here, have translated the phrase to read seventy *weeks*. But this translation is not totally accurate and has caused some confusion about the meaning of the passage. Most Jews know the Hebrew word for "weeks" (*shavuot*) because of the observance of the Feast of Weeks. However, the word that appears here in the Hebrew text is *shavuim*, which means "sevens." This word refers to a "seven" of anything, with the context determining the content of the "seven." It is similar to the English word "dozen," which means twelve of anything based upon context.

It is obvious here that Daniel had been thinking in terms of years—specifically the seventy years of captivity. He had assumed that the captivity would end after seventy years and that the kingdom would be established. However, Gabriel was using a play upon words in the Hebrew text, pointing out that, insofar as Messiah's kingdom was concerned, it was not seventy "years," but seventy "sevens" of years, or a total of four hundred ninety years (70 × 7).

This period of four hundred ninety years had been *decreed* for the Jewish people and for the holy city of Jerusalem. The Hebrew word translated "decreed" literally means "to cut off" or "to determine." In chapters 2, 7, and 8, God revealed to Daniel the course of future world history, in which Gentiles would have a dominant role over the Jewish people. This lengthy period began with the Babylonian Empire and was to continue until the establishment of Messiah's kingdom. For that reason, it is often referred to as *the times of the Gentiles* (Lk.

21:24). Now the prophet was told that a total of four hundred ninety years was to be "cut out" of the times of the Gentiles. This four hundred ninety-year period had been "determined" or "decreed" for the accomplishment of the final restoration of Israel and the establishment of Messiah's kingdom.

The focus of the program of the seventy sevens was *your people* and *your holy city*. The *people* were Daniel's people, the Jewish people, and the *holy city* was Daniel's city, Jerusalem. Although he had spent the vast majority of his life in the city of Babylon, Jerusalem was still Daniel's city. For Jews, whether they are in the land or outside the land, their city is always Jerusalem—not any other. It is important to note that the program of the seventy sevens does not concern the Gentiles or the church; it concerns the Jewish people and the city of Jerusalem. The program of the seventy sevens concerns both the First Coming and the Second Coming of the Messiah, but it is primarily the First Coming that will be our concern here.

e. The Purpose of the Seventy Sevens—9:24b

Next, Daniel was told by Gabriel that the seventy sevens are to accomplish six purposes. The first three are negative and undesirable elements which will be removed. The second three are positive and desirable elements to be effected.

(1) To finish the transgression

The Hebrew text has the word "the" in front of the word "transgression." It means this period is intended to "finish" a specific sin, **the** *transgression*. In the context of New Testament teaching, this specific, singular transgression is the national sin of Israel, which was the rejection of the Messiahship of *Yeshua* on the grounds that He was demon-possessed. So where it says to *finish the transgression*, it means to put an end to Israel's national sin as just described.

(2) To make an end of sins

The word "sins" is plural and refers to sins in general. The point here is that the second purpose of the seventy sevens is to end sinning among the people of Israel. There will be a total cessation of sinning in Israel, so that Jews will no longer commit sin. This is in keeping with the New Covenant, in Jeremiah 31:34, where there is the clear promise of God that sinning in Israel will cease because all Israel will be saved, down to its smallest member.

(3) To make reconciliation for iniquity

The word "iniquity" refers to internal sin, or the sin-nature, while the word "sins" in the previous phrase refers to external acts of sin. The point here is, that Israel is to be reconciled back to God.

Now, these first three purposes of the program of the seventy sevens relate to the First Coming of the Messiah. They deal with finishing Israel's national sin of rejecting the Messiahship of *Yeshua*, they deal with ending Israel's external acts of sin, and they deal with purging Israel's internal sin-nature, for within the program of the seventy sevens is the final atonement for sin. This all relates to the First Coming of the Messiah. The last three purposes will be accomplished by the program of the Second Coming.

(4) To bring in everlasting righteousness

The Hebrew text reads, "to bring in an age of righteousness." This "age of righteousness" is the Messianic Kingdom.

(5) To seal up vision and prophecy

The term "vision" has to do with oral prophecy, and the term "prophecy" has to do with written prophecies. So this purpose of the seventy sevens is that all prophecy will cease and all Old Testament prophecies will be fulfilled, and they will be fulfilled with the establishment of the Messianic Kingdom. Remember, in Old Testament prophecy, the kingdom was the high point. In New Testament prophecy, the eternal state is the high point, but no Old Testament prophet saw beyond the kingdom to the eternal state.

(6) To anoint the most holy

The Hebrew would be better translated as "to anoint the most holy place." This is a reference to the Millennial Temple, or the fourth Temple (Ez. 40–48).

So these are the six specific things to be accomplished by the program of the seventy sevens, and this program includes the First and the Second Coming of the Messiah.

f. The Start of the Seventy Sevens—9:25a

Daniel was clearly told when the seventy sevens would begin. Gabriel said, *Know therefore and discern, that from the going forth of the commandment to restore and to build Jerusalem.* Thus the seventy sevens would begin with a decree involving the rebuilding of the city of Jerusalem. Not everything in Persian chronology is as clear as we would like to have it, and there are still some gaps in our knowledge of history. However, from what biblical and historical records we do have, there are four possible answers to the question of which decree the passage refers to.

One is the decree of Cyrus, issued somewhere between 538–536 B.C., which concerned the rebuilding of the Temple (II Chron. 36:22–23; Ezra 1:1–4, 6:1–5) and of the city of Jerusalem (Isa. 44:28, 45:13). Another option is the decree of Darius Hystaspes (Ezra 6:6–12), issued in the year 521 B.C., which was a reaffirmation of the decree of Cyrus. A third possibility is the decree of Artaxerxes to Ezra (Ezra 7:11–26), issued in 458 B.C., which contained permission to proceed with the Temple service. The last option is the decree of Artaxerxes to Nehemiah (Neh. 2:1–8), issued in the year 444 B.C. This decree specifically concerned the rebuilding of the walls around Jerusalem. Of these four possibilities, only the first and fourth decrees have any real validity in fulfilling the wording that Gabriel gave to Daniel. It is not necessary for our purpose here to deal with the various arguments of either option, but one thing is certain: by the year 444 B.C., the countdown of the seventy sevens had begun.

g. The First Sixty Nine Sevens—9:25b

The seventy sevens are divided into three separate units: seven sevens, sixty two sevens, and one seven. During the first time period of seven sevens, or forty nine years, Jerusalem would be *built again, with street and moat, even in troublous times.* The second block of time, sixty two sevens, or a total of four hundred thirty four years, immediately followed the first for a total of sixty nine sevens, or four hundred eighty three years. There is no implication of a gap of time between the first and second subdivisions of the seventy sevens.

It is at this point that we are told that the ending point of the sixty nine sevens is to be *unto the anointed one, the prince*, or as the NASB puts it, *until Messiah the Prince.* As clearly as Daniel could have stated it, he taught that Messiah would be here on earth 483 years after the decree to rebuild Jerusalem had been issued.

The obvious conclusion is this: If Messiah was not on earth 483 years after a decree was issued to rebuild Jerusalem, then Daniel was a false prophet and his book has no business being in the Hebrew Scriptures; but if Daniel was correct, and his prophecy was fulfilled, then who was the Messiah of whom he spoke?

h. The Events between the Sixty-Ninth and the Seventieth Seven—9:26

There is going to be a gap of time between the sixty ninth seven and the seventieth seven, and this passage makes it quite clear what will happen. Stepping back in time and looking ahead from Daniel's perspective, we see first that the Messiah will *be cut off, and shall have nothing* (v. 26). The Hebrew word translated as *cut off* is a common word used in the Mosaic Law and simply means "to be killed." The implication of the term is that the Messiah would not only be killed, but also that He would die a penal death by execution.

The Hebrew expression translated *and shall have nothing* has two possible meanings. It may mean "nothingness," emphasizing Messiah's state at death. It can also be translated "but not for Himself," and the meaning would then be that He died for others rather than for Himself," a substitutionary death. The latter meaning would be much more consistent with what the Prophets had to say about the reason for Messiah's death (e.g., Isa. 53:1-12).

The first three purposes of the seventy sevens—to finish the transgression, to make an end of sin, and to make reconciliation for iniquity—have all to be accomplished by some means of atonement. The Law of Moses decreed that atonement is made by blood (Lev. 17:11). It appears that Messiah's death, "not for himself" but for others, would atone for Israel's transgression, sin, and iniquity. The point of this phrase is that between the end of the second subdivision, the sixty ninth seven, and before the start of the seventieth seven, Messiah would be killed and would die a penal, substitutionary death.

During this interim period, it would also happen that *the people of the prince that shall come shall destroy the city and the sanctuary; and the end thereof shall be with a flood.* The city and the Temple which were to be rebuilt because of the decree by which the seventy sevens began would now be destroyed, sometime after the Messiah was *cut off*, Jerusalem and the Temple would suffer another destruction. Our knowledge of history during this period is extensive: The people responsible for this deed were the Romans, and Jerusalem and the Temple were destroyed in the year A.D. 70.

Based upon this verse, it is also clear that the Messiah should have both come and died prior to the year A.D. 70. If such an event did not take place, then Daniel was a false prophet. If such an event did occur, then the question must be answered: Who was that Messiah who was killed before A.D. 70?

Verse 26 closes with the prediction that *even unto the end shall be war; desolations are determined.* For the remainder of the interval between the sixty ninth seven and the seventieth seven, the land would be ravaged by war, and its resulting condition would be desolation. All this would set the stage for the final, or seventieth, seven.

i. The Seventieth Seven—9:27

From where we stand in time today, the last seven years of Daniel's prophecy are still future, but it is with their conclusion that all six purposes of verse 24 will reach their fulfillment.

Four key observations can be made about this verse. First, the seventieth seven will begin only with the signing of a seven-year covenant, or treaty, between Israel and a major Gentile political leader. The pronoun "he" in verse 27 goes back to its nearest antecedent, in verse 26, which is not the Messiah but *the prince that shall come*. This *prince* has been a topic of Daniel's earlier prophecies, in chapters 7-8. This political leader is better known to Christians as the Antichrist.

Second, in the middle of the seventieth seven, that is, after three and a half years, this Gentile leader will break his treaty with Israel and cause a cessation of the sacrificial system. The implication here is that by this time, a temple in Jerusalem will have been rebuilt; the sacrificial system of Moses will have been re-instituted, then be stopped by force.

Third, the result of the breaking of this covenant is that this third Temple will now be desecrated. The "abomination" refers to an image or an idol. Just as it was in the days of Antiochus Epiphanes, so it will be again in the future when a Gentile ruler will defile the third Temple by means of idolatry.

Fourth, the "abomination" is to be followed by wrath and desolation, persecution and warfare, for the remaining half of the seventieth seven, or the final three and a half years. This is similar to the trials and tribulations the rabbis spoke of as preparation for the establishment of the Messianic Kingdom. They referred to these terrible days as "the footsteps of the Messiah," and also as "the birth-pangs of the Messiah." Once those days have run their course, the last three things predicted in verse 24 will occur. The age of righteousness will be brought in; the most holy place will be anointed; and every vision and prophecy will be fulfilled. At this point the Messianic Kingdom for which the Prophet Daniel yearned will be set up.

Obviously, the Messianic Kingdom requires the Messiah to rule as king. This means the Messiah will come after the seventieth seven. Yet earlier, Daniel stated that the Messiah would come and be killed after the sixty ninth seven. This would appear to be a contradiction unless Daniel was speaking of two comings of the Messiah. The first time was to be after the sixty ninth seven, when He would die a penal, substitutionary death for the sins of Israel and accomplish the first three purposes listed in verse 24. The second time, still future, was to be after the seventieth seven, when He will establish the Messianic Kingdom and accomplish the last three things of verse 24. There is also an important implication here that should not be missed: The Messiah would be killed after His First Coming, yet He would be alive at His Second Coming. The implication is that the Messiah would be resurrected from the dead after He was killed.

j. Summary

This dramatic prophecy features certain things in very clear and unmistakable terms:

1. The Messiah was to be on earth four hundred eighty three years after the decree to rebuild Jerusalem.
2. After His appearance on earth, He was to be killed—not for His own sins, but rather for those of others—and the death He would die was to be the death of the penalty of the law.
3. The death of the Messiah had to come sometime before Jerusalem and the Temple were destroyed again; this occurred in the year A.D. 70.
4. Some time after the destruction of Jerusalem and the Temple, and following a long period of warfare, the seventieth seven will commence. Once it has run its course, Messiah's kingdom and age of righteousness will be established. For that to occur, the implication is that the Messiah who was killed would return.

But who is this Messiah? Only one man fulfills all that is required in this passage: *Yeshua* of Nazareth. He was born into the Jewish world and proclaimed His Messiahship four hundred eighty three years after the decree to rebuild and restore Jerusalem was issued. In the year A.D. 30, *Yeshua* was executed by crucifixion. Daniel indicated that He would be cut off—not for Himself, but rather for others. Isaiah 53 also prophesied the death of the Messiah, pointing out that He would die a substitutionary death on behalf of His people Israel. The teaching of the New Testament is that *Yeshua* died a penal death by taking upon Himself the penalty of the law as a substitute for His people. In keeping with Daniel 9:24, He died for the purpose of making an atonement for sins. Three days after His death, He was resurrected. Finally, the New Testament proclaims the fact that He will someday return to set up His kingdom and the age of righteousness.

If Daniel was right, then Messiah came and died prior to the year A.D. 70. If Daniel was right, then there are no other options for who the Messiah is: *Yeshua* of Nazareth. If Daniel was right, this *Yeshua* is destined to return and to set up the Messianic Kingdom.

7. First Chronicles 17:10b-14

> [10b] *Moreover I tell you that Jehovah will build you a house.* [11] *And it shall come to pass, when your days are fulfilled that you must go to be with your fathers, that I will set up your seed after you, who shall be of your sons; and I will establish his kingdom.* [12] *He shall build me a house, and I will establish his throne for ever.* [13] *I will be his father, and he shall be my son: and I will not take my lovingkindness away from him, as I took it from him that was before you;* [14] *but I will settle him in my house and in my kingdom for ever; and his throne shall be established for ever.*

The Davidic Covenant promised to David an eternal dynasty, an eternal throne, and an eternal kingdom (II Sam. 7:11b-16). The verses above now tell us that a distant seed of David will be an eternal person (v. 14); this guarantees that David's dynasty, kingdom, and throne will last forever. So, in the progressive revelation of Scripture, the seed concept has been narrowing. As the seed of the woman, Messiah had to come out of humanity; He could not be an angel. As the seed of Abraham, He had to be of the nation of Israel; He could not be a Gentile. As arising out of Judah, He had to be of the tribe of Judah. As being of the seed of David, He had to specifically be of the family of David.

There is one further limitation put upon Messiah's descent. In Jeremiah 22:24-30 the family of Jeconiah is cursed by God; no descendant of his could ever sit on the throne of David. So Messiah will be descended from David but not from the line of Jeconiah.

D. Conclusion

Having studied the Messianic prophecies of the Hebrew Scriptures, we should now be able to present the entire gospel purely from the pages of the Old

Testament, just the way the apostles did. This is Messianic Christology, and this now brings us to the next main division of Christology: the names of the Messiah.[8]

[8] Pop-Quiz on page 56.

E. Questions and Study Suggestions

Study Suggestion 1: Read Acts 8:26-40. Would you be able to preach *Yeshua* as Philip did—which is, by only using the Hebrew Scriptures? Many believers are seeking to hear from God, always wondering what it might be He would have them do. What if He wanted you to know the Messianic prophecies of the Old Testament so well that you could use them to teach as Philip taught?

Study Suggestion 2: Many people take notes in the margins of their Bibles to remind them of things they have learned. A list of the Old Testament prophecies about the Messiah, small enough to be inserted in your Bible, might be a useful tool as well. Why not develop such a list with the help of this book?

Pop-Quiz: Having carefully studied the Old Testament prophecies which give a clear picture of Messiah's First Coming, can you now answer the following questions?

a. Was *Yeshua's* mother, Miriam, really a virgin? Where was this prophesied and why is it important?

b. Which of the prophecies predicts that He would be born in Bethlehem?

c. Where do the Hebrew Scriptures predict the death and resurrection of the Messiah?

Chapter III

The Names and Titles of the Messiah

Altogether there are fifteen names of the Messiah which will be discussed in this chapter. Some are proper names, some are descriptive names, and some are titles.

A. Names

1. *Yeshua*–Jesus

By far the most common name of the Messiah among English speakers is Jesus. This name originates from the Greek *Iesous*, which, in turn, comes from the Hebrew name *Yeshua*, meaning "salvation." This is the point of Matthew 1:21, when the angel told Joseph to call *his name Yeshua; for it is he that shall save his people from their sins.*

Yeshua is a human name, thus emphasizing the Messiah's humanity. The root of this name is *Yashah*, which is the same root of some other biblical names, such as Joshua, Isaiah, and Hosea. These are all closely related names, coming from the same Hebrew root, meaning "to save." The name *Yeshua* emphasizes not only His humanity, it also emphasizes the work He came to do: the work of salvation.

2. *Christos*–Christ

The second name of the Messiah for English speakers is "Christ," a term which comes from the Greek word *Christos*. This term is simply the Greek equivalent of the Hebrew word for "Messiah," *Mashiach*. Both *Christos* and *Mashiach* mean "anointed" or "anointed one." While *Mashiach* becomes "Messiah" in English, *Christos* transliterates as "Christ."

The Greek term may be used as a title to designate the "fulfiller of Israelite expectation of a deliverer, *the Anointed One, the Messiah, the Christ*."[9] In these examples, "Jesus the Christ" would be a good rendering in English. At other times, *Christos* "does not mean the Messiah in general, but a very definite Messiah, *Yeshua*, who now is called Christ, not as a title but as a name:"[10] Examples of this are Acts 24:24 where we find *Christ Jesus* (Messiah *Yeshua*) and Romans 1:4 where it says *Jesus Christ* (*Yeshua* Messiah). The first century Jewish audience understood in any case that *Christos*, when applied to *Yeshua*, was not His last name, but indicated that He was the awaited deliverer. He was called *Iesous Christos* (Jesus Christ). Gentiles might have confused this even back then, and English speakers today certainly make the mistake of assuming that "Christ" is Jesus' last name by not understanding the meaning or significance of the word "Christ."

The name is used of *Yeshua* in many places, such as Luke 2:11. It emphasizes His office, and there are three specific implications concerning this office of *Christos*, or Messiah. First, it implies that *Yeshua* was appointed. In fact, according to Acts 2:36, He was appointed by God the Father: *Let all the house of Israel therefore know assuredly, that God has made him both Lord and Christ, this Jesus whom ye crucified.*

The second implication of the name *Christos* is that there is a sacred relationship between the Anointed One and God. God did the appointing, and He also did the anointing. This sacred and special relationship is a Father-Son relationship.

---

[9] Walter Bauer, Frederick Danker, W. F. Arndt, and F. W. Gingrich, *A Greek-English Lexicon of the New Testament and Other Early Christian Literature*. 3rd Edition (Chicago: University of Chicago Press, 2000), p. 1091.

[10] Ibid.

The third implication of the name *Christos* is that the anointing communicates the Spirit's authority, a point made in Psalm 2:2, 45:7, Acts 4:27, and 10:38. This special communication of the Spirit's authority happened at *Yeshua's* baptism.

3. *Logos*–Word

The third name of the Messiah is *Logos*. This Greek name means "word." It emphasizes the Messiah as the expression, the revealer, and the one who manifests God. The key verses are John 1:1-2, 14, and 18:

> [1] *In the beginning was the Word, and the Word was with God, and the Word was God.* [2] *The same was in the beginning with God.*
>
> ***
>
> [14] *And the Word became flesh, and dwelt among us (and we beheld his glory, glory as of the only begotten from the Father), full of grace and truth.*
>
> ***
>
> [18] *No man has seen God at any time; the only begotten Son, who is in the bosom of the Father, he has declared him.*

This particular title implies five important truths about the Messiah. The first implication is in verse 1: He was *In the beginning*. This teaches His preexistence. He existed time itself. Furthermore, this verse points out that He has existed as long as God has existed. Since God has existed for all eternity past, this would mean that *Yeshua* has existed for all eternity past.

The second implication of the name *Logos* is that He was *with God*. The statement in John 1:1, *the Word was with God*, means that in some sense, He is distinct from God. He is distinct from God in that He is not God the Father, nor is He God the Holy Spirit.

The third implication of the name *Logos* is that He is God. Verse 1 not only states, *the Word was with God*, it also states, *the Word was God*; therefore, He is deity. On one hand, He is distinct from God in that He is neither the Father nor the Holy Spirit; on the other hand, He is the same as God because He is the second member of the Trinity, God the Son.

The fourth implication of the name *Logos* is that He reveals God the Father to man. Being the Father's manifestation, man can know God by knowing His Son.

The fifth implication of the name *Logos* is that *the Word became flesh* (Jn. 1:14). He was the God-Man in that He was both God and man at the very same time. He was the visible God.

4. Begotten

The fourth name of the Messiah is *Begotten*, or in Greek *to gennomenon hagion*. The name is used in the context of the virgin birth and found in Luke 1:35:

> *And the angel answered and said unto her, The Holy Spirit shall come upon you, and the power of the Most High shall overshadow you: wherefore also the holy thing which is begotten shall be called the Son of God.*

5. The Only Begotten

The fifth name of Messiah is *Only Begotten*, or in Greek *monogeneis*. When the Messiah is called the Only Begotten, the eternal relationship between the Father and the Son is emphasized. This name is found in the following passages:

- ✡ John 1:14: *And the Word became flesh, and dwelt among us (and we beheld his glory, glory as of the only begotten from the Father), full of grace and truth.*
- ✡ John 1:18: *No man has seen God at any time; the only begotten Son, who is in the bosom of the Father, he has declared him.*
- ✡ John 3:16: *For God so loved the world, that he gave his only begotten Son, that whosoever believes on him should not perish, but have eternal life.*
- ✡ John 3:18: *He that believes on him is not judged: he that believes not has been judged already, because he has not believed on the name of the only begotten Son of God.*
- ✡ I John 4:9: *Herein was the love of God manifested in us, that God has sent his only begotten Son into the world that we might live through him.*

Some cultic groups teach that the very fact Messiah is called Begotten or Only Begotten means that He Himself did not eternally exist, but was brought into existence by God the Father. This is a misunderstanding of how such terms are used. When *Yeshua* is called by the term "Begotten," it emphasizes His human, virgin birth, but says nothing about His deity. When He is called the Only Begotten, the *monogeneis*, His eternal relationship with God the Father and His uniqueness are emphasized.

It is necessary to understand what is being emphasized by these two names because the terms "son" or "sons" of God are applied to creatures other than the Begotten or Only Begotten Son. For example, angels were created by God, so they are called "the sons of God" (Job 38:4-7; Col. 1:16). Israel was formed by God, so Israel is the national son of God (Ex. 4:22; Is. 64:8; Hos. 11:1). Adam was created by God, so Adam is called "the son of God" (Lk. 3:38). Believers are a new creation by virtue of the regeneration of the Holy Spirit, so they, too, are called "the sons" or "children of God" (Jn. 1:12; Rom. 8:14; II Cor. 6:18; Gal. 3:26; I Jn. 3:1).

To distinguish *Yeshua* as the eternal Son of God from those who became sons by virtue of God's creation, such as the angels, Israel, and believers, the term "Only Begotten," or *monogeneis*, is used. It emphasizes His uniqueness as the Son of God. He had this relationship through all eternity. Rather than *Only Begotten* being evidence that *Yeshua* Himself was created, it is actually evidence against it. This term emphasizes His eternal relationship with God the Father.

6. The First Begotten

The sixth name for the Messiah is *First Begotten*. The Greek word for this name is *prototokos*, meaning "first-begotten." It has four slightly different implications than the names *Begotten* and *Only Begotten*. The first implication is that *Yeshua* is the elder in relation to all creation—not in the sense that He was created first, but in the sense that all things were created through Him. Because all things were created through Him, He is the elder in relation to all creation. The second implication is that He is antecedent to all things, meaning He existed before all creation. The third implication is that He is also the cause of all things in that all things were created through Him. The fourth implication is that He has preeminence above all other things (Col. 1:15-18; Heb. 1).

Three aspects are embodied within the concept of *Yeshua* as the *prototokos*. First, He is the firstborn of all creation in that He pre-existed the material universe (Col. 1:15).

The second quality embodied in the concept of *Yeshua* as the *prototokos* is that He was Miriam's first child (Lk. 2:7). Miriam had at least six other children, four sons and at least two daughters. *Yeshua* was the first of her brood, so He is the *First Begotten* in this sense.

The third quality related to *Yeshua's* being the *First Begotten* is that He is also *the firstfruits of them that are asleep* (I Cor. 15:20), or *the firstborn of the dead* (Rev. 1:5). This has caused some confusion. How could *Yeshua* be called "the Firstborn of the Resurrection" when others were resurrected before Him? The difference is found in the two types of resurrections. The first type of resurrection is a restoration back to natural life. Those who experienced this type of resurrection were restored back to natural life, but died again later. All those who were resurrected before the resurrection of *Yeshua* experienced this first type of resurrection. The second type of resurrection is the kind that leads to true resurrection life, when one is no longer subject to death. It means that "corruption has put on incorruption and mortality has put on immortality." *Yeshua* was the first one to be resurrected in this type of true resurrection (Col. 1:18; Rev. 1:5). In that sense, He is "the Firstborn of the Resurrection."

7. *Kurios*–Lord

The seventh name for the Messiah is *Lord*. The Greek word for "Lord" is *kurios*, which traditionally is used in one of two ways. First, it is used as a title of respect. Sometimes *Yeshua* is called "Lord" only in the sense of having a title of respect. This usage of *kurios* is applied to both God and man. The second usage is that of ownership in that one is a lord because he owns something. For example, he is "lord of the house" because he owns a house, or he is "lord of a slave" because he owns a slave. The name *kurios*, Lord, with this usage is also used of both God and man. However, there is a third usage of the term *kurios* that is only used of God, never of man. This usage emphasizes deity. Sometimes *Yeshua* is clearly called "Lord" not only as a title of respect and not only to emphasize His ownership of something, but also to emphasize His deity. In this case, *kurios* becomes a unique name of *Yeshua*. A few examples of this usage in the New Testament are Matthew 8:2, Luke 2:11, Acts 2:36, and Revelation 19:16.

8. *Theos*–God

The eighth name of the Messiah is *Theos*, which is a Greek word meaning "god." *Yeshua* is called by the term *Theos* in various passages of the New Testament.

Perhaps the most famous example is John 1:1: *In the beginning was the Word, and the Word was with God, and the Word was God.*

Other passages include John 1:18 and 20:28, where Thomas stated, *my Lord* [*Kurios*] *and my God* [*Theos*]. *Yeshua* is also called *Theos* in Romans 9:5, Titus 2:13, Hebrews 1:8, and I John 5:20.

9. *Elohim*–God

The ninth name for the Messiah is *Elohim*. Just as the Greek word *Theos*, the Hebrew name *Elohim* means "God." Isaiah 9:6 states, *For unto us a child is born, unto us a son is given; and the government shall be upon his shoulder: and his name shall be called Wonderful, Counsellor, Mighty God* [*Elohim*], *Everlasting Father, Prince of Peace.* We know that this verse refers to the Messiah, so the Messiah is *Elohim*. We also know that *Yeshua* is *Elohim* by looking at Old Testament passages which are quoted by the New Testament. Isaiah 40:3 is one example; it speaks of preparing the way for God. Luke 3:4 says that this Old Testament prophecy was fulfilled by John the Baptist as he came to prepare the way for *Yeshua*. Hebrews 1:8, 9 says that Psalm 45:6 is speaking of God (*Elohim*) the Son. So it is quite clear that *Elohim* is used of the Son, as well as the Father and the Spirit.

10. *YHVH*

The tenth name of the Messiah is the unique name of God Himself that is comprised of four Hebrew letters. These Hebrew letters transliterate into the English letters YHVH and are called the Tetragrammaton. This unique name of God is often translated as *Yahweh* or *Jehovah*. However, because of the Jewish people's strict adherence to the commandment, *You shall not take the name of Jehovah your God in vain*, the proper pronunciation has been forgotten.

The Messiah is given this name in Jeremiah 23:5-6:

> [5] *Behold, the days come, says Jehovah, that I will raise unto David a righteous Branch, and he shall reign as king and deal wisely, and shall execute justice and righteousness in the land.* [6] *In his days Judah shall be saved, and Israel shall dwell safely; and this is his name whereby he shall be called: Jehovah our righteousness.*

In verse 5, a descendant of David sits upon David's throne, and in verse 6, Jeremiah says that this human descendant of David has God's name in that He is called *Jehovah our righteousness*.

A second passage where the name Jehovah is clearly applied to the Messiah is Zechariah 12:10, in which Jehovah states, *they shall look unto me whom they have pierced*. Of course, the One who was pierced was the Second Person of the Trinity, the God-Man, *Yeshua* the Messiah.

Another way to see that the Messiah is given the name *YHVH* is to note how the Old Testament passages in which the name is used are quoted in the New Testament and applied to *Yeshua*. Several examples can be listed. Psalm 68:18 speaks about *YHVH*, and this verse is quoted and applied to the Messiah in Ephesians 4:8-10. The same is true for Psalm 102:25-27 in Hebrews 1:10-12, Isaiah 6:1-13 in John 12:38-41, and Isaiah 8:13-14 in I Peter 2:7-8. These quotations show that God's personal name, *YHVH*, is applied to *Yeshua*.[11]

B. Titles

There are a total of twelve different titles given to the Messiah. The first five are general titles relating either to His person or to His work. The remaining seven titles all deal with the aspect of His Sonship. They will be dealt with in chapter five.

1. Lamb of God

This title of the Messiah is found in John 1:29 and 36:

> [29] *On the morrow he sees Yeshua coming unto him, and says, Behold, the Lamb of God, that takes away the sin of the world!*
>
> * * *
>
> [36] *and he looked upon Yeshua as he walked, and said, Behold, the Lamb of God!*

---

[11] Study Suggestion 1 on page 67.

By giving Him the title of *the Lamb of God*, John connected *Yeshua* with two Old Testament elements: the paschal lamb of Exodus 12 and the Messianic Lamb of Isaiah 53. The title *Lamb of God* emphasizes that He is the fulfillment of the Feast of Passover and that He will be the final Passover sacrifice.[12]

2. Mediator

There are two aspects to *Yeshua's* role as mediator. First, He is the mediator between God and man (I Tim. 2:5). Second, He is the mediator of the New Covenant. In Hebrews 8:6, He is called *the mediator of a better covenant*, and in Hebrews 9:15 and 12:24, He is *the mediator of a new covenant*. The point here is that, on one hand, He is the mediator between God and man, so He is functioning as a priest. On the other hand, as the mediator of the New—and better—Covenant, He is functioning as the covenant-sealer or signatory.

3. Intercessor

That *Yeshua* is our intercessor is brought out in Romans 8:34: *who is he that condemns? It is Messiah Yeshua that died, yea rather, that was raised from the dead, who is at the right hand of God, who also makes intercession for us.* Hebrews 7:25 says, *Wherefore also he is able to save to the uttermost them that draw near unto God through him, seeing he ever lives to make intercession for them.*

Functioning as our intercessor is part of His high priestly ministry in that He intercedes on behalf of the believer before God. The picture is that as mediator, He represents God to man, and as intercessor, He represents man to God.

4. Advocate

The title of *Advocate* is applied to *Yeshua* in I John 2:1: *My little children, these things write I unto you that ye may not sin. And if any man sin, we have an Advocate with the Father, Yeshua Messiah the righteous.*

---

[12] Study Suggestion 2 on page 67.

The term *advocate* has the concept of being a lawyer. The reason that believers need *Yeshua* as their advocate is because of Satan's title as the accuser of the brethren (Job 1:1-12; 2:4-5; Zech. 3:1-2; Rev. 12:10). Satan still has access to heaven to appear before the very presence of God. He does so for one reason, which is to accuse the brethren. If a believer falls into a state of unconfessed sin, sooner or later Satan will appear before God the Father to accuse that believer. This is the exact reason why believers still need the ministry of *Yeshua* as an advocate. Whenever Satan has any grounds to accuse a saint, *Yeshua* can say, "Lay that sin upon my account. I have already paid the penalty for that sin when I died for that person on the cross."[13]

5. Savior

This particular title emphasizes the Messiah's work of salvation in that He is the One who saves. As Messiah, He is able to save. By the shedding of His blood, He has provided the basis of salvation. He is viewed as the Savior throughout the New Testament in verses such as Luke 2:11, John 4:42, Acts 5:31, I Timothy 1:1, Titus 2:13, and II Peter 2:20.

[13] Study Suggestion 3 on page 67.

C. Questions and Study Suggestions

Study Suggestion 1: Knowing the names of *Yeshua* gives us an insight into who He really is. Meditate on the names we have looked at so far and develop a working definition of what you know about His person, work, and role in God's plan of the ages.

Study Suggestion 2: It is impossible to fully understand the idea of the Lamb of God without understanding the Jewish roots of this title. Read Exodus 12 and Isaiah 53. If at all possible, try to watch a Passover *Seder* presentation by Dr. Fruchtenbaum or other Messianic Jews. These presentations are available online or can be bought as DVDs. They will greatly broaden the horizon in regards to this wonderful title of *Yeshua*.

Study Suggestion 3: By way of application, believers should live the kind of spiritual lifestyle that will not give Satan any basis for accusations. Try to develop an idea of what such a lifestyle could look like.

Chapter IV

The Preexistence of the Messiah

The Scriptures clearly teach that the Messiah existed before His actual physical appearance on the earth. He existed as the Second Person of the triune God, and so His preexistence is inseparable from His deity. Those who deny His eternality also deny His deity. We will be discussing the topic in four categories and look at theophanies, statements in the Old and the New Testaments, and Messiah's own assertions.

A. THEOPHANIES

The word "theophany" describes the visible manifestations of God that we find throughout the Old Testament. The rabbinic/Jewish term of these manifestations is *Shechinah*. They came in various forms. Sometimes God appeared as the Angel of Jehovah, or the Angel of the Lord. At other times, He appeared as light, fire, or cloud. Sometimes He used a combination of these things. Lightning and thunder and various other manifestations could be theophanies when the invisible God decided to take on visible form and His omnipresence became localized. Whenever this visible, localized presence of God took place, it is known as a theophany.

The Angel of Jehovah is of unique interest for Messianic Christology. It is quite evident from the Hebrew Scriptures that this Angel was the Second Person of the Trinity, the Messiah Himself. The term "Angel of Jehovah" is not to be taken as a title, but, following Hebrew grammar, it always functions as a proper name. This individual is always considered distinct from all other angels and is unique. The term never appears in the plural as "the angels of Jehovah" or "the angels of the God," but rather there are three—and only three—different expressions which are used:

1. The Angel of Jehovah—*Malach YHVH*, always singular.
2. The Angel of the God—*Malach Ha-Elohim*, always singular with the definite article.
3. The angels of God—*Malachei Elohim*, plural, and never with a definite article.

The third of these expressions is used in general terms of ordinary angels. The first two expressions are both used to describe a very special and distinct individual—the Angel of Jehovah. We can see this in Judges 6:20–21, where the same person is described first, in verse 20, as "the Angel of the God," and then, in verse 21, as "the Angel of Jehovah." This is also brought out in Judges 13:3, where we find a reference to "the Angel of Jehovah," and later, in verse 9, this same individual is called "the Angel of the God."

Consistently throughout the Hebrew text, there is a distinction made between ordinary angels and this unique person referred to as both "the Angel of *YHVH*" and "the Angel of the God." He is clearly revealed as being different in stature, nature, person, and essence from ordinary angels.

1. The Angel of Jehovah is Jehovah

What the Hebrew grammar is trying to show is that this unique individual is in fact God Himself. In virtually every context in which He appears, He is referred to as both the Angel of Jehovah and Jehovah Himself. There are many examples which show this:

- ✡ In Genesis 16:7–14, there are four references to the Angel of Jehovah (vv. 7, 9, 10, and 11). But then in verse 13, the reference is to Jehovah Himself, and so Hagar names the place "You are a God that sees."
- ✡ In Genesis 22:9–16, the Angel is called the Angel of Jehovah (vv. 11 and 15). In verse 12, He is also referred to as God, and in verse 16, He is called Jehovah.

- ✡ In Genesis 31:11–13, the reference is literally to "the Angel of the God" (v. 11), but when He speaks in verse 13, He says, *I am the God of Beth-el.*
- ✡ Genesis 32:24–30 is the very famous passage which describes Jacob wrestling with the Angel. But with whom is he really wrestling? Verse 28 states, *for you have striven with God*. After this, in verse 30, Jacob declares, *I have seen God face to face.* The Angel with whom he wrestled is recognized to be God Himself.
- ✡ In Exodus 3:1–5, it is the Angel of Jehovah who is in the burning bush (v. 2), but verse 4 says that *God called unto him out of the midst of the bush*.
- ✡ In Judges 2:1, the Angel of Jehovah claims to be responsible for the Exodus and for making the covenant with Israel. A comparison with Exodus 19:4 clearly shows that it was God Himself who was responsible for both these things; the two are synonymous.
- ✡ In Judges 6:11–24, He is said to be the Angel of Jehovah four times (vv. 11, 12, 20, 21), and four times He is described as Jehovah Himself (vv. 14, 16, 22, 23).
- ✡ In Judges 13:2–24, He is referred to as the Angel of Jehovah nine times (vv. 3, 9, 13, 15, 16, 17, 18, 20, 21). But then in verse 22, He is said to be God Himself. Note also in verse 18 that this Angel's name is *Wonderful*. In our study of Isaiah 9:6, it was pointed out that *pele*, the Hebrew word for "wonderful," is only used of God, never of man or an angel. The very fact that He claims this name for Himself shows that He is not a common angel, but God Himself.

Beyond the book of Judges, the Angel of Jehovah virtually disappears from Jewish history. He only appears twice more in the Scriptures. In Isaiah 37:36, He slaughters the Assyrian army, and in the first six chapters of Zechariah, He is the One who gives Zechariah his eight visions.

2. The Uniqueness of His Person

In Isaiah 42:8, God says of Himself, *I am Jehovah, that is my name; and my glory will I not give to another, neither my praise unto graven images.* When we compare this statement with Exodus 23:21, we are better able to understand the unique nature of the Angel of Jehovah. In Exodus 23:20–23, it is God who is speaking, and He says:

> [20] *Behold, I send an angel before you, to keep you by the way, and to bring you into the place which I have prepared.* [21] *Take ye heed before him, and hearken unto his voice; provoke him not; for he will not pardon your transgression: for my name is in him.* [22] *But if you shall indeed hearken unto his voice, and do all that I speak; then I will be an enemy unto your enemies, and an adversary unto your adversaries.* [23] *For mine angel shall go before you, and bring you in unto the Amorite, and the Hittite, and the Perizzite, and the Canaanite, the Hivite, and the Jebusite: and I will cut them off.*

In Exodus 23:20, God says that this Angel will lead the people of Israel throughout the Exodus until they come into the land. This is consistent with Judges 2:1, as discussed above in point 1.

In verse 21, several commands are given. Israel is commanded to be obedient to this Angel and not to provoke Him to anger. This Angel commands the people's absolute obedience. Why? Because *my Name is in him*.

This Angel is very special for several reasons:

1. He *will not pardon your transgression* (v. 21). He has the power to forgive sins, a prerogative that only God has.
2. God's name is in Him (v. 21). The name is Jehovah, a name given only to members of the Godhead; this Angel has that name.
3. There are blessings for obeying Him (v. 22)
4. He is the Angel of the Exodus (v. 23)

Later, in Exodus 32:34–35, we read that despite the warnings, the people did indeed rebel against this Angel and were punished for it.

Hosea 12:3–5 also says that this Angel has the very name of God in Him. The fact that He has all four letters of God's name within His name indicates that He is actually God Himself.

When Isaiah 63:7–14 describes Him as "the Angel of God's presence," it is in fact saying that He is the Second Person of the Trinity.[14]

---

[14] Question 1 on page 78.

B. Old Testament Statements

There are two key statements in the Old Testament that support the concept of the preexistence of Messiah.

The first one is found in Isaiah 9:6. The first part of the verse emphasizes His humanity—*a child is born, a son is given*. In the second part of the verse, we learn about the names given to Him—*Wonderful, Counsellor, the Mighty God, the Father of Eternity, the Prince of Peace*. These are divine names.[15] They emphasize His preexistence in that, although He was born in His humanity at a given point in history, through His deity He was, of course, preexistent.

A second Old Testament statement about the preexistence of the Messiah is Micah 5:2: *But you, Bethlehem Ephrathah, which are little to be among the thousands of Judah, out of you shall one come forth unto me that is to be ruler in Israel; whose goings forth are from of old, from everlasting.* The first part of the verse talks about His birth in Bethlehem, but the verse goes on to say that His existence has been *from of old, from everlasting*. These are the strongest Old Testament terms for eternity past. So as to His humanity, *Yeshua* had a definite beginning in Bethlehem, yet He existed before His actual birth in Bethlehem.[16]

C. New Testament Statements

The New Testament makes very clear statements about the preexistence of Messiah. John 1:1-2 states: *1 In the beginning was the Word, and the Word was with God, and the Word was God. 2 The same was in the beginning with God.*

Here the point is made that *the Word*, the *Logos*, was always with God. He was in the very beginning with God. As long as God has existed, the Son has existed. He existed before His physical birth of a virgin in Bethlehem.

John 1:14-15 gives more detail about the Word:

[15] These names were discussed in chapter 2 of this book.

[16] Question 2 on page 78.

> [14] *And the Word became flesh, and dwelt among us (and we beheld his glory, glory as of the only begotten from the Father), full of grace and truth.* [15] *John bears witness of him, and cries, saying, This was he of whom I said, He that comes after me is become before me: for he was before me.*

In verse 14, John points out that the Word, who was *in the beginning with God*, at some point in human history took on human form by becoming "flesh," or a man. So while His human nature had a definite beginning, His divine nature was preexistent. In verse 15, John elaborates on this and says that while *Yeshua* was in one sense after him, He was also before him. In what way was the Messiah both after John and before him? *Yeshua* was after John in the sense that He was born six months after him. So in His humanity, He was six months younger than John. But as to His deity, He was preexistent, so He was also before John.

In John 1:30, John repeats this point when he says, *This is he of whom I said, After me comes a man who is become before me: for he was before me.*

Paul makes a similar point in Ephesians 1:4: *even as he chose us in him before the foundation of the world, that we should be holy and without blemish before him in love.* We were chosen in Him—that is, in *Yeshua*—before the foundation of the earth. This requires the Messiah's preexistence.

Another example is Philippians 2:6-8. Verse 6 says, *who, existing in the form of God, counted not the being on an equality with God a thing to be grasped.* Verses 7 and 8 add, *He was made in the likeness of men and found in fashion as a man.* This passage clearly states that *Yeshua* existed in the form of God before He became man.

Finally, Colossians 1:16-17 states that the Messiah preceded everything:

> [16] *for in him were all things created, in the heavens and upon the earth, things visible and things invisible, whether thrones or dominions or principalities or powers; all things have been created through him, and unto him;* [17] *and he is before all things, and in him all things consist.*

Verse 16 gives us various facets of the creation account, but verse 17 points out that He preceded everything. Hence, this verse emphasizes once again the preexistence of the Messiah.

There are those who would claim that these statements were made about *Yeshua* by others, but that Messiah Himself never said these sorts of things about Himself. This is not true, as we shall now consider.

D. Messiah's Assertions

Several times *Yeshua* asserted His own preexistence, and we are going to look at a number of examples, beginning with John 3:16-17:

> [16] *For God so loved the world, that he gave his only begotten Son, that whosoever believes on him should not perish, but have eternal life.* [17] *For God sent not the Son into the world to judge the world; but that the world should be saved through him.*

It is the Messiah Himself who speaks these words, and the very fact that God sent Him into the world presupposes that He existed before the sending. The Messiah was sent into the world by virtue of His virgin birth, but in order for Him to have been sent by God, He had to have already existed.

In John 6, *Yeshua* elaborates on the "bread of heaven" theme. In verse 33, He says, *For the bread of God is that which comes down out of heaven, and gives life unto the world.* The Messiah is "the bread of heaven," and here He tells us that He existed in heaven before coming down to the earth. Then, in verse 38, He says, *For I am come down from heaven, not to do mine own will, but the will of him that sent me.* Again, to come down from heaven means He must have existed in heaven.

In verses 41-42 of this chapter, it is very clear that the Jewish audience understood *Yeshua's* claims:

> [41] *The Jews therefore murmured concerning him, because he said, I am the bread which came down out of heaven.* [42] *And they said, Is not this Yeshua, the son of Joseph, whose father and mother we know? how does he now say, I am come down out of heaven?*

The people clearly understood that He did not merely claim to have been born in a unique way. They knew He was claiming to have come down from heaven. This is why they murmured, why they were upset. Knowing who His parents were, His claims made them uncomfortable.

In verses 50-51 of the chapter, *Yeshua* repeats His claim:

> [50] *This is the bread which comes down out of heaven, that a man may eat thereof, and not die.* [51] *I am the living bread which came down out of heaven: if any man eat of this bread, he shall live for ever: yea and the bread which I will give is my flesh, for the life of the world.*

Again, *Yeshua* says that He is the bread out of heaven and that He came down to earth from heaven. This presupposes His preexistence. He existed before He was born in Bethlehem. *Yeshua* repeats this assertion in John 6:58.

In verse 62, He adds a little variation to the same theme: *What then if ye should behold the Son of man ascending where he was before?* He plans to ascend into heaven, which, of course, He did after His forty days of post-resurrection ministry. Furthermore, He points out that when He ascends into heaven, He will be simply returning to the place where He was before. Once again, His preexistence is clearly taught.

In the next chapter of John, He moves away from the "bread of heaven" theme and says about God the Father, *I know him; because I am from him, and he sent me* (Jn. 7:29). He knows the Father because He came from the Father who had sent Him. This is another clear statement of preexistence.

In the eighth chapter of the Gospel of John, *Yeshua* asserts three times that He came from heaven. In verse 23, He says, *Ye are from beneath; I am from above: ye are of this world; I am not of this world.*

In verse 42 of the same chapter, He adds, *If God were your Father, ye would love me: for I came forth and am come from God; for neither have I come of myself, but he sent me.* For the second time in this chapter, *Yeshua* asserts that He came from God; He was with God and was sent by God.

The strongest statement in this chapter is found in verse 58: *Yeshua said unto them, Verily, verily, I say unto you, Before Abraham was born, I am.* Here the Messiah asserts that He existed even before the birth of Abraham. There is no denying the fact that He claimed preexistence. In fact, His Jewish audience clearly understood what He was saying, because in the very next verse they try to stone Him for blasphemy.

The next passage where the Messiah asserts His own preexistence is found in John 16:27-28:

> [27] *for the Father himself loves you, because ye have loved me, and have believed that I came forth from the Father.* [28] *I came out from the Father, and am come into the world: again, I leave the world, and go unto the Father.*

In preparation for His ascension, *Yeshua* explains to His disciples that He will be departing to the Father. Additionally, He points out that He had been with Him before. He came from the Father, and now He was going back to the Father.

Finally, in chapter 17 of the Gospel of John, *Yeshua* asserts His preexistence twice. In verse 5, He prays, *And now, Father, glorify you me with your own self with the glory which I had with you before the world was.* Here the Messiah clearly states that He was with the Father not only before Abraham was, but even before the world was. In verse 24, He speaks about the love His Father has for Him: *Father, I desire that they also whom you have given me be with me where I am, that they may behold my glory, which you have given me: for you loved me before the foundation of the world.* The Father loved the Son before the foundation of the world. This means that the Son preexisted the foundation of the world.[17]

E. The Importance of the Doctrine

The teaching of the preexistence of Messiah is foundational to the biblical faith. Other doctrines depend on it. If the Messiah had come into existence at the time of His birth, then His incarnation, His atoning work on the cross, His resurrection, and therefore our hope of eternal life would be in question.

Our understanding of His preexistence clearly affects our perspective of God, the Trinity, Messianic Christology, and even topics such as creation. To put it in simple terms, there would be no eternal Trinity if the Son of God came into existence at His physical birth in Bethlehem. His deity would be in question, since being God implies eternality. He simply could not be God if He did not exist before He became a human being. Furthermore, if *Yeshua* did not preexist, He was a liar, since He clearly claimed to have preexisted in heaven. If He lied about this topic, everything He ever said about creation, the state of man, sin, salvation, and things to come would be in question as well. Hence, our understanding of the preexistence of the Messiah is vitally important to our faith.

[17] Study Suggestion on page 78.

F. Questions and Study Suggestions

Question 1: With the help of a concordance, try to find out if the Angel of the Lord also appears in the New Testament. Why or why not is He part of the narrative of the Gospels or the book of Acts?

Question 2: The Lutheran theologian Rudolf Bultmann described the preexistence of Messiah as "not only irrational but utterly meaningless."[18] Having studied the Old Testament statements that speak of His preexistence, how would you respond to a person like Bultmann?

Study Suggestion: You might have noticed that *Yeshua's* statements regarding His preexistence are all taken from the Gospel of John. A worthy challenge for the earnest Bible student is to find evidence of His preexistence in the Synoptic Gospels.

[18] Robert Bultmann, "New Testament and Mythology: The Mythological Element in the Message of the New Testament and the Problem of its Re-interpretation," in *The Historical Jesus: Critical Concepts in Religious Studies, Volume 1*, (Craig A. Evans ed.; New York: Routledge, 2004), 328.

Chapter V

The Sonships of the Messiah

In chapter three, we discussed the five general titles of the Messiah and said that in a separate chapter, we would look more closely at the seven titles that pertain to His Sonship. Each of these titles deals with either His nature, His person, or His work.

A. Son of Abraham

Yeshua is called *the Son of Abraham* in Matthew 1:1. This title emphasizes His Jewishness; it teaches that *Yeshua* was a Jew. In fact, it teaches that He **is** a Jew because He is still very much alive. He is still the God-Man, and in His humanity, He is still a Jew, the King of the Jews.

The title "Son of Abraham" also relates Him to the Abrahamic Covenant. He lived under this covenant because He was born a Jew, and He had certain obligations as a descendant of Abraham. For example, it was mandatory for *Yeshua* to be circumcised on the eighth day, as commanded by the Abrahamic Covenant. The title also relates Him to the Abrahamic Covenant as the One who will fulfill all the blessings and promises that have been made to the Jewish people through this covenant.[19]

---

[19] Question 1 on page 84.

B. The Son of David

Yeshua is called *the Son of David* in Matthew 1:1. This title emphasizes His royalty. Furthermore, it relates Him to the Davidic Covenant. As with the Abrahamic Covenant, His relationship to the Davidic Covenant is also twofold. First, He is under the Davidic Covenant in that He Himself is a direct descendant of David. Certain aspects of the Davidic Covenant were applicable to those who were members of the Davidic dynasty. The second relationship of *Yeshua* to the Davidic Covenant is that He will be the One to finally fulfill it. He will fulfill it when He sits upon David's throne and rules over Israel from the city of Jerusalem. This relationship of the Messiah to the Davidic Covenant is taught in Isaiah 9:6-7, Jeremiah 23:5-6, and Luke 1:30-33.

C. The Son of Adam

The Messiah is called *the Son of Adam* in Luke 3:38. The title emphasizes His humanity. He was fully man and fully God. The title relates the Messiah to the Adamic Covenant as the "last Adam" (Rom. 5:12-21). While with the first Adam came death, with the last Adam will now come the resurrection from the dead (I Cor. 15:14-28).

D. The Son of God

The Messiah is called *the Son of God* in Luke 3:38. This is a very common title for *Yeshua*, and it emphasizes the fact that He is God.

The title is used in three different senses in the New Testament. The first is the nativistic[20] sense that emphasizes His human nature as a product of the work of

[20] "Nativistic" is a term used by theologians like Louis Berkhof and George Eldon Ladd. It expresses the thought that the name "Son of God" is given to *Yeshua* "in view of the fact that He owed His birth to the paternity of God. He was begotten, according to His human nature, by the supernatural operation of the Holy Spirit, and is in that sense the

God (Lk. 1:35). Because Miriam conceived by the overshadowing work of the Holy Spirit, therefore, that *which is begotten shall be called the Son of God.*

The second usage of "the Son of God" is as a Messianic title. This was one of the titles of the Messiah in the Old Testament, and it is used as one of His Messianic titles in the New Testament as well (Mt. 8:29; 14:28-33; 24:36).

The third way this title is used is in its Trinitarian sense, in which He is distinguished from the Father and from the Holy Spirit (Mt. 11:27; 16:16; 22:41-46; Jn. 5:18).

In summary, the three different usages of the title "the Son of God" emphasize His virgin conception, His Messianic title, or His membership in the Trinity.

There were two particular occasions when *Yeshua* was declared to be the Son of God. This was not **when** He became the Son of God—He has been the Son of God for all eternity. But He was declared to be the Son of God on two occasions. The first occasion was at His baptism (Mt. 3:16-17; Mk. 1:10-11; Lk. 3:21-22; Jn. 1:32-34). The second occasion was at the transfiguration (Mt. 17:5; Mk. 9:7; Lk. 9:35; II Pet. 1:17).

Finally, *Yeshua's* resurrection proved that He was indeed the Son of God. He was declared to be the Son of God by God the Father (Ps. 2:7), and He was proven to be the Son of God by virtue of His resurrection (Acts 13:32-33; Rom. 1:3, 4). *Yeshua* is the Son of God.[21]

E. The Son of Man

The Messiah is called "the Son of Man" in numerous passages. This title has four specific emphases. First, it stresses His human nature (Mk. 2:27-28; Jn. 5:27; 6:53 and 62).

Second, it emphasizes His sufferings as the Son of Man, because it calls attention to the frailty of His humanity. It is used that way in places such as Matthew 12:40, 17:22, 20:18-19 and 28.

Son of God." (Louis Berkhof, *Systematic Theology*, Wm. B. Eerdmans Publishing Co., 1996, p. 92)

[21] Question 2 on page 84.

The third emphasis of His title as "the Son of Man" is unique to the Gospel of John. When John uses the term "Son of Man," he uses it to emphasize the super-human character of the Messiah and His preexistence. His super-human character is emphasized in John 1:51: *And he said unto him, Verily, verily, I say unto you, Ye shall see the heaven opened, and the angels of God ascending and descending upon the Son of man.*

His preexistence is emphasized in John 3:13-14: *13 And no one has ascended into heaven, but he that descended out of heaven, even the Son of man, who is in heaven. 14 And as Moses lifted up the serpent in the wilderness, even so must the Son of man be lifted up.* This same kind of usage is found in John 6:27, 53, 62, and 8:28.

The fourth emphasis of this title is in reference to *Yeshua's* Second Coming. Prophetically, this is the way the term is used in Daniel 7:13. This is where the term "Son of Man" originates, and it is also where the term is given its prophetic meaning. In the New Testament, this is applied to *Yeshua* in Matthew 16:27-28, Mark 8:38, and 13:26.

In summary, the title "Son of Man" either stresses *Yeshua's* human nature or His sufferings, accounts for His super-human side and preexistence, and stresses His Second—the eschatological—Coming.[22]

F. The Son of Mary

The Messiah is called *the son of Mary* in Mark 6:3.[23] When He is called the Son of Mary, it emphasizes His human origin, or more specifically, the origin of His humanity in that His humanity came from Miriam. Miriam was His real mother, and this makes Him a member of the House of David through her.[24]

---

[22] Question 3 on page 84.

[23] As noted before, Mary is the English name for the Hebrew *Miriam*, so this name of the Messiah should really be "Son of Miriam."

[24] Question 4 on page 84.

G. The Son of Joseph

The Messiah is called *the son of Joseph* in John 1:45 and 6:42. This title emphasizes His human father Joseph. Joseph was His legal father by means of adoption; he was not *Yeshua's* natural father because *Yeshua* did not have a natural father. But because Joseph adopted the Messiah, *Yeshua* could be listed legally as the son of Joseph in the genealogies.

H. Questions and Study Suggestions

Question 1: Believers in the Western world often envision *Yeshua* as a blond haired, blue-eyed man who slightly resembles a young Charlton Heston or Brad Pitt, depending on the age of the beholder. The artists of the last five centuries did not help either with their depictions of the Son of God as a haloed, long-haired, white man. Looking at *Yeshua's* title "the Son of Abraham," what does the fact that He was a Jew mean for your perception of Christianity?

Question 2: There are some conservative, Bible-believing men who have denied that *Yeshua* is God's eternal Son. Instead, they believe that He became the Son of God at the moment of His incarnation. Thus, their doctrine is called the incarnational Sonship. These believers do not deny *Yeshua's* deity or His eternality. They base their theory on Hebrews 1:5, which speaks of God the Father begetting God the Son, an event that took place at a specific point in time. From what you have learned so far in this book, how would you respond to these people?

Question 3: In your perception, are the titles "Son of God" and "Son of Man" contradictory? If you were challenged to prove that both titles are true and valid, what arguments would you bring forward?

Question 4: What do Matthew 12:46-47, 13:55, Mark 6:2-3, John 2:12, Acts 1:14, I Corinthians 9:4-5, and Galatians 1:19 tell us about *Yeshua's* mother, Miriam (or Mary, as she is called in English)?

Chapter VI

The Incarnation

The term "incarnation" comes from the Latin and literally means "embodied in flesh" or simply "in flesh." Theologically, it means that God took on human nature. Because it was God the Son, the Second Person of the Trinity, who became incarnate, it is probably more correct and proper to say that it was the *Logos* or the Word that became flesh, rather than saying that God became a man, though both statements are actually true. The incarnation of the Messiah means that suddenly, there were two natures in this one person. The two natures were always distinct and never mixed.

A. The Doctrine of the Incarnation

There are five main passages of Scripture that deal with the doctrine of the incarnation.

1. John 1:1-14

The most extended passage is John 1:1-14. Insofar as the incarnation is concerned, there are four key elements, all spelled out in verses 1 and 14:

> [1] *In the beginning was the Word, and the Word was with God, and the Word was God.*

***

> [14] *And the Word became flesh, and dwelt among us (and we beheld his glory, glory as of the only begotten from the Father), full of grace and truth.*

The first key element is that the Word was *In the beginning* (v. 1a). The second element is that *the Word was with God* (v. 1b). As long as God has been, the Word has been. If God is eternal, the Word is eternal. The third element is that *the Word was God* (v. 1c). How the Word could be with God, which is the second element, and yet be God, which is the third element, is explainable only in terms of the Trinity. The Word was with God and, therefore, distinct from God, because the Word is not the Father, nor is the Word the Holy Spirit. However, the Word was God in that the Word is the Son. And the fourth element is that *the Word became flesh* (v. 14). The Word that was in the beginning with God, that was God, at a certain point in human history took on flesh, became man, and that is the incarnation.

2. Romans 1:3-4

> [3] *concerning his Son, who was born of the seed of David according to the flesh,* [4] *who was declared to be the Son of God with power, according to the spirit of holiness, by the resurrection from the dead; even Yeshua Messiah our Lord.*

Two key phrases concerning the incarnation are found in this passage: *according to the flesh* (v. 3) and *according to the spirit of holiness* (v. 4). This is the incarnation. He became man according to the flesh. It was accomplished by the power of the Holy Spirit; therefore, it was according to the Spirit as well.

3. Philippians 2:6-8

> [6] *who, existing in the form of God, counted not the being on an equality with God a thing to be grasped,* [7] *but emptied himself, taking the form of a servant, being made in the likeness of men;* [8] *and being found in fashion as a man, he humbled himself, becoming obedient even unto death, yea, the death of the cross.*

Three key elements concerning the incarnation are found in this passage. First, the Messiah always existed *in the form of God* (v. 6); for all eternity past, He existed in the form of God, because He was the Second Person of the Trinity, God the Son. Second, He that existed in the form of God for all eternity at some point in human history was made into *the likeness of men* (v. 7). That is the statement of the incarnation: He was made into the likeness of sinful men. The use of the term "likeness" does not mean He was not really a man. Rather, the term emphasizes the similarity to sinful men in that by mere observation, He did not look any different than any other human being. However, He never committed a single sin. He absolutely was an real human being, a real man, but not a sinful man. Third, He was found *in fashion as a man* (v. 8). He looked like all other human beings. The incarnation means that He took on flesh and became man.

4. I Timothy 3:16

> *And without controversy great is the mystery of godliness: God was manifest in the flesh, justified in the Spirit, seen of angels, preached unto the Gentiles, believed on in the world, received up into glory.*

The emphasis of this verse is that He was manifested in the flesh, a statement of the incarnation.

5. Hebrews 2:14

> *Since then the children are sharers in flesh and blood, he also himself in like manner partook of the same; that through death he might bring to nought him that had the power of death, that is, the devil;*

Concerning the incarnation, the key phrase in this verse is *sharers of flesh and blood*. The Greek word for "sharer" means "to take hold of." The picture is that He was always God, but at a certain time in human history, He took hold of human nature.[25]

---

[25] Question 1 on page 95.

B. The Means of the Incarnation

What are the means of the incarnation? How did God become a man? The means of the incarnation involved three things.

First, it involved the Holy Spirit. In Luke 1:35, we read: *And the angel answered and said unto her, The Holy Spirit shall come upon you, and the power of the Most High shall overshadow you: wherefore also the holy thing which is begotten shall be called the Son of God.* When Miriam asked how conception was possible, because she was a virgin, the angel answered that the Holy Spirit would overshadow her and bring about a miraculous conception. The generator of the incarnation was the Holy Spirit. The Holy Spirit came upon Miriam, and the power of the Most High overshadowed her. The Spirit worked to beget, or conceive, the humanity of the Messiah. He was always God, so deity did not need to be generated; only His humanity needed to be generated. Deity partook of Miriam's humanity, but at the same time, precluded Miriam's sin-nature. By means of the overshadowing of the Holy Spirit with the power of the Most High, the Holy Spirit generated the humanity of *Yeshua* the Messiah. The Holy Spirit generated the conception. The product, according to Luke 1:35, was to be two things: He was to be holy, and He was to be the Son of God, the God-Man.

Second, the incarnation involved the Virgin Miriam. Her virginity was affirmed by two of the four Gospels (Mt. 1:18; 22-23; Lk. 1:27; 34). The conception was supernatural. Because Miriam was a virgin, it was necessary that there be a supernatural conception. People often speak of the miracle of the virgin birth, but technically, it was not the actual birth that was the miracle; *Yeshua* was born just like any other baby. It was not the birth that was miraculous, but the conception. The female egg was that of Miriam, so *Yeshua* was the real son of Miriam, but there was a total absence of the male sperm. Therefore, the Messiah did not have a natural father, and that is why the conception required the generating power of the Holy Spirit. On one hand, the Holy Spirit was the means, but on the other hand, the Virgin Miriam was a means as well.

Third, the incarnation involved the virgin birth which produced the incarnate man. This was predicted in Genesis 3:15 and Isaiah 7:14 and finally came into fulfillment in Matthew 1:16.

C. Reasons and Purposes

What are the reasons for and the purposes of the incarnation? There are twelve specific reasons why the incarnation occurred.

First, the incarnation was conditioned by human sin. Luke 19:10 states, *For the Son of man came to seek and to save that which was lost.* A more extended passage that states this as a reason for the incarnation is John 3:13-21. The purpose of the incarnation was to save sinners. In order to pay the penalty for sin, *Yeshua* had to be made "like unto" or "in the likeness of" sinful flesh. As mentioned in the previous paragraph, He was not made sinful, but, in outward appearance, He looked like any other man. It was necessary for Him to be made in the likeness of sinful flesh because He came for the purpose of dying for sinners. The incarnation was conditioned by human sin in that human sin necessitated the incarnation. As Hebrews 2:14 states, it was necessary for Him to become a sharer in flesh and blood in order to deal with the issue of sin.

Second, the incarnation was to reveal God to man concerning the truths of the Father (Mt. 11:27). According to John 1:18, He came for the purpose of revealing the Father: *No man has seen God at any time; the only begotten Son, who is in the bosom of the Father, he has declared him.* He revealed the nature of the Father in His sermons and discourses. In John 14:8-9, when one of His own disciples eventually asked *Yeshua, Show us the Father,* He answered, *he that has seen me has seen the Father.* Everything that is true of the nature of the Father is true of the Son.

Third, the incarnation was to provide believers with an example for living (I Pet. 2:21; I Jn. 2:6). In His humanity, *Yeshua* lived a lifestyle that the believer should imitate. This includes not only the good times, but also the bad times. Both His strength and His sufferings are to be an example. Just as He underwent suffering in a meek manner, we, too, should undergo our sufferings in the same way. He became a man to provide an example for living.

Fourth, the incarnation was to provide a sacrifice for sin (Heb. 2:9; 10:1-10; I Jn. 3:5). He came as a man to provide a sacrifice for sin. While animal sacrifices were allowed temporarily, all they could ever do was cover the sins of the Old Testament saints; they could never take them away. The removal of sin required better blood than animal blood. The better blood was human blood, but it had to be sinless human blood. This ruled out every human being that had existed since the fall of Adam with one exception, and that was the God-Man, *Yeshua.* As a result of the incarnation, He became a man. Being in the form of a man, He had human blood and, therefore, better blood than animal blood. He had sinless human blood; for that reason, He was able to become the sacrifice for sin.

Fifth, the incarnation was to destroy the works of the devil (Jn. 12:31; 16:11; Col. 2:15; Heb. 2:14; I Jn. 3:8).

Sixth, the incarnation enabled *Yeshua* to become a merciful high priest. This is especially stressed in the book of Hebrews. Hebrews 2:17-18 follows the statement on the incarnation in verse 14 and explains that it made Him a merciful and faithful high priest. Hebrews 5:1-2 emphasizes that for one to be a genuine priest, he had to be human. Thus, if *Yeshua* had not become a real man, He could not have been a high priest. By becoming a man, by becoming incarnate, He could become, and continues to be, the High Priest of believers. This also enabled Him to offer sacrifices, as only priests could do. He was able to offer a better sacrifice—His own blood—not animal blood.[26]

Seventh, the incarnation was to fulfill the Davidic Covenant. The Davidic Covenant promised that a descendant of David would sit upon David's throne forever. It was necessary for *Yeshua* to become a real man through the Virgin Miriam because she was a member of the House of David; therefore, her son was a member of the House of David. Because He is both God and man, He now lives forever, and He will rule upon David's throne forever (Lk. 1:31-33, 68-70).

Eighth, the incarnation was to confirm the promises of God (Rom. 15:8-9) that were given in the Old Testament. In order for these prophecies to be fulfilled, the incarnation was necessary.

Ninth, the incarnation provided for *Yeshua* the Messiah to become highly exalted (Phil. 2:9-11). The exaltation could come only by means of suffering. God is incapable of suffering. But when God the Son became a man, He became capable of suffering. He certainly did suffer; He suffered humiliation and much more. As a result, He became highly exalted. This, too, was a purpose of the incarnation.

Tenth, the incarnation was to restore dominion over the earth to man (Heb. 2:5-9). It was to man that God gave dominion over the earth, but man lost it when Satan caused him to fall; Satan usurped the authority over the earth which had been given to man (Jn. 12:31; 14:30; 16:11; II Cor. 4:4; I Jn. 5:19). The

[26] Hebrews 8:1, 9:11-12 and 14 shed additional light on this topic.

Messiah defeated Satan; now, as a man, He must restore man's dominion over the earth, which He will do in the future kingdom.

Eleventh, the incarnation was to bring many sons to glory (Heb. 2:10-11). This, too, required the incarnation.

Twelfth, the incarnation was to deliver believers from the fear of death (Heb. 2:15). This, too, was accomplished through the incarnation.[27]

D. The Hypostatic Union

One of the greatest theological implications of the incarnation is referred to as the hypostatic union. What does this term mean? And what do theologians imply when they refer to Messiah as the Theanthropic Person?

"Hypostatic union" is a term which describes the union of the Messiah's humanity and divinity in one hypostasis,[28] or individual existence. The term describes the idea that God the Son took on human nature yet remained fully God. Theanthropic[29] is another term which comes from the Greek and expresses the same idea; it describes a person who embodies two distinct natures, the nature of both God and man.

When we speak about *Yeshua's* hypostatic union, we mean five things:

1. He is undiminished deity. He is fully God. He never was less than God.
2. He is fully human. He has full humanity.
3. His undiminished deity and full humanity have been united into one person forever. There is still only one person, but He has two distinct and separate natures. These two natures can never be separated. They have been united into one person forever.
4. The product of this union is the Theanthropic Person, the One who is fully God and fully man—the God-Man.

---

[27] Question 2 on page 95.

[28] The term "hypostasis" comes from a Greek word meaning "subsistence" or "substance."

[29] The term "theanthropic" comes from the two Greek words *theos* (god) and *anthropos* (human being).

5. This is the great mystery spoken of in Colossians 2:2-3 as *the mystery of God, even Messiah*—that *Yeshua* is fully God and fully man.

So hypostatic union simply means that two natures were combined into one person creating a union that was never to be separated. This union results in six noteworthy truths. The first truth is that there are two natures in Messiah. One is human; one is divine. The term "nature" needs to be seen as the sum total of all His attributes in relation to each other. *Yeshua* has all of the attributes that are the sum total of deity. He also has all those that are the sum total of humanity.

The second truth is that these two natures are united in the one person of Messiah, but they remain distinct. This means they are never mingled; they are never confounded; they are not a mixture, producing some kind of a third substance. The person of *Yeshua* is not part deity and part humanity. Rather, He is theanthropic: fully God and fully human. It is the person who is theanthropic, not His nature. As to His person, He is the God-Man. He does not have one nature, which would be the God-Man-nature. He has two natures: one human nature and one divine nature. So it is His person that is theanthropic, not His nature. In fact, there is no theanthropic nature. He has two natures: human and divine. This means that He is fully God and fully man at the same time. This one person, then, has two sets of attributes—divine attributes and human attributes.

The third truth of the hypostatic union in the person of Messiah is that there is no transfer of the attributes of one nature to the other. Each set of attributes must remain compatible with the nature to which they correspond, and they cannot be absorbed into the other nature. In other words, there are certain things which are true of the divine nature of the Son. For example, He is omniscient, omnipresent, and omnipotent. These are attributes of a divine nature. There is no way the human nature can absorb these divine attributes. They are foreign to the human nature. On the other hand, the human nature is characterized by limited knowledge, limited space, and limited ability. God can never be limited in these areas, and so the divine nature cannot absorb these attributes of the human nature and become limited in that way. Hence, the third truth of the hypostatic union is that the attributes of one nature are not being transferred to the other.

The fourth truth is that the hypostatic union is a personal union. It is hypostatic, meaning it pertains to an individual existence. It is personal and person-centered. It is not merely a divine nature "indwelling" the human nature or a human nature indwelling the divine nature. The union is such that *Yeshua* is only one person. He is not deity possessing humanity; neither is He humanity indwelt by deity. He is one person in whom this union has taken place.

The fifth truth is that there is only one person. The Son of God did not unite with a human person. He united with a human nature and became man. This is a crucial biblical distinction. There was no interchange between "I" and "Thou," as would have been the case if the union had resulted in two persons. We would find an I/Thou interchange in Scripture in the person of *Yeshua* if the union resulted in two persons. But we do not find this. The two natures are united in one person.

The sixth and last truth of the hypostatic union in the person of Messiah is that this union is eternal. Having been united, it is now permanent. That is the point of Matthew 26:64b, where *Yeshua* said, *Henceforth ye shall see the Son of man sitting at the right hand of Power, and coming on the clouds of heaven.* At present, He is the Son of Man sitting at the right hand of God the Father. In the future, He will be the Son of Man coming in the clouds of heaven. He is not only always the Son of God, He is also always the Son of Man—both in the present in heaven and in the future when He comes in the clouds of heaven. So this union is eternal.

From a theological standpoint, the concept of the hypostatic union is foundational. A better understanding of the biblical teaching about the God-Man allows us to correctly correlate *Yeshua's* humanity and deity. It helps us avoid many of the pitfalls, errors, and heresies that have cropped up in church history and are still propagated by various cultic groups today.[30]

E. The Character of Messiah

The incarnation provided Messiah with a specific character. In studying this character, seven elements or traits become important:

1. He was absolutely holy (Lk. 1:35; Jn. 14:30; Acts 2:27; 3:14; 4:27; Heb. 7:26).
2. He was sinless (Jn. 8:46; II Cor. 5:21; Heb. 4:15; I Pet. 2:22; I Jn. 3:5).

[30] Question 3 on page 95.

3. He had genuine love. Because He was both God and man, He could love in a divine way and also in a human way. In either case, it was a real and genuine love that He expressed (Mk. 10:21; Jn. 13:1; 14:31; 19:25-27; Gal. 2:20; Eph. 3:19; 5:25).
4. He was truly humble (II Cor. 8:9; Phil. 2:5-8).
5. He was truly meek (Mt. 11:29; II Cor. 10:1).
6. He lived a life of prayer (Mt. 14:23; Mk. 1:35; Lk. 6:12; 22:44; Jn. 17:1-26; Heb. 5:7).
7. He was an incessant worker (Jn. 5:17; 9:4). However, He was not a "workaholic," for He knew when to step aside and rest. He knew when to withdraw from the masses, and He knew when to go into the desert for a time of rest and prayer.

These are the seven characteristics of *Yeshua* which resulted from the incarnation. As previously mentioned, one of the purposes of the incarnation was to set an example for living. These seven characteristics do exactly that, and they should be imitated by believers in their day-to-day spiritual lives.

F. Questions and Study Suggestions

Question 1: In an article published online by Jews for Judaism, the following statement is made about the incarnation: "The Jew equates worship of Jesus with idolatry. A Jew sees no room for discussion of this issue. A man cannot be God and that's all there is to it." Is there anything in the verses we just studied which might be able to help Jewish people understand what happened when the Word became flesh?

Question 2: In the year 386, one of the early church fathers, John Chrysostom, preached the following words: "O ineffable grace! The Only Begotten, Who is before all ages, Who cannot be touched or be perceived, Who is simple, without body, has now put on my body, that is visible and liable to corruption. For what reason? That coming amongst us he may teach us, and teaching, lead us by the hand to the things that men cannot see. For since men believe that the eyes are more trustworthy than the ears, they doubt of that which they do not see, and so He has designed to show Himself in bodily presence, that He may remove all doubt." After having studied the reasons for the incarnation, which points did Chrysostom miss in his explanation of why God took on the form of a man? What does this example teach us about half-truths being taught by man?[31]

Question 3: According to Malachi 3:6, one of God's attributes is His immutability. He cannot change. How do you reconcile the teaching of the hypostatic union with the immutability of God? In other words, did God not change when He became man?

[31] *The Sunday Sermons of the Great Fathers: A Manual of Preaching, Spiritual Reading and Meditation, Volume 1.* (M. F. Toal ed.; San Francisco: Ignatius Press, 2000), 112. It should be noted that John Chrysostom's teaching about what he called Judaizing Christians has led to much anti-Semitism in the church. This should show us how important it is to carefully compare man's teaching with God's Word.

Chapter VII

The Humanity of the Messiah

The incarnation resulted in a being who was both God and man: *Yeshua* was very man and very God. In His being, He united both a divine nature and a human nature.

A. The Proof of His Humanity

What proof do we have that the Messiah was truly human, that He was a real man and did not merely have the appearance of a man?

1. His Human Nature

His humanity is seen in that He had all the essentials of the human nature: body, soul, and spirit. From passages like Matthew 26:12 and Luke 24:39, we know that He had a real body. Verses like Matthew 26:38 and John 12:27 prove that He had a soul. Mark 2:8 and John 11:33 speak about His human spirit. *Yeshua* clearly had all the essentials of the human nature.

2. His Human Birth

His humanity is also evidenced by the fact that He had a normal, human birth. Again, it is not His birth that was miraculous, but His conception. His birth was like that of any other human being (Mt. 1:18-2:12; Lk. 1:26-38; 2:1-20). This is stated as a doctrine in Galatians 4:4, where Paul wrote that Messiah was born of a woman.

3. His Human Ancestry

His humanity is seen in that He had a human ancestry, being a descendant of Abraham and David (Mt. 1:1; Rom. 1:3).

4. His Human Names

The fact that He had human names further demonstrates His humanity. He was named *Yeshua*, or "Joshua," a common human name of that day. He was also called the "Son of Man," a title that clearly emphasizes His humanity.

5. Others Saw Him as Man

He was actually called a man by others. This, too, is evidence that He did not merely have the appearance of a human being. John the Baptist called Him a man in John 1:30. The multitudes called Him a man in John 10:33. Peter called Him a man in Acts 2:22. And Paul called Him a man in Acts 13:38, Romans 5:15, I Corinthians 15:21 and 47, Philippians 2:8, and I Timothy 2:5.

6. He Called Himself a Man

His humanity is seen in that He called Himself a man (Jn. 8:40) and in the fact that He was subject to all the laws of human development (Lk. 2:40, 52). Like every other human being, He developed in four areas: mental, physical, spiritual, and social.

7. His Human Experience

He was subject to all human experiences: He was hungry (Mt. 4:2; 21:18). He was thirsty (Jn. 19:28). He was weary (Jn. 4:6). He was sleepy (Mt. 8:24). He was subject to all human emotions: love (Mk. 10:21), compassion (Mt. 9:36), anger and grief, which He demonstrated in weeping and shedding tears (Mk. 3:5; Jn. 11:35; Heb. 5:7). Furthermore, He agonized (Lk. 22:44). He was troubled

(Jn. 12:27). He was tested (Heb. 2:18; 4:15). He needed to pray (Mt. 14:23; Mk. 1:35; Lk. 6:12). These are all evidences of His humanity.

8. His Limited Knowledge

In His humanity, He had limited knowledge; there were things He did not know. Two examples of this limited knowledge are Mark 13:32 and John 11:34.

9. His Suffering and Death

Finally, His humanity is evidenced by the fact that He suffered and died (Jn. 19:30, 34; Heb. 2:14; 5:8).[32]

B. The Humiliation of the Messiah

Part of the humanity of *Yeshua* involved His humiliation. In dealing with this theologically, it involves twelve elements.

First, the very incarnation was a humiliation because God had to take on human nature with all of its limitations. The fact that He had to become a man was a "stepping-down," a humiliation (Gal. 4:4; Phil. 2:6-7; Heb. 2:14).

Second, His humiliation is seen in that He was made in the likeness of sinful flesh. He looked like a sinful human being. This, too, is part of His humiliation (Rom. 8:3; Phil. 2:7).

Third, His humiliation is seen in that He was born in a lowly condition. We see this in several ways. Matthew 2:23 states He was raised in Nazareth. He was called a Nazarene, and that was not considered a favorable title. "Can any good thing come out of Nazareth?" was a popular saying (Jn. 1:46). Of all the places He could have been raised, He was raised in one of the most denigrated towns in Galilee. Nazareth was a city of disrepute. To make matters worse, He was not born into a wealthy family, but into a family that was poverty-stricken. According to Matthew 8:20, He had no wealth of His own. Luke 2:7 says He was born in a

[32] Question 1 on page 105.

stable and laid in a manger. Luke 2:22-24 teaches that He was born into a family that was so poverty-stricken that the only offering the parents could afford to give was two turtledoves, a sign of their economic destitution (Lev. 12:1-8). Second Corinthians 8:9 finally states that by means of the incarnation, He became poor.

Fourth, His humiliation is seen in that He was born under the law (Gal. 4:4). He had to subject Himself to a law that He Himself had originated (Lk. 2:22-24). This, too, was part of the humiliation of *Yeshua*.

Fifth, His humiliation is seen in that He had to be in submission to the limitations of humanity. This is the point of Philippians 2:5-11. It means that while He did not lose any of His divine attributes, He did have limited use of them. This was also part of His humiliation and is known as the doctrine of the kenosis which will be discussed in depth in chapter nine.

Sixth, His humiliation is seen in that He had to undergo all the miseries of human life (Jn. 7:5; Heb. 4:15; 12:3).

Seventh, His humiliation is seen in that He became a servant and ministered as a servant. This is illustrated in John 13:1-11, when He washed the disciples' feet. It is also stated in Philippians 2:7.

Eighth, His humiliation is seen in that He bore man's sins. That was humiliating for One who was absolutely holy and sinless (II Cor. 5:21; I Pet. 2:24).

Ninth, His humiliation is seen in that He endured the curse of death on the cross. Of all the ways He could have been executed, the most ignoble execution, the most humiliating way to die, was by hanging on a tree (Deut. 21:22-23). This was considered by Jewish culture and custom to be the most degrading death of all. So this, too, was a part of His humiliation (Gal. 3:13; Heb. 12:2).

Tenth, His humiliation is seen in His death. The very fact that the God-Man, the holy and sinless One, had to undergo death was a part of His humiliation (Phil. 2:8).

Eleventh, His humiliation is seen in His burial. The fact that He had to be buried like every other man was a sign of His humiliation (Mt. 27:59-60; Jn. 19:40; Acts 13:34-35; I Cor. 15:4). None of those who were close to *Yeshua* throughout His life and ministry were involved in the burial. The fact that they kept their distance was an additional humiliation. The Son of God was buried by two men who, up until then, were secret, distant believers: Joseph of Arimathea and Nicodemus.

Twelfth, His humiliation is seen in His descent into Sheol or Hades. He, too, had to descend to that temporary place of confinement for the saints (Acts 2:27, 31; Eph. 4:9; I Pet. 3:18-19).

These are the twelve elements that clearly teach the concept of the humiliation of the Messiah. His humiliation is very much a part of His humanity, and His humanity is very much part of the concept of the incarnation.[33]

C. The Offices of the Messiah

In His humanity, *Yeshua* holds three offices: prophet, priest, and king. Although He holds these three offices eternally, He does not function in all three simultaneously, but chronologically. For example, when *Yeshua* was here on the earth during His First Coming, He functioned in His role of a prophet. But in the closing week of His life, He went through a transition from the office of prophet to the office of priest. To this day, He is functioning as our High Priest in heaven. *Yeshua* has not as yet functioned in His third office, the office of king. That awaits the day when He will return to function as King.

1. The Office of Prophet

A prophet is one who receives direct revelation from God: he speaks from God to man. He is a spokesman for God and speaks the words of the One who sent him. A prophet is not someone who merely teaches the Scriptures. That is the role of a teacher. For someone to fulfill the function of a prophet, he must be receiving direct revelation from God. We see this in the commissioning of both the Prophet Jeremiah (Jer. 1:9) and the Prophet Ezekiel (Ez. 3:4, 10, 11).

The role of the prophet involved two things. The first was the area of foretelling, meaning "the prediction of future events." He would first have to predict events to be fulfilled in the near future so that his prophetic office could be tested. Only if his near prophecies were fulfilled could his distant prophecies be trusted and believed. The prophet, then, would function in the area of

---

[33] Read Dr. Fruchtenbaum's note to believers about a possible application of *Yeshua's* humiliation on page 105.

foretelling future events, both near and distant. The second role of a prophet would be that of forthtelling. By forthtelling, he would proclaim exactly what God was saying and what God's will was in any matter. It is the first function, that of foretelling, which authenticated the second function, that of forthtelling.

Yeshua clearly fulfilled the office of prophet. Deuteronomy 18:15-19 predicted that the Messiah would be a prophet like Moses, and the New Testament teaches that He fulfilled this role (Mt. 21:11, 46; Lk. 7:16; 24:19; Jn. 4:19; 6:14; 7:40; 9:17; Acts 3:20-26). *Yeshua* was clearly recognized to be a prophet while He was ministering during His First Coming. He fulfilled both roles of the prophetic office: forthtelling and foretelling. An example of forthtelling is the Sermon on the Mount in Matthew 5–7. As Prophet, *Yeshua* spelled out exactly what the will of God was in various situations. An example of foretelling is the Olivet Discourse in Matthew 24–25, when *Yeshua* predicted future events. He predicted some near events, such as Jerusalem's destruction in A.D. 70. He also foretold some distant events, such as the Tribulation and His Second Coming. Thus, *Yeshua* fulfilled the first office, the office of prophet, the office in which He functioned during His First Coming.

2. The Office of Priest

Today, *Yeshua* no longer functions in the office of prophet. Today, He is functioning in His second office, the office of priest. Whereas a prophet speaks from God to man, a priest speaks for man to God.

The office of a priest is that of a mediator. In the Old Testament, the mediator was required to do two things. Just as a prophet's office had two facets, foretelling and forthtelling, so also the priest's office had two facets, sacrificing and interceding. A priest was someone who was duly qualified to minister in sacred things, as spelled out in Hebrews 5:1. This ministry involved two things: first, he was to offer a sacrifice at the altar, and second, he had to act as a mediator between God and man.

Just as the Old Testament predicted that the Messiah would be a prophet, it also predicted that the Messiah would be a priest (Ps. 110:4; Zech. 6:13). The fact that He fulfilled the priestly office is taught throughout the book of Hebrews, especially in Hebrews 3:1. In fact, the only book in the New Testament that actually calls *Yeshua* a priest is the book of Hebrews, and it does so twelve times. Furthermore, it teaches thirteen things about the priesthood of Messiah:

1. It is a Melchizedekian priesthood, which means that *Yeshua* can be both priest and king (5:6; 6:19-20; 7:1-28).
2. It is a sinless priesthood, which was not true of the Levitical priesthood (4:15).
3. It is eternal (7:25).
4. It began at the cross (9:14; 12:24).
5. It is not transitory (7:11-14).
6. It is immutable (7:20-22).
7. It is uninterrupted (7:23-25).
8. It is not temporary; *Yeshua* is going to hold it forever (7:15-19).
9. He clearly qualified for this office (1:3).
10. He was divinely appointed by God to this office (5:5-10).
11. His priesthood is efficacious in that it will accomplish what it sets out to do, and that is to remove sin (10:4).
12. It was to continue after the ascension and so endures to this day (4:14; 6:20; 8:1).
13. It is an exalted priesthood (9:14).

Yeshua fulfilled both functions of the priesthood. In the area of sacrifice, He was both the sacrifice and the sacrificer (Heb. 9:11-15, 24-28; 10:12-14; I Cor. 5:7). The sacrifice of the Messiah accomplished redemption (Rom. 3:24-25), propitiation (I Jn. 2:2), and reconciliation (Rom. 5:10; II Cor. 5:18-21). When *Yeshua* fulfilled the first function of a priest, it was with a once and for all sacrifice, and He is no longer offering sacrifices. The second function of a priest was to intercede. That is what *Yeshua* is doing to the present day: He is interceding for us (Rom. 8:34; Heb. 7:25). Because He offered Himself as a once for all sacrifice, He is not sacrificing anymore; however, He is still interceding and will continue to intercede until the Second Coming.

3. The Office of King

Messiah's third office of king is still future. His first office was fulfilled in history by His First Coming. He presently holds His second office. His third office is future, and He will begin to function as king only with His Second Coming.

The office of king, as far as its relationship to *Yeshua* is concerned, is His right to rule over Israel and the world. Just as His prophetic and priestly offices were predicted by the Old Testament, His kingly office was also predicted by the Old Testament and much more frequently than the other two (Gen. 49:10; Num. 24:17; I Chron. 17:10-14; Ps. 45; 72; Isa. 9:6-7; 11:1-10; 33:17; Jer. 23:5-6; Dan. 7:13-14; Mic. 5:2; Zech. 9:9).

The New Testament clearly teaches the future fulfillment of this office by *Yeshua* when He returns. Even within the scope of the Gospels, during the time of His First Coming, He was declared to be King of the Jews. In Matthew 2:1-2, the wise men came looking for Him, asking the question, *Where is he that is born King of the Jews?* He is also referred to as king in Matthew 21:4-5, Luke 1:30-33, John 1:49, and 18:37.

Yeshua offered Himself as king at His First Coming, but He could not rule as such unless He was accepted by His own nation. Unfortunately, at His First Coming, He was rejected (Mt. 27:37; Mk. 15:16-20; Lk. 19:11-14; 23:38; Jn. 19:19-22). All of these specific passages emphasize not just the rejection of *Yeshua* as Messiah, but, in particular, the rejection of Him as King of the Jews. Since He cannot fulfill that function until He is accepted by His own nation, He did not become king during His First Coming, nor is He functioning in that office today. Instead, at His First Coming, He remained within the scope of prophet, and today He remains within the scope of priest. Someday, He will function in that third office, the office of King of the Jews and King of the world. Indeed, when *Yeshua* comes back, He is returning for the purpose of setting up His kingdom. The prerequisite to the Second Coming is the Jewish request for Him to return. Someday, all Israel will be saved and accept *Yeshua* as king. Once they do, He will come again to set up His kingdom. This particular aspect of His Second Coming—for the purpose of setting up a kingdom to rule over as king—is brought out in Matthew 25:34 and Revelation 19:15-16.[34]

[34] Study Suggestions 1 and 2 on page 106.

D. Questions and Study Suggestions

Question 1: Generally speaking, the fact of *Yeshua's* deity is met with more resistance than the fact of His humanity. We won't have any problem finding people from all walks of life and with various religious convictions who will readily admit that He was a "wonderful man," "a prophet," "a saint," or "a great example for all sorts of life choices and ideas." Do you think the same people would be equally willing to admit His ***perfect*** humanity? Why do you think that is?

Application: Dr. Fruchtenbaum writes:

> As believers look at all the things to which *Yeshua* submitted Himself, as they look at all the points of His humiliation, they should not miss the opportunity to remind themselves of exactly why He did all this. The reason was so that He could become their substitute. He lived as a man and died as a man, but He died a substitutionary death for man's sins. As believers undergo the sufferings of human life, as they undergo deprivation or humiliation, they should always have this picture in their minds: that they have not suffered anything nor will ever suffer anything that is anywhere near comparable to the sufferings of *Yeshua* the Messiah. If this is kept in mind, they will see what a great thing He did and will understand that He did it for them. Believers should always be grateful that He was willing to be humiliated in order to provide salvation and power for living in this life. When they suffer, let them not react against God. Let them remember that when they suffer, they are co-suffering with Him. The Bible promises that if they suffer with Him, they shall also be glorified with Him.

Study Suggestion 1: On the next page, you will find a chart with a few empty fields for you to fill in.[35]

Study Suggestion 2: Take the online test for this section of the study of the Messiah found on http://ariel.org/come-and-see.htm under "The Incarnation (054)."

The Ministries of the Messiah

Title	Bible Reference	His Ministry as Man	His Ministry as God
Savior	Romans 1:3-4		To give death meaning
High Priest		To represent man as a sacrifice for sin	
Judge	John 5:22		
Source of Christian Living			To empower our lives

[35] The chart is taken from Dr. Charles C. Ryrie's book, *Basic Theology*, Moody Press, Chicago, 1999, p. 283.

Chapter VIII

The Deity of the Messiah

The incarnation resulted in One who was both man and God. In the previous chapter, it was shown that He was a real man, who had real humanity. The other side of the coin is Messiah's deity. The incarnation does not mean that He gave up any portion of His deity. It was not a lessening of deity; it was perfect deity taking hold of and adding to Himself a human nature. To merely prove His preexistence does not by itself prove that He is God. It only proves that He existed before all creation, be it angels, man, or the material universe. What, then, is the evidence for the deity of Messiah?[36]

A. The Divine Names

The first area of evidence encompasses *Yeshua's* divine names. In chapter three, we studied His names and titles. This means some of the names included here will be familiar to the reader. Others will be new. There are a total of seven names which emphasize His deity:

1. God (Jn. 1:1; 20:28; Heb. 1:8);
2. The Son of God (Mt. 16:16);

[36] Question 1 on page 119.

3. Lord (Mt. 22:43-45; Acts 9:17);
4. The Alpha and the Omega (Rev. 1:8), an expression meaning "the beginning and the end;"
5. The First and the Last (Rev. 1:17);
6. The Image (Col. 1:15). The Greek word for "image" means "prototype," the image in its revealed reality; He is the visible manifestation of the invisible God.
7. The Very Image (Heb. 1:3), meaning the exact impress of the divine nature.

B. The Attributes of Deity

Messiah has all divine attributes, of which there are ten. Each attribute describes something that God is, and it is something that is characteristic of Him, not something He merely possesses. This means that He is also God. Looking at the list of attributes, the reader will note and might be confused by the usage of nouns. Each noun can be expressed as an adjective though, and each adjective could be expressed as a verb. Abstract nouns do not imply a stagnant God. Nevertheless, over the centuries, most theologians have agreed to the usage of certain nouns, and this book follows this tradition.

1. Eternality

Yeshua is eternal. Eternality does not merely mean that He will exist eternally in the future—something that is true of angels and saints. Eternality also means that He eternally existed in the past.

Concerning the Messiah, Micah 5:2b states that His *goings forth are from old, from everlasting.* In this verse, Micah uses the strongest possible Hebrew term for eternity past to emphasize the eternality of the Messiah.

John 1:1 states, *In the beginning was the Word, and the Word was with God, and the Word was God.* The point of this verse is that for as long as God has been in existence, the Messiah has been in existence. Because God has existed forever, even so, the Son has existed forever.

Other passages that teach the eternality of the Son include John 8:58, Colossians 1:17, and Hebrews 1:11.

2. Immutability

Yeshua is immutable; He never gets old. The fact that He is immutable means that He is changeless. He stays the same in His divine nature without any decrease in His divine power. The immutability of the Messiah is taught in two passages of the book of Hebrews. The first passage is Hebrews 1:10-12:. Here, the writer of Hebrews applies verses 25-27 of Psalm 102 to *Yeshua*:

> [10] *And, You, Lord, in the beginning did lay the foundation of the earth, And*
> *the heavens are the works of your hands:* [11] *They shall perish; but you*
> *continue: And they all shall wax old as does a garment;* [12] *And as a mantle*
> *shall you roll them up, As a garment, and they shall be changed: But you are the same, And your years shall not fail.*

The second passage is Hebrews 13:8: *Jesus Christ is the same yesterday and to-day, yea and for ever.* Contextually, this refers to His divine nature. *Yeshua* has the attribute of immutability.

3. Self-Existence

Yeshua is self-existent; His existence does not depend upon any other subject. Our existence is dependent upon God's work of preservation, but John 1:1-3 says that the Son is self-existent:

> [1] *In the beginning was the Word, and the Word was with God, and the Word*
> *was God.* [2] *The same was in the beginning with God.* [3] *All things were made through him; and without him was not anything made that has been made.*

These verses emphasize His self-existence in that He was not created; He always existed. In fact, everything that was created, everything that now exists, was created through Him.

A second passage that emphasizes His self-existence is John 5:26 which states, *For as the Father has life in himself, even so gave he to the Son also to have life in himself.* The fact that the Son has life in Himself shows that He is self-existent.

4. Life

Yeshua has the attribute of life. John 1:4 states, *In him was life; and the life was the light of men.* This was not a life that was created. It was not a life that was generated through natural means; He has life within Himself. This emphasizes deity. The same point is taught in John 14:6 and Acts 3:15.

5. The Fullness of the Godhead

This divine attribute is found in Colossians 2:9: *for in him dwells all the fulness of the Godhead bodily.* It emphasizes that everything that is obligatory to deity, everything that proves the deity of the Father and the deity of the Spirit, is also true of the Son; therefore, He, too, is deity. Everything that is true of the divine nature of the Father and the Spirit is therefore also true of the divine nature of the Son.

6. Holiness

Yeshua is holy. This is found in Hebrews 7:26 which states, *For such a high priest became us, holy, guileless, undefiled, separated from sinners, and made higher than the heavens.* This verse clearly teaches that *Yeshua* has holiness within Himself. The holiness that the saints have is an applied holiness; it is a holiness that comes from the Messiah. It is a holiness that is imputed to us when we are "reckoned righteous." *Yeshua* does not have a righteousness that was applied to Him or that was reckoned to Him; His holiness is a holiness that is true within Himself. Therefore, He has this attribute of holiness.

7. Sovereignty

Yeshua is sovereign; He is in total control. For example, in Matthew 5:27-28, He has the authority to execute judgment. The fact that *Yeshua* has the authority to do the work of divine judgment proves that He is sovereign.

This is taught in Matthew 28:18: *And Yeshua came to them and spoke unto them, saying, All authority has been given unto me in heaven and on earth.* The Messiah stated that His authority is not only on earth, but in heaven also.

This is also taught by John 17:2: *even as you gave him authority over all flesh, that to all whom you have given him, he should give eternal life.* A created being, such as an angel or a man, could never give eternal life to someone else.

The sovereignty of the Son is further taught in Acts 2:36, Philippians 2:9-10; Colossians 1:18, I Peter 3:22, and Revelation 19:16.

8. Omnipotence

Yeshua is omnipotent; He is all-powerful. To be all-powerful means that He must be God. The fact that He is omnipotent is taught in John 10:18, where He says about His life, *No one takes it away from me, but I lay it down of myself. I have power to lay it down, and I have power to take it again. This commandment received I from my Father.*

The fact that He has the power over His own life, both to take it and to raise it, shows a unique degree of omnipotence. All men have authority to take their own life, but not to raise themselves back to life.

The omnipotence of the Son is also taught in Luke 8:25, I Corinthians 15:25, 28, Philippians 3:21, Colossians 1:16-17, Hebrews 1:3, Jude 24, and Revelation 1:8.

9. Omniscience

Yeshua is omniscient; He knows all there is to know; He knows all realities and possibilities. While He has limited knowledge in His humanity, in His deity, He is all-knowing.

The fact that *Yeshua* is omniscient is taught by Matthew 11:27, John 1:48, 2:25, 10:15, 13:1 and 11, 16:30, 18:4, 19:28, Colossians 2:3, and Revelation 2:23.

10. Omnipresence

Yeshua is omnipresent; He is everywhere at the same time. To be everywhere at the same time is something that can only be true of God.

The fact that *Yeshua* is omnipresent is taught in Matthew 18:20, 28:20, John 3:13, 14:18, 20, and 23.[37]

C. The Works of God

Another evidence of *Yeshua's* deity is that He does the work of God. In other words, He accomplishes works only God can perform. There are six works of God to be considered.

1. Creation

Creation is a work that only God can do. Yet it is stated in John 1:3 that *Yeshua* performed the work of creation: *All things were made through him; and without him was not anything made that has been made.* This truth is repeated in John 1:10: *He was in the world, and the world was made through him, and the world knew him not.* In I Corinthians 8:6, Paul reaffirmed what John had taught: *yet to us there is one God, the Father, of whom are all things, and we unto him; and one Lord, Yeshua Messiah, through whom are all things, and we through him.* Paul repeats this truth in Colossians 1:16: *for in him were all things created, in the heavens and upon the earth, things invisible, whether thrones or dominions or principalities or powers; all things have been created through him, and unto him.* The same truth is taught by the writer of the book of Hebrews in 1:3 and 10.

From these passages, it is clear that the Son does the work of creation, which means that He is God.[38]

2. Preservation

Preserving that which has been created is another work only God can perform. Yet two New Testament passages teach that *Yeshua* does this work. The first passage is Colossians 1:17, which states that He *is before all things, and in him all things consist.* This verse teaches that the Messiah is the One who is holding the

[37] Question 2 on page 119.

[38] Question 3 on page 119.

universe together and preserving it. He is the "atomic glue" that scientists talk about, which mysteriously holds the atoms together and keeps them from exploding in all directions.

The second passage is Hebrews 1:3: *who being the effulgence of his glory, and the very image of his substance, and upholding all things by the word of his power, when he had made purification of sins, sat down on the right hand of the Majesty on high.*

Not only is the creation of the universe a work of God, but its preservation is a work of God. *Yeshua* does the work of preservation, which means that He must be God.

3. Forgiveness of Sin

Only God can forgive sins in a salvation sense. Yet *Yeshua* has the authority to forgive sins, a fact which emphasizes His deity. He is seen forgiving sins in Matthew 9:2, 6, Luke 5:24, and 7:47-48.

4. Sending of the Holy Spirit

Only God can send forth the Holy Spirit. Yet this is a work which, according to John 15:26, Messiah does: *But when the Comforter is come, whom I will send unto you from the Father, even the Spirit of truth, which proceeds from the Father, he shall bear witness of me.* For someone to be able to send the Holy Spirit, He must either be an equal of or greater than the Spirit. The Holy Spirit is God, and for *Yeshua* to be able to send Him means that He must also be God.

5. Resurrection

According to the New Testament, the Messiah will be responsible for raising people from the dead. This, too, is a work only God can do. In John 6:40, we read that He will be responsible for raising both the righteous and the unrighteous from the dead: *For this is the will of my Father, that every one that beholds the Son, and believes on him, should have eternal life; and I will raise him up at the last day.* Since the resurrection of the dead is a work of God, it means that *Yeshua* Himself must be God.

6. Final Judgment

Throughout the Old Testament, it is clearly taught that someday God will render final judgment. The work that was ascribed to God the Father in the Old Testament is ascribed to *Yeshua* in the New Testament. Obviously, if the Old Testament says that God is responsible for final judgment, and the New Testament says that Messiah is responsible for final judgment, then He must be God.

One passage that teaches that *Yeshua* will be responsible for final judgment is Matthew 25:31-46, which deals with the judgment of the Gentiles, and it is the Son who is doing the judging. In John 5:22-27, it says that the Son has been given the right to judge the righteous and the unrighteous. In Acts 17:31, Paul announced that someday God would judge all men through the Son. This is also taught by Acts 10:42, II Corinthians 5:10, and II Timothy 4:1.

D. Worship Accorded to Him

Another evidence of *Yeshua's* deity is that worship is accorded to Him. He is worshipped in a way only God can be worshipped. Furthermore, when He was worshipped, He received it and welcomed it, showing that He claimed to be God and accepted worship as God.

Some examples of this in action are Matthew 14:33, John 9:38, and 20:28. In John 20:28, Thomas, the doubting disciple, is finally convinced concerning the resurrection. He not only believed that *Yeshua* was a man resurrected from the dead, he believed He was his Lord and his God. In that context, *Yeshua* did not correct Thomas by saying that he should not call Him God or worship Him. On the contrary, He accepted Thomas' worship.

Yeshua is worshipped as God in Philippians 2:10 and Hebrews 1:6, which reads: *And when he again brings in the firstborn into the world he says, And let all the angels of God worship him.*

Not only is *Yeshua* worshipped by other men such as Thomas, He is also worshipped by the angels. To be worshipped by the angels clearly implies deity.[39]

---

[39] Question 4 on page 119.

E. Immortality

The Messiah's deity is evidenced by the fact that He gives immortality. The very power to provide eternal life belongs to God alone. Yet we find *Yeshua* having the ability to do so in four passages.

The first passage is John 5:28-29:

> [28] *Marvel not at this: for the hour comes, in which all that are in the tombs*
> *shall hear his voice,* [29] *and shall come forth; they that have done good, unto*
> *the resurrection of life; and they that have done evil, unto the resurrection of*
> *judgment.*

The second passage is John 6:39-40:

> [39] *And this is the will of him that sent me, that of all that which he has given*
> *me I should lose nothing, but should raise it up at the last day.* [40] *For this is*
> *the will of my Father, that every one that beholds the Son, and believes on*
> *him, should have eternal life; and I will raise him up at the last day.*

The third passage is John 17:2:

> *even as you gave him authority over all flesh, that to all whom you have given him, he should give eternal life.*

And the fourth passage is Philippians 3:21:

> *who shall fashion anew the body of our humiliation, that it may be conformed to the body of his glory, according to the working whereby he is able even to subject all things unto himself.*

F. Association with the Trinity

The Messiah is closely associated with the Trinity, a fact that proves His deity. He is associated with God the Father in the closest possible way. This is taught in two passages.

The first passage is John 10:30, where *Yeshua* says, *I and the Father are one.* This verse teaches that the Father and the Son are one in essence, the essence of divinity itself.

The second passage is John 14:23, which reads, *Yeshua answered and said unto him, If a man love me, he will keep my word: and my Father will love him, and we will come unto him, and make our abode with him.* Notice that the Father will indwell the believer and, at the same time, the Son will indwell the believer. He is associated with the Father in the closest possible way. Such an association is only possible by sharing the same divine essence.

Yeshua is also closely associated with the Trinity in that He is associated with both the Father and the Holy Spirit. This is taught in Matthew 28:19, where the Great Commission is given. *Yeshua* says that after one leads a person to the Lord, he should baptize him in the name of the Father and the Son and the Holy Spirit. In this passage, the Messiah is clearly associated with both the Father and the Holy Spirit.

Another example that shows the association with the Father and the Holy Spirit is in II Corinthians 13:14, which says, *The grace of the Lord Yeshua Messiah, and the love of God, and the communion of the Holy Spirit, be with you all.*

G. Divine Declarations

Finally, *Yeshua's* deity is seen in the declarations He made regarding His divinity. In light of these declarations, there are only three options from which to choose. The first option is that *Yeshua* was a false teacher; He was deceptive. He knew what He was teaching was not true. The second option is that He was self-deceived. While He really believed the statements He made, the statements were not true and He deceived Himself. The third option is the only biblical option. What *Yeshua* said of Himself was true.

What are some of these declarations of divinity?

1. To Have the Closest Possible Relationship with God

Yeshua said that He enjoyed the closest possible relationship with God. He explained that to know Him was to know God. He made this statement to unbelievers in John 8:19: *They said therefore unto him, Where is your Father? Yeshua answered, Ye know neither me, nor my Father: if ye knew me, ye would know my Father also.*

He made a very similar statement to believers in John 14:7: *If ye had known me, ye would have known my Father also: from henceforth ye know him, and have seen him.*

Yeshua also said that to see Him was to see God. He made this declaration in John 12:45: *And he that beholds me beholds him that sent me.* The Messiah was sent by God. He said that anyone who saw Him also saw the One who sent Him, and that was God.

He stated this again in John 14:9b, where He asked, *Have I been so long time with you, and do you not know me, Philip? he that has seen me has seen the Father; how say you, Show us the Father?*

Yeshua also declared He had the closest possible relationship with God by stating that to receive Him was to receive God. This is found in Mark 9:37: *Whosoever shall receive one of such little children in my name, receives me: and whosoever receives me, receives not me, but him that sent me.* The One who sent the Messiah was God. To receive the Messiah is to receive God.

Yeshua taught that to honor Him is to honor God. He stated this in John 5:23, *that all may honor the Son, even as they honor the Father. He that honors not the Son honors not the Father that sent him.* Not to honor the Son meant not to honor the Father, but to honor the Son meant to honor the Father.

Finally, *Yeshua* said that He enjoyed a unique oneness with the Father. He stated this in John 10:30, a verse we already looked at in the previous point and which reads, *I and the Father are one.*[40]

2. To Be the Object of Saving Faith

Yeshua said that He is the object of saving faith, and as only God can save, this is a statement of divinity. In Matthew 11:28-29, He gave this invitation:

> [28] *Come unto me, all ye that labor and are heavy laden, and I will give you rest.* [29] *Take my yoke upon you, and learn of me; for I am meek and lowly in heart: and ye shall find rest unto your souls.*

He stated this again in John 3:36, *He that believes on the Son has eternal life; but he that obeys not the Son shall not see life, but the wrath of God abides on him.*

[40] Question 5 on page 119.

He also taught this in John 14:1, *Let not your heart be troubled: believe in God, believe also in me.*

In John 17:3, He confirms this, *And this is life eternal, that they should know you the only true God, and him whom you did send, even Yeshua Messiah.*

3. To Have Absolute Dominion over His Followers

Yeshua said that He has absolute dominion over His followers, thus claiming a position only God can have. This is brought out in Matthew 10:37-39:

> [37] *He that loves father or mother more than me is not worthy of me; and he that loves son or daughter more than me is not worthy of me.* [38] *And he that does not take his cross and follow after me, is not worthy of me.* [39] *He that finds his life shall lose it; and he that loses his life for my sake shall find it.*

4. To Have Sovereignty over the Laws and Institutions of God

Yeshua declared His deity when He said He has sovereignty over the laws and institutions of God. Some examples of this are:

- ✡ He is *greater than the temple* (Mt. 12:6).
- ✡ He is *lord of the Sabbath* (Mt. 12:8).
- ✡ He has *the keys to the kingdom of heaven* (Mt. 16:19).
- ✡ He is Lord of the covenant because His is the *blood of the covenant* (Mt. 26:28). [41]

---

[41] Question 6 and Study Suggestion on page 119.

H. Questions and Study Suggestions

Question 1: Many people believe that *Yeshua* never declared He was God. Read Mark 14:61-64. How does the high priest's reaction to what the Messiah said prove that *Yeshua* indeed proclaimed to be God?

Question 2: Read Mark 13:32. How would you answer a person who says this verse contradicts *Yeshua's* omniscience?

Question 3: Read Colossians 1:15. Some claim this verse teaches that *Yeshua*, as the firstborn of every creature, was Himself created. How would you reply to this, taking into consideration what we learned about His ability to create?

Question 4: Read John 17:3. In this verse, *Yeshua* calls God the only true God. Does this contradict His deity? How would you help someone who struggles with this to understand the verse?

Question 5: Read John 14:28. How can He be Almighty God if God is greater than He?

Question 6: Read John 20:17. How can *Yeshua* be God if He has a God?

Study Suggestion: Take the online test for this section of the study of the Messiah found on http://ariel.org/come-and-see.htm under "The Deity of the Messiah (063)."

Chapter IX

The Kenosis

The study of the deity of Messiah and topics like His incarnation will lead the student of the Word to something which theologians call "the kenosis." This term is based upon a Greek word and can be defined loosely as *Yeshua's* self-emptying. In order to fully comprehend biblical Christology, we must deal with this subject in greater depth than we did preliminarily in chapter seven.

A. Meaning

The word "kenosis" comes from the Greek verb *kenoo*, which means "to empty," "to make void," or "to evacuate."

There are several forms of this verb in the Greek New Testament. As *ekenosen*, it is found in Philippians 2:7, where it is translated as "emptied." As *kekenotai*, it is found in Romans 4:14, where it is translated as "is made void." As *kenosei*, it is found in I Corinthians 9:15, where it is translated as "should make void." Finally, as *kenothe*, the term is found in I Corinthians 1:17 and II Corinthians 9:3, where it is translated as "should be made void."

When the Son became incarnate, some kind of "emptying" took place. Certain theologians have taught that what *Yeshua* emptied Himself of, what He gave up when He became a man, was being God. If it were possible for someone to give up being God, then that person was not God to begin with. Nevertheless, kenosis means that somehow, in some way, deity adjusted to humanity. This adjustment took place without the Son of God giving up any of His deity and, at the same time, without reducing any of His humanity.

So while "kenosis" basically means "to empty oneself," in its theological relationship to Messiah, it means that a kenosis of some sort took place at the incarnation, where deity somehow adjusted to humanity, yet without giving up deity or reducing humanity.

B. PHILIPPIANS 2:5-11

The key Scripture on the kenosis of Messiah is Philippians 2:5-11. To fully understand all that is involved in the doctrine, a short exposition of this passage is in order. It will allow us to better understand what the kenosis is about and of what it was that *Yeshua* emptied Himself at the incarnation. The passage reads as follows:

> [5] *Have this mind in you, which was also in Messiah Yeshua:* [6] *who, existing in the form of God, counted not the being on an equality with God a thing to be grasped,* [7] *but emptied himself, taking the form of a servant, being made in the likeness of men;* [8] *and being found in fashion as a man, he humbled himself, becoming obedient even unto death, yea, the death of the cross.* [9] *Wherefore also God highly exalted him, and gave unto him the name which is above every name;* [10] *that in the name of Yeshua every knee should bow, of things in heaven and things on earth and things under the earth,* [11] *and that every tongue should confess that Yeshua Messiah is Lord, to the glory of God the Father.*

Verse 5 is a transitional statement. In the Greek, it begins with a word that means "be minding." It is in the present tense, and so the point is: "keep on minding," "strive to imitate Him," "strive to reproduce His image." We are to follow the pattern of *Yeshua's* humanity and His unselfishness. So the point of verse 5 is to teach the imitation of Messiah, the habitual, daily directing of the mind to the distinctive virtue of Messiah-likeness. Therefore, Paul says, *Have this mind in you, which was also in Messiah Yeshua.* In our minds, we are to be imitating what Messiah is all about.

The first part of verse 6 emphasizes His preexistence when it says, *who, existing in the form of God.* The way He has always existed in eternity past is *in the form of God*. Before He became a man, His existence has been continuous, eternal, *in the form of God*. To exist *in the form of God* means to be God.

Indeed, in the second part of verse 6, His deity is clearly taught when it says that He *counted not the being on an equality with God a thing to be grasped.* While the first part of verse 6 teaches the preexistence of *Yeshua*, the second part teaches His *equality with God*. He existed in a form that naturally made Him an equal with God. To be an equal of God means to be God. The mind of the Messiah was exercised in such a way that He did not consider His exalted God-equal existence a warrant for seizing and grasping the glory for Himself—the glory that comes with being God. In other words, He did not count *equality with God* as something to be used selfishly for His own enrichment. He was willing to exist in a form other than the form of God.

What that form was is brought out in verse 7, where the incarnation of the Messiah is taught. According to this verse, He *emptied himself, taking the form of a servant, being made in the likeness of men.*

There are two things to notice here. First, we need to note what this verse does not say concerning the act of self-emptying. The Messiah did not empty Himself of the form of God, nor did He exchange the form of God for the likeness of men. The concept is not "to give up;" rather, it is "to add to." The statement of the Greek text *emptied himself* (*ekenosen*) is in itself an incomplete thought. What follows next in the sentence is describing the nature of His humiliation—He took upon Himself *the form of a servant* and was made *in the likeness of men*. The *form of a servant* was not exchanged for the form of God, not exchanged for equality with God, but added to it. The picture is that He added to His divine form; He took upon Himself the addition of humanity.

Second, the verse goes on to explain of what He did empty Himself. He emptied Himself of the right to have the independent use of those ten divine attributes that were discussed in chapter eight of this book. As God, He had the perfect right to independently use those attributes, but He would no longer use them except in accordance with the will of God the Father.

That is why the writer says that He not only took upon Himself *the likeness of men*, but specifically, He took upon Himself *the form of a servant*, the servant role. Of course, a servant is someone who obeys a lord. This is the picture of what He emptied Himself—He emptied Himself of the right to independently use His divine attributes. He now became an earthly servant of God the Father. He would use His attributes only in accordance with the will of God the Father. He would not use His omnipotence unless God the Father willed it. He would not use His omniscience unless God the Father willed it. Consequently, there were things *Yeshua* did not know in His humanity. For example, He did not know when He was coming back. The reason He did not know this is because He did not use the attribute of omniscience; it was not God the Father's will for Him to do so. When *Yeshua* became a man, He did not become less than God. Rather, by becoming a man, He took on humanity in addition to His divinity.

Having said all this about verse 7, let us paraphrase it to try and bring the thoughts together and make it more understandable: "He did not count the state of equality with God as something to be grasped at all costs and used as a means of self-enrichment, but willed to give up the independent use of the attributes of deity to stoop down in order to take on the form of a servant and so become a man by means of the virgin birth and the incarnation." If we can grasp this paraphrase, we will get all of the implications that are taught in this passage.

Verse 8 describes His crucifixion: *and being found in fashion as a man, he humbled himself, becoming obedient even unto death, yea, the death of the cross.* When humankind saw *Yeshua*, they did not see Him in a divine essence; they saw Him as a human being. He was recognized by all to be a man. This was part of His humiliation, part of His obedience to God the Father. He emptied Himself of His omnipotence in that He did not use His omnipotence to keep people from putting Him to death. Because the Son was willing to give up existing only in the form of God—not in exchange of existing in the form of God, but in addition to that form—He took on the form of a man.

Because He was willing to empty Himself in that way, there is a promise of His exaltation in verses 9-11. As a result of His kenosis, He was exalted when He ascended into heaven.

Verse 9 states, *Wherefore also God highly exalted him, and gave unto him the name which is above every name.* He was raised from the dead to unusual dignity and power.

Verse 10 goes on to explain *that in the name of Yeshua every knee should bow, of things in heaven and things on earth and things under the earth.* His universal sovereignty is recognized.

Verse 11, finally, concludes the thought with these words: *and that every tongue should confess that Yeshua Messiah is Lord, to the glory of God the Father.* There will eventually be universal homage to the Messiah as Lord.

To summarize what has been said so far, the kenosis does not imply that He divested Himself of the form of deity. Rather, it means that He laid aside the independent exercise of His divine attributes by which the form of God expresses itself. Instead, He took on and assumed human form, flesh, and nature by means of the incarnation and the virgin birth. The self-emptying brought about a change of status from the position of God to the position of a servant. In the exchange, He did not divest Himself of or give up His deity. In His human form, He retained all the attributes of His deity, but He never manifested His deity apart from the will of the Father. Thus, even in His earthly sojourn as a man, He was still God.[42]

C. False Views

There are eight false views of the kenosis, which in some shape or form reduce the Messiah to something less than God. A so-called kenotic theologian would hold to these false views. While the kenosis is a biblical reality, kenotic theology, as presented below, has many errors. This is what is being taught:

1. Messiah laid aside deity to become man.
2. Messiah's deity was veiled and limited only in certain important respects.
3. Messiah actually limited Himself, so that His self-limitation was real, but inconsiderable.
4. Messiah was in possession of all of His attributes, but acted as though He was not.
5. Messiah gave up certain relative attributes, such as being omniscient, omnipotent, and omnipresent.
6. Messiah gave up His essential attributes of deity.
7. Messiah emptied Himself of all of His attributes so that His deity was non-existent.
8. The entire event of the kenosis is to be placed merely within the earthly life of Messiah.

[42] Study Suggestion 1 on page 129.

D. The True View

The true view of the kenosis can be determined from the exposition of the Philippians passage.

1. The Facets

The true view of the kenosis has six facets:

1. *Yeshua* did not divest Himself of the form of deity.
2. He laid aside the independent exercise of the divine attributes by which the form of God expresses itself.
3. He assumed human form, flesh, and nature by the incarnation.
4. His self-emptying brought about a change of state, from the position of God to the position of a servant. It did not change His being God; it changed His position.
5. In this change, He did not divest Himself of deity.
6. In His human form He retained the possession of deity, but He never manifested this apart from the will of the Father.

2. Specific Truths Included

This biblical view of the kenosis includes specific truths. It includes the veiling of Messiah's pre-incarnate glory. It is not His deity that was veiled, but His glory (Jn. 17:5). There were two times when He manifested His glory during the time of His earthly life. One was at His transfiguration, the second at the time of His arrest when He spoke and the arresting group fell to the ground. These were the only two occasions when His pre-incarnate glory was revealed. So the kenosis involved the veiling of His pre-incarnate glory.[43]

The biblical view of the kenosis also includes His condescension to take upon Himself the likeness of sinful flesh (Rom. 8:3).

[43] Question on page 129.

Finally, it includes His voluntary non-use of some of His attributes of deity during the time of His earthly life. We see this, for example, in Matthew 24:36, where He did not use His attribute of omniscience. It is not so much what *Yeshua* gave up as what He gained that needs to be considered. He gained human nature. This simply involved a change of position. It does not mean that He was not God anymore, just that He changed His position. He did not give up deity; rather, He gained humanity. He did not cease to exist in the form of God, but added the form of a servant.

3. Answers for Kenotic Theologians

Kenotic theologians, generally speaking, agree in their view that *Yeshua* gave up being God in some way or in some capacity. They teach that He laid aside His deity in order to become man. In answer to these claims, we should point out that it is impossible to surrender an attribute by changing the character of the essence to which it belongs. To remove an attribute of deity is to destroy deity. So once *Yeshua's* attributes of deity are removed, He ceases to be God. It is also impossible to distinguish between relative and absolute attributes, because both are absolutely essential to deity. Lastly, we can point out that the Gospel of John greatly emphasizes the deity of Messiah during His earthly life. This shows that He was God, even while in human form. It is wrong to set aside His deity and teach that He was less than God.

4. Conclusion

Having discussed the biblical view of the kenosis, three conclusions can be drawn. First, with the incarnation, the Messiah did not cease to be God, nor did He give up His divine attributes. What He did was to add to His divine nature human nature so as to be able to take on the role of a servant and to die for the sins of the world.

Second, He gave up the independent use of His divine attributes and exercised them only in accordance with the will of God the Father. Furthermore, in His humanity, He functioned with power of the Holy Spirit.

Third, He voluntarily accepted a life of suffering and abuse, leading to His death by crucifixion.[44]

[44] Study Suggestion 2 on page 129.

E. Questions and Study Suggestions

Study Suggestion 1: Some terms seem very technical to us, yet the concepts they describe are not difficult to understand. This is true of the kenosis of *Yeshua*. Try to develop a definition which you can use when you explain this marvelous truth to others.

Question: Read II Peter 1:16-18. When Peter states that he was an eyewitness of *Yeshua's* majesty, to which event is he referring? How does the account of this event (in Matthew 17:1-8) help you make sense of the kenosis?

Study Suggestion 2: We can study biblical truths and gain great intellectual knowledge. Often, it takes a while until this knowledge moves from the brain to the heart. Take a moment—or two—and consider what the Lord had done for you by emptying Himself. Meditate on the beauty of this truth and tell Him how grateful you are that He was willing to add humanity to His deity.

Chapter X

Messiah's Impeccability

So far, we have established a few important truths about the Messiah. *Yeshua*, we learned, is fully God and fully man. He existed before His incarnation, and though He took on the form of man, He never gave up His deity. The next question to consider is if He could have sinned. If the answer is that He was impeccable, that is unable to sin, how then could He truly "sympathize with our weaknesses" as Hebrews 4:15 tells us?

The theological term "impeccability" comes from the Latin *impeccabilis*, in which the words *in* and *peccare* (to sin) are combined to express the inability to sin. Impeccability needs to be distinguished from the term "peccability." While peccability means that Messiah was able to sin (though He chose not to), impeccability means He was not able to sin. These terms indicate differences of view. Even some firm Bible-believing evangelicals hold to the peccability of Messiah, while others believe in His impeccability. However, both agree that *Yeshua* never sinned. Those who believe He was peccable believe that He could keep Himself from sinning. He was able to sin. Those who believe that He was impeccable are saying He was not even able to sin. This author holds the view that *Yeshua* was impeccable.[45]

---

[45] Study Suggestion on page 136.

A. The Doctrine

The doctrine of impeccability teaches that the temptations of Messiah were real. As a man, He experienced real temptation because of His human nature. God, on the other hand, cannot be tempted to sin. Hence, in relation to His divine nature, the temptations He experienced as man would not have been real. However, since He was fully God and fully man, His temptations were very real to Him because of His real human nature.

The doctrine of impeccability also teaches that the possibility of sin is removed by the presence of divine nature. Messiah, we need to remember, was a unique being who had two natures. His human nature made Him temptable, making the temptations real, but His divine nature precluded any possibility of His sinning.

The distinctions between the first Adam and the last Adam need to be discussed here (I Cor. 15:45). The first Adam was temptable and peccable because he was human only. But the last Adam—*Yeshua*—is perfectly human and perfectly divine, meaning that two natures joined in one person. The question as to the possibility of sin has to be addressed to the whole person of the last Adam, and not to any one particular nature. So as to His divine nature, *Yeshua* was neither temptable nor peccable. As to His human nature He was both temptable and peccable. Because we are dealing with the person of Messiah, who had two natures, He was indeed temptable as regards His human nature; but as to His divine nature, He was impeccable. Since both natures are joined in the one person of Messiah, peccability would have implied something less than God, since God is not able to sin.

The conclusion of the doctrine, then, is not that *Yeshua potuit non peccare,* meaning in Latin that "it was possible for Him not to sin," but that He *non potuit peccare,* meaning "it was impossible for Him to sin." That is what the doctrine of impeccability teaches. *Yeshua* was temptable, but impeccable—He simply was not able to sin because He was the God-Man.

B. The Proof

The proof of the doctrine of impeccability is to be found in four ways. First, it is evidenced in the divine attribute of immutability. God is immutable, and so is His

Son, the Messiah. As *Yeshua* could not change, He was holy both before and after His incarnation.

A second proof of His impeccability is His omnipotence. The very possibility of sin implies weakness. However, because Messiah was omnipotent, He had no weaknesses whatsoever and therefore did not possess the capability of sinning.

A third attribute which provides evidence for the doctrine of impeccability is omniscience. Sin appeals to the ignorance of the one tempted. But by His omniscience, *Yeshua* always knew the results of sin. This militates against His peccability.

Fourth, there are Scriptures directly concerning Messiah's inability to sin. These are Hebrews 4:15, James 1:13, and I John 3:5, which all point to the fact that God is unable to sin. *Yeshua*, being God, cannot sin.[46]

C. Objections and Answers

There are many fine believers and teachers of the Word who hold to the view that Messiah was peccable. They would raise specific objections to the doctrine of impeccability, which will be examined and answered here.

1. The Temptations Were not Real

How could an impeccable person really be tempted? It would appear that the temptation could not be very real. In answer to this objection, we need to remember that Messiah did not have a sin-nature. The nature of His temptation was different than ours, and so it had to be, because our temptations are aimed at our sin-nature. He did not have a sin-nature, and so His temptations must have been different. Nevertheless, He really was tempted, and His temptation set forth His sinlessness. He was tempted as to His person, which was both human and divine. His human nature was temptable, but His divine nature was not. He was tempted as a man, since, of course, God could not be tempted.

[46] Study Suggestion 2 on page 136.

Furthermore, there are three points of agreement between those who believe in His impeccability and those who believe in His peccability. Both groups believe that *Yeshua* never sinned, that He had no sin-nature, and that He really was tempted.

Another answer we can give to those who believe in the peccability of Messiah is that it really is possible to attempt the impossible! An invincible army can still be attacked, for example. A row-boat can attempt to attack a battleship, although its chances of success are virtually nil. So Messiah's inability to sin does not preclude the possibility of temptation. Satan could still attempt the impossible by tempting the impeccable person to sin.

Furthermore, temptability does not imply susceptibility. Even a person who is not susceptible to a specific temptation might still be tempted to do it.

A final answer is that the temptation may be real, but if there is infinite power to resist, the person is impeccable.

2. Messiah's Humanity Demands Temptability

The second objection claims that the humanity of the Messiah, the very fact that He was truly man, militates against impeccability. We can answer this objection in four points:

1. Temptations come by virtue of the fact that man has a sin-nature.
2. Messiah was not tempted through a sin-nature, although He was *tempted in all points like as we are* (Heb. 4:15).
3. He had to be tempted as to His human nature since He could not be tempted as to His divine nature (Jam. 1:13).
4. Hebrews 4:15 does not say that He was tempted with a view to His succumbing to sin, but rather He was tested with a view to proving that He was sinless.

3. Impeccability Rules out the Genuineness of the Temptation

The third objection to the doctrine of impeccability is that it rules out the reality and the genuineness of the temptation. We can answer this objection by saying two things.

First, the reality of a test does not lie in the moral nature of the one tested or in his ability or inability to yield to it.

Second, *Yeshua's* ability to sympathize with us does not demand or depend on a one-to-one correspondence in the problems that call forth sympathy. To say that Messiah could not sympathize if He could not sin is not true. For example, we can sympathize with a person although we ourselves have not suffered in a similar situation. We can be sympathetic towards someone facing a divorce even though we have never faced divorce. The ability to sympathize simply does not require this kind of one-to-one correspondence. Sympathetic people can sympathize whether or not they have ever suffered the specific things others suffer.

D. Conclusions

Having defined the doctrine of impeccability and having answered the most common objections to this doctrine, there are two basic conclusions to note. First, the testing proved the sinlessness of the Messiah. The purpose of His temptation was not to prove that He was able not to sin, but to prove that He was unable to sin to begin with. Second, it made Him a sympathizing high priest.[47]

[47] Study Suggestion 3 and Application on page 136.

E. Questions and Study Suggestions

Study Suggestion 1: You might have never even asked yourself the question if you believe in the peccability or the impeccability of *Yeshua*. Now is the time to make up your mind and see if Dr. Fruchtenbaum's explanation lines up with your beliefs.

Study Suggestion 2: Here is another point to consider when we try to wrap our minds around the idea of *Yeshua's* impeccability. Read Romans 1:20, 2:14-15, Mark 1:13, and Hebrews 4:15. What role does our conscience play in determining what sin is?

Study Suggestion 3: Temptation in itself is not sinful. It only becomes sin when we start acting upon it, even in our minds. Though sins like pride, greed, lust, and covetousness are not necessarily evident to others, they can be sins of the heart (Mk. 7:21-22). Read James 1:13-15 and discover the path of unrighteousness. According to Romans 13:13-14, what tools are available to you to not allow a temptation to turn into a sinful action?

Application: Dr. Fruchtenbaum writes:

> When *Yeshua* resisted temptations, He did not rebuke Satan or call him names, nor did He "bind" him. He always resisted Satan by means of Scripture; He simply quoted appropriate Scripture. Even when Satan misapplied and misused Scripture, *Yeshua*, by the proper use of the Scriptures, was able to resist Satan. This is the way all believers should resist Satan as well. In Luke's account of the temptation of *Yeshua*, he states that *when the devil had completed every temptation, he departed from him* (Lk. 4:13). Here, we can see the biblical principle that if one resists Satan, he will flee. We also see that resisting always comes by Scripture. The key passage on resisting Satan is Ephesians 6:10-18, which emphasizes the use of Scripture. Luke adds one last phrase, *for a season*. Every spiritual victory is always temporary. There will be more spiritual battles later, and the spiritual warfare must be fought until the day of death.

Chapter XI

The Life of the Messiah

The life of Messiah is an important theological topic. However, it is a study in its own right, and due to its immensity, it would have to be detailed in a separate book. In a study devoted to Christology, the study of the life of the Messiah will need to concentrate on the points that affect the theology of this doctrine. What are the theological implications of Messiah's birth, His childhood, His baptism, and so on?

A. The Birth

The Scriptures which speak of the birth of Messiah are Matthew 1:18-25, Luke 1:26-38, and 2:1-20. In previous chapters, it was pointed out that the miracle was in the conception, not in the actual birthing process. Galatians 4:4 says, *but when the fulness of the time came, God sent forth his Son, born of a woman, born under the law.* The fact that *Yeshua* was *born of a woman* simply shows that while He was miraculously conceived and born of a virgin, His birth was normal. Technically, we are not talking about the miracle of the virgin birth, but the virgin conception.

Several Old Testament prophecies—which were discussed in chapter two—provided important information about *Yeshua's* birth. The first one, found in Genesis 3:15, spoke of Messiah being of the seed of the woman, and Isaiah 7:14 adds the important truth that He would be conceived and born of a virgin.

Without doubt, the virgin birth, which was predicted long before the New Testament was written, is a crucial element of New Testament theology.

There is a misconception that the virgin birth was necessary to keep the Messiah from inheriting the sin-nature of His mother Miriam. It is based upon the false assumption that the sin-nature is transmitted only through the father. However, the sin-nature is actually transmitted through both the father and the mother. What protected the Messiah from inheriting the sin-nature of Miriam was not the lack of a human father, but rather, it was the overshadowing work of the Holy Spirit. So it was not the absence of a male sperm, but the actual work of the Holy Spirit in His conception that protected *Yeshua* from inheriting the sin-nature of man. God could have done this through normal conception. If God had wanted to, His omnipotence would have allowed Him to produce a sinless being, using both a male sperm and a female egg. So again, it was not the absence of a human father that protected *Yeshua* from the sin-nature, but the overshadowing of the Holy Spirit. The reason the Messiah was conceived in a virgin's womb was not that God had no other options.

Messiah's unique birth resulted in four things:

1. It made Him a member of humanity.
2. It made Him a member of the seed of Abraham, making Him a Jew.
3. It made Him a member of the House of David, making Him a king.
4. It is the means by which Messiah became the God-Man.[48]

B. The Childhood

There are seven theologically relevant events which happened during Messiah's childhood. The first event was His circumcision, which is recorded in Luke 2:21: *And when eight days were fulfilled for circumcising him, his name was called Yeshua, which was so called by the angel before he was conceived in the womb.* Two covenants demanded that the Messiah would be circumcised on the eighth day: the Abrahamic Covenant and the Mosaic Covenant. Under the Abrahamic Covenant, His circumcision was a sign of His Jewishness. Under the Mosaic Law,

[48] Question 1 on page 163.

His circumcision was a sign of submission to the law. On the day of His circumcision, He was also officially named *Yeshua*.

The second event was His presentation, which is recorded in Luke 2:22-25. The first three verses of this passage set the scene:

> [22] *And when the days of their purification according to the law of Moses were fulfilled, they brought him up to Jerusalem, to present him to the Lord* [23] *(as it is written in the law of the Lord, Every male that opened the womb shall be called holy to the Lord),* [24] *and to offer a sacrifice according to that which is said in the law of the Lord, A pair of turtledoves, or two young pigeons.*

The presentation occurred when *Yeshua* was forty days old. This was the occasion when, according to the Law of Moses, the price of the redemption of the firstborn had to be paid (Ex. 13:12-15). While at the Temple, two Jewish individuals, Simeon and Anna, recognized His Messiahship (Lk. 2:25-38).

The third theologically relevant event was the Messiah's sojourn in Egypt, which is recorded in Matthew 2:1-18. It was brought about by the visit of the Magi. These Gentile astrologers from Babylonia recognized His Messiahship.

The fourth element of the Messiah's childhood was His upbringing in Nazareth, which is recorded in Matthew 2:19-23 and Luke 2:39. From at least the age of four onward, He was largely brought up in a town whose reputation was more than questionable.

The fifth event was His development from the age of four to the age of twelve. This development is recorded in two passages. It is simply summarized in Luke 2:40, but the details are given in Isaiah 50:4-9. From this passage, we know that God the Father would wake up His Son early in the morning to train Him for His Messianic mission. This took place on a daily basis for eight years until *Yeshua* was twelve years old.

The sixth event was *Yeshua's* visit to Jerusalem, which is recorded in Luke 2:41-50. This occurred when the Messiah was twelve years old, and what happened shows the results of His divine training. By this age, He already recognized His Sonship-relationship to God the Father.

The seventh theologically relevant element of Messiah's childhood was His further development from the age of twelve to about the age of thirty. It is summarized in Luke 2:51-52. Here we learn two things: *Yeshua* remained in submission to His earthly parents, and He developed mentally, physically, spiritually, and socially.[49]

C. The Baptism

There are three passages of Scripture that discuss the details of *Yeshua's* baptism. These are Matthew 3:13-17, Mark 1:9-11, and Luke 3:21-23. From these and other passages, one can derive six reasons why the baptism was necessary.

1. The Reasons

The first reason for His baptism was to fulfil all righteousness (Mt. 3:15). To be righteous means "to live consistently with a standard," "to conform perfectly to a standard." The standard at this point was the Mosaic Law. *Yeshua* was baptized to show that He would fulfill the righteous demands of the law. This would identify Him with righteousness.

Second, *Yeshua* was baptized to identify with John the Baptist's preaching of the kingdom; thus He was identified with a message.

Third, He was to be publically identified to Israel; shortly, there will be a public verbal and visible authentication of His Messiahship.

Fourth, He was to be identified with the believing remnant being prepared by John. Those who were responding to John's message made up the believing remnant of Israel of that day; thus He was identified with a group.

Fifth, He was to be identified with sinners, as Paul puts it in II Corinthians 5:21: *Him who knew no sin he made to be sin on our behalf; that we might become the righteousness of God in him.*

Sixth, at His baptism, *Yeshua* was to receive His special anointing by the Holy Spirit. This is brought out by Acts 10:38: *even Yeshua of Nazareth, how God anointed him with the Holy Spirit and with power: who went about doing good, and healing all that were oppressed of the devil; for God was with him.*

[49] Question 2 on page 163.

2. The Presence of the Trinity

At His baptism, the entire Triune God appeared, both visibly and audibly. God the Son was seen in the person of *Yeshua*. Matthew 3:16 describes how the Holy Spirit made His appearance: *And Yeshua, when he was baptized, went up straightway from the water: and lo, the heavens were opened unto him, and he saw the Spirit of God descending as a dove, and coming upon him.* Obviously, this was not a real dove. Neither was it some ghostly form, because Luke 3:22 specifies He came down *in bodily form, as a dove.*

Of all the various ways the Holy Spirit could have made His appearance, why did He choose a bird? And why specifically a dove? There is something in the Jewish background about this that would communicate to a Jewish audience. The first time the Holy Spirit is mentioned in Scripture is Genesis 1:2b, where *the Spirit of God moved upon the face of the waters.* The Hebrew word is *merachephet*, meaning that He was "brooding over the waters like a mother bird." It is a word used to describe what mother birds do when they hover over their young or over the nest. The Hebrew word in Genesis 1:2 gives the Holy Spirit the function of a mother bird. The ancient rabbinic commentary on Genesis 1:2 states that the Spirit that brooded over the waters was "like a dove." The rabbis themselves specified the bird to be a dove, so the Holy Spirit was already connected with the concept of a dove in the Jewish mindset. To communicate that clearly during *Yeshua's* baptism, the Holy Spirit does come down in the bodily form of a dove. So now, the Son and the Spirit are visible.

The final member of the Trinity to make His appearance does not do so visibly, but audibly, as it says in Matthew 3:17: *and lo, a voice out of the heavens, saying, This is my beloved Son, in whom I am well pleased.*

The account of the voice out of heaven also has a rabbinic background. Rabbinic writings refer to what is called in Hebrew a *bat kol. Bat kol* literally means "the daughter of a voice." In rabbinic theology, the voice of the prophets closed with Malachi and the next prophet would be Elijah, who would return to announce the coming of the Messiah. However, while the prophetic voice ended, the voice of God did not cease, and periodically, He spoke a short sentence out of heaven. This was the *bat kol.*

What God the Father spoke audibly out of heaven at the baptism of *Yeshua* was: *This is my beloved Son, in whom I am well pleased.* With these words, He identified *Yeshua* as the Messianic Son of Psalm 2, where He said, *You are my son; This day have I begotten you.*[50] While God the Father verbally identified Him at the baptism, the Holy Spirit anointed Him for service.[51]

D. The Temptation

The clear relationship between the baptism of *Yeshua* and His temptation should not be missed. This connection is seen in two ways. First, at His baptism, He said that He had come *to fulfil all righteousness* (Mt. 3:15); at His temptation, this righteousness was tested. Second, at His baptism, God the Father declared Him to be the *beloved Son* (Mt. 3:17); at His temptation, He was challenged to prove it.

All three Gospel accounts make the point that the temptation of *Yeshua* was very much a part of the divine plan. Mark 1:12-13 tells us that He was tempted of Satan in the wilderness: [12] *And straightway the Spirit drove him forth into the wilderness.* [13] *And he was in the wilderness forty days tempted of Satan; and he was with the wild beasts; and the angels ministered unto him.* In these verses, Mark states four basic facts: first, the Spirit drove the Messiah *into the wilderness*; second, *Yeshua* fasted for *forty days*; third, during the forty days, He was *tempted of Satan*; and fourth, He was *with the wild beasts*.

Matthew and Luke both give the details, but there is a difference in the order of the temptations in the two Gospels. Matthew arranged his order based upon his theme, the kingship of *Yeshua*. For him, the key temptation was that of the kingdoms of the world, so he saved the best for last, so to speak. Matthew 4:1 states: *Then was Yeshua led up of the Spirit into the wilderness to be tempted of the devil.*

Luke, who was historically minded, gave the actual order in which the temptations occurred. Therefore, this study follows his account because he is the only Gospel writer who claimed to have put his material in chronological sequence. His account of the temptation is found in Luke 4:1-13:

> [1] *And Yeshua, full of the Holy Spirit, returned from the Jordan, and was led in the Spirit in the wilderness* [2] *during forty days, being tempted of the devil.*

[50] A more detailed analysis of this Messianic title can be found on page 40.

[51] Question 3 on page 163.

And he did eat nothing in those days: and when they were completed, he hungered. [3] *And the devil said unto him, if you are the Son of God, command this stone that it become bread.* [4] *And Yeshua answered unto him, It is written, Man shall not live by bread alone.* [5] *And he led him up, and showed him all the kingdoms of the world in a moment of time.* [6] *And the devil said unto him, To you will I give all this authority, and the glory of them: for it has been delivered unto me; and to whomsoever I will I give it.* [7] *If you therefore will worship before me, it shall all be yours.* [8] *And Yeshua answered and said unto him, It is written, You shall worship the Lord your God, and him only shall you serve.* [9] *And he led him to Jerusalem, and set him on the pinnacle of the temple, and said unto him, If you are the Son of God, cast yourself down from hence:* [10] *for it is written, He shall give his angels charge concerning you, to guard you:* [11] *and, On their hands they shall bear you up, Lest haply you dash your foot against a stone.* [12] *And Yeshua answering said unto him, It is said, You shall not make trial of the Lord your God.* [13] *And when the devil had completed every temptation, he departed from him for a season.*

1. The Purpose

As to the purpose of the temptation, we can summarize what we have already said in the previous chapter, which dealt with the doctrine of impeccability. The temptation Messiah experienced was to prove that He was impeccable, meaning He was not able to sin.

God's aim in allowing these temptations was to prove the sinlessness of His Messiah. Satan's aim in these temptations was to cause Messiah to sin. He simply tried to accomplish the impossible. Messiah was impeccable, but that did not discourage the fallen one from attempting the impossible. Satan's subsidiary aim was to keep *Yeshua* from the cross by offering Him a shortcut to His Messianic goal. If *Yeshua* had succumbed to this temptation, it would have been a good example of the attainment of a legitimate end by illegitimate means.

2. Messiah's Resistance

Messiah resisted all the temptations Satan offered. It is noteworthy that *Yeshua* always resisted temptation by citing Scripture, even when Satan misused Scripture by quoting it clearly out of context.

3. Messiah Representing Israel

In His temptations, *Yeshua* played a representative role for Israel. There are five ways in which this can be seen. The first way is that He was addressed as the Son of God, a title which relates Him to God's Chosen People. Israel, as a nation, is "the son of God," according to Exodus 4:22-23 and Hosea 11:1. *Yeshua* is called "the Son of God" in Matthew 2:15, which cites the Hosea account. In Matthew 4:3 and 6, Satan addresses Him in that way. So this very title "the Son of God" relates Messiah to Israel.

The second way which attests to *Yeshua's* representative role with Israel is that His testing took place in the wilderness. Just like Israel was tested in the wilderness (I Cor. 10:1-13), Messiah's temptation also took place in the wilderness (Lk. 4:1).

The third way which shows this relationship between Israel and her Messiah is in the use of the figure forty. Israel spent forty years in the wilderness (Num. 32:13; Hos. 13:5); Messiah spent forty days in the wilderness (Lk. 4:2). Though forty is a common figure in the Bible, here it relates the Messiah to His people.

The fourth way this relationship can be seen is that in both cases the Holy Spirit was present. The Holy Spirit was present with Israel during the wilderness wandering (Isa. 63:7-14). Just so, the Spirit was present with Messiah (Lk. 4:1).

The fifth way which demonstrates Messiah's representative role is that He responded to all three of Satan's temptations by citing Scripture from one book, the book of Deuteronomy, which is God's covenant book with the people of Israel.

Now, the point of all this is to show that where Israel as a nation has failed, the ideal Israelite, *Yeshua* the Messiah, has succeeded.

5. Messiah Representing Humanity

Not only did Messiah play a representative role with Israel, He also represented all of humanity. Hebrews 4:15 says that Messiah *was tempted in all points like as we are, yet without sin*. This, then, becomes the basis for His priesthood. Because He was tempted as we are, He could become our sympathetic High Priest. This does not mean that *Yeshua* suffered every type of temptation we experience, just as we do not suffer every type of temptation He did. For example, we are never going to be tempted to turn stones into bread. On the other hand, *Yeshua* was never tempted to waste His whole day watching talk shows on television or using social media. He was never tempted to do these things.

Hebrews 4:15 can be explained by I John 2:16, which reads, *For all that is in the world, the lust of the flesh and the lust of the eyes and the vain glory of life, is not of the Father, but is of the world.* This verse points out that there are three areas of temptation: the lust of the flesh, the lust of the eyes, and the pride of life. Every specific type of temptation will fit into one of these categories. When *Yeshua* was tempted to change stones into bread, it was after He had fasted for forty days. He was extremely hungry, and His flesh cried out to be satisfied with food. This was a temptation in the area of the lust of the flesh. Of course, it was God's will for *Yeshua* to satisfy His own hunger, but it was not God's will for Him to use His Messianic power to achieve this. The second temptation was when He was asked to throw Himself off the pinnacle of the Temple to prove He was the Son of God. This was a temptation in the area of the pride of life, because He was asked to prove that He was the Messiah. His third temptation was when He was shown all the kingdoms of the world and was told He could have it all by simply worshipping Satan just once. This was a temptation in the area of the lust of the eyes. The fact that *Yeshua* was tempted in all three areas of I John 2:16 proves that He indeed "suffered in all points like as we are, yet without sin."

E. The Transfiguration

Three of the Gospel accounts tell us of Messiah's transfiguration. They are Matthew 17:1-8, Mark 9:2-8, and Luke 9:28-36. Though it is recommended that all three accounts are read together, only Luke's Gospel will be cited here:

> [28] *And it came to pass about eight days after these sayings, that he took with*
> *him Peter and John and James, and went up into the mountain to pray.*
> [29] *And as he was praying, the fashion of his countenance was altered, and his*
> *raiment became white and dazzling.* [30] *And behold, there talked with him*
> *two men, who were Moses and Elijah;* [31] *who appeared in glory, and spoke of*
> *his decease which he was about to accomplish at Jerusalem.* [32] *Now Peter*
> *and they that were with him were heavy with sleep: but when they were fully*
> *awake, they saw his glory, and the two men that stood with him.* [33] *And it*
> *came to pass, as they were parting from him, Peter said unto Yeshua,*
> *Master, it is good for us to be here: and let us make three tabernacles; one*

for you, and one for Moses, and one for Elijah: not knowing what he said.
[34] And while he said these things, there came a cloud, and overshadowed
them: and they feared as they entered into the cloud. [35] And a voice came
out of the cloud, saying, This is my Son, my chosen: hear ye him. [36] And when
the voice came, Yeshua was found alone. And they held their peace, and told no man in those days any of the things which they had seen.

1. What Happened during the Transfiguration

From the Gospel accounts, we can derive six descriptive factors of the transfiguration:

1. Matthew and Mark tell us that *Yeshua was transfigured*, or metamorphosed (Gr. *metamorphoo*).
2. Luke describes this as *the fashion of His countenance was altered.*
3. Matthew says His *face did shine as the sun*, very brightly.
4. Matthew describes His garments as becoming *white as the light.*
5. Luke says His *raiment became white and dazzling.*
6. Mark describes His garments as glistening, exceeding white, *as no fuller on earth could whiten them.*

Taking into consideration these six descriptive factors, the question arises what exactly happened at the transfiguration. What happened is that the veiled *Shechinah* Glory[52] was unveiled and the three disciples saw the glory the Son of Man will have in the kingdom. Just before this account, *Yeshua* had promised that some of His disciples would not die until they saw His glory. He said in Luke 9:27, *But I tell you of a truth, There are some of them that stand here, who shall in no wise taste of death, till they see the kingdom of God.* In other words, they would not die until they had seen the kind of glory He will have in His Messianic Kingdom. The transfiguration is a fulfillment of this promise. The "some" who would not see death until this happened were Peter, James, and John. When

---

[52] The *Shechinah* Glory of God is a term which was transliterated from a Hebrew noun meaning "dwelling" or "settling." As such, the word does not appear in the Bible, but the concept clearly does. The Jewish rabbis used it to express a moment of divine visitation of the presence of God. It was the visible manifestation of an invisible God and happened, for example, in form of light, a cloud, or a pillar of fire.

Yeshua lived in the presence of God the Father in heaven, He had the glory of the *Shechinah*, so that He was always seen in the brightness of His glory. But with the incarnation, the brightness of His glory was veiled by His physical body. At His transfiguration, that glory became visible, and just for a short moment, His body was no longer a veil; the *Shechinah* Glory penetrated through the veil, and these disciples did indeed see the glory the Son of Man is going to have in His kingdom. So the event of the transfiguration is that the veiled *Shechinah* Glory became unveiled.

Appearing with *Yeshua* were Moses and Elijah, and the point of their discussion was Messiah's approaching death in Jerusalem. Then a cloud, the *Shechinah* Glory, enveloped all three men, and once again the *bat kol* came from heaven. It repeated what was declared at *Yeshua's* baptism, but then added the phrase: *hear ye him*. They have heard Moses and the Prophets, now they must hear the Messianic Son who is God's final revelation to man.

2. Theological Implications

All of the major events in the life of the Messiah have theological implications, and the same is true of the transfiguration. We can point out five such implications. First, the transfiguration authenticated the Messiahship of *Yeshua*, who was rejected by men, but accepted by God the Father. When God the Father spoke audibly, He said: *This is my beloved Son in whom I am well pleased; hear ye him.*

Second, the transfiguration anticipated the earthly kingdom of the Messiah. Before the transfiguration, *Yeshua* had promised His disciples that some of them—Peter, James and John—would not die until they had seen the glory that the Son of Man would have in the kingdom. This occurred when they witnessed the transfiguration. After the transfiguration, Peter wrote in II Peter 1:16-18:

> [16] *For we did not follow cunningly devised fables, when we made known unto you the power and coming of our Lord Yeshua Messiah, but we were eyewitnesses of his majesty.* [17] *For he received from God the Father honor and glory, when there was borne such a voice to him by the Majestic Glory, This is my beloved Son, in whom I am well pleased:* [18] *and this voice we ourselves heard borne out of heaven, when we were with him in the holy mount.*

As Peter reflected upon the experience, he pointed out that the transfiguration was in anticipation of the future power and return the Messiah, the coming of *Yeshua* in His kingdom.

Third, the transfiguration guaranteed the fulfillment of all Scripture. According to Luke 9:31, *Yeshua's* discussion with Moses and Elijah concerned His coming *exodus*, His coming death, which would fulfill the Law and the Prophets. Moses was there representing the Law, and Elijah was there representing the Prophets. *Yeshua* had come to fulfill all that Moses and the Prophets said. Peter reflects on this in II Pet. 1:19-21:

> [19] *And we have the word of prophecy made more sure; whereunto ye do well that ye take heed, as unto a lamp shining in a dark place, until the day dawn, and the day-star arise in your hearts:* [20] *knowing this first, that no prophecy of scripture is of private interpretation.* [21] *For no prophecy ever came by the will of man: but men spoke from God, being moved by the Holy Spirit.*

Fourth, the transfiguration was a pledge of life beyond the grave. Moses, who did die, was there, representing the resurrected saints. Elijah, who did not die, was there, representing the translated saints. For church saints, this will happen at the Rapture. For millennial saints, it will be sometime during or at the end of the Millennium. The fact that these two men continue to exist—one in spirit form only, and the other in a translated body that has been glorified—shows the continuation of life beyond death. So whether by resurrection or translation, there is, and will be, life beyond death.

Fifth, the transfiguration is a measure of God's love for humanity. It shows what it cost *Yeshua* to come to earth. It meant He had to veil His glory twice: first, at the incarnation, and second, after the transfiguration. Only at His ascension was His glory unveiled forever. When John saw Him again in the vision of Revelation 1:12-16, He was in the fullness of His *Shechinah* Glory, no longer veiled. When the Messiah returns at His Second Coming, it will be with unveiled glory. He will come with power and great glory in the clouds of heaven, the *clouds* representing the *Shechinah* Glory.[53]

---

[53] Study suggestions 1 and 2 on page 163.

F. THE TEACHINGS

Yeshua was called a teacher forty-five times in the Gospels. His fundamental teachings are found in the three major discourses—the Sermon on the Mount, the Olivet Discourse, and the Upper Room Discourse. Of equal importance are the parables, which will also be considered in this chapter on the teachings of Messiah.

1. The Major Discourses

a. The Sermon on the Mount

The Sermon on the Mount is found in Matthew 5:1–8:1 and Luke 6:17-49. Since we are studying the theological implications of the life of Messiah, the sermon itself will not be detailed.

As a unit, exactly what is the Sermon on the Mount?

(1) What it is Not

Starting with the negative, there are three things the Sermon on the Mount is not. First, it is not the constitution of the future Messianic Kingdom, a common interpretation in some circles. That would require the reinstitution of all 613 commandments of the Mosaic Law. However, this will not happen, because the Law of Moses was forever rendered inoperative when the Messiah died.

Second, it is not a way of salvation. This has been a common interpretation in more liberal circles that wish to avoid the narrow way of entry into heaven, namely, that a person must believe in *Yeshua* to be saved. They try to provide an alternative by teaching that keeping the high standards of the Sermon on the Mount ensures entrance into eternal glory. However, even if a person were capable of keeping these standards consistently, he still would not make it to heaven, because that would mean salvation is based on works, not by grace through faith. This sermon is a rule of life for those already saved, not a means of earning salvation.

Third, the sermon as a unit does not provide Christian or church ethics for this age. Some of the things mentioned in it did indeed become the rule of life for the believer, and it is possible to determine which ones those are because they were repeated later by the apostles. However, if it was the purpose of the Sermon on the Mount to provide moral standards, believers would be obligated to keep all 613 commandments of the Mosaic Law because, as we will see in the next paragraph, the sermon was Messiah's interpretation of the law. So it presents the Law of Moses in its purest form. Matthew 5:19 states that a person must keep even the *least commandment* of the Mosaic Law. If the sermon was given to teach church ethics for this age, it would require all believers to keep the dietary code. They would have to abide by the clothing laws, such as the prohibition of mixed threads and tassels, and men's beards would have to be cornered, not rounded. The church would have to obey many other *least commandments*, not to mention the priesthood and the sacrificial system. So as a unit, it was not the intent of the Sermon on the Mount to provide the church with ethics.

(2) What it Is

On the positive side, the sermon is the Messiah's interpretation of the true righteousness of the Law of Moses in contradistinction to the pharisaic interpretation of the righteousness of the law. The basic distinction was this: Did the law require only external conformity or did it require both external and internal conformity, both external and internal righteousness? In the Sermon on the Mount, *Yeshua's* purpose was to set forth the righteousness of God as demanded by the Mosaic Law. The Mosaic Law did not end with the coming of the Messiah; it ended with His death. As long as He was alive, all 613 commandments of the Mosaic Law had to be kept.

The purpose of the Sermon the Mount, or Messiah's interpretation of the law, then, was twofold: to set forth the righteousness of God and to convict men of their unrighteousness.

b. The Olivet Discourse

A second major example of the teaching of *Yeshua* is the Olivet Discourse, which is found in three Gospels: Matthew 24:1–25:46, Mark 13:1-37, and Luke 21:5-36. Again, the purpose here is to look at the theological implications of the Olivet Discourse, not at its details. The Sermon on the Mount was addressed to Israel as a whole, while the discourse was given to the disciples privately.

As to its significance, two points can be made. First, with the Olivet Discourse, the Messiah concluded the longest prophetic discourse of His public ministry. The Olivet Discourse is the most detailed of His teachings concerning future things. It was His last great discourse as a prophet. From this point on, He transitioned to His office as priest. He offered a sacrifice—that of His own blood—and then began to function as high priest after the order of Melchizedek. When He returns to fulfill the rest of the Olivet Discourse, He will come as king.

The second significance of the Olivet Discourse is that it answered the question: What will be the circumstances for the setting up of the kingdom?

The Olivet Discourse contains words for believers today: to *look up, for your redemption draws nigh* (Lk. 21:28). It contains words for unbelievers today: to believe on the Messiah. And it contains words for those who will be living during the Great Tribulation: for Jews to flee; and for Gentiles to watch, to be ready, and to labor.

c. The Upper Room Discourse

The Upper Room Discourse is a lengthy teaching session that *Yeshua* had with His disciples. It began at the conclusion of the Passover observance in the Upper Room and ended just prior to their arrival at the Garden of Gethsemane. In the Scriptures, it is found only in the Gospel of John, comprising four chapters: John 13, 14, 15, and 16.

The Upper Room Discourse contains various promises and admonitions and is significant for four key reasons, which will be described in the following paragraphs.

(1) The Transition from Prophet to Priest

The Upper Room Discourse marks the transition for *Yeshua* from the office of prophet to the office of priest. While the Messiah has the three offices of prophet, priest, and king, He does not function in all three offices simultaneously, but chronologically. During His First Coming, He functioned in the office or role of prophet; now He is functioning in the office or role of priest; at His Second Coming, He will function in the office or role of king. *Yeshua* was a prophet; He is now a priest; He will be a king.

His prophetic office ended a couple of days before the Upper Room Discourse. In Matthew 23, *Yeshua* denounces scribes and Pharisees for leading the nation to reject His Messiahship. With this denunciation, His public ministry ended and He concluded His prophetic office. The Upper Room Discourse is the transition from the office of prophet to the office of priest. His first priestly act was that of the shedding of His own blood as the final sacrifice for sin.

(2) The Transition from Law to Grace

The Upper Room Discourse also marks the beginning of the transition from the dispensation of law to the dispensation of grace. Technically, the dispensation of law ended with the death of the Messiah, while the dispensation of grace began with the birth of the church and the coming of the Holy Spirit's ministry of Spirit-baptism in Acts 2. Between the two dispensations, there is a transitional period. The dispensation of law should be pictured as slowly fading out, and the dispensation of grace as beginning to fade in. By the time of Acts 2:1-4, the dispensation of law had totally faded away and the dispensation of grace totally faded in. The Upper Room Discourse begins this transition.

(3) The Planting of Doctrinal Seeds

In the Upper Room Discourse, *Yeshua* planted many seeds of church doctrine that were further developed in the Epistles. Many of the things He taught in seed form in the Upper Room Discourse are given expositions, elaborations, and doctrinal formulations by the apostles in the Epistles.

(4) The New Relationship with the Messiah

The Upper Room Discourse begins to describe the new relationship that believers will have with *Yeshua* following His death and resurrection. Even the disciples had one type of relationship with Him before His death and resurrection. Afterwards, they entered into a new relationship with Him. This new relationship is the same type of relationship all believers now have with Him.

Believers today can never have the same type of relationship the apostles had with *Yeshua* before His death. They enjoyed a rather unique experience available only during His earthly ministry, when He still had His mortal body. But believers are all participants in the relationship that the apostles had with Him after His death and resurrection. This relationship is developed later by the Apostle Paul in the concept of being in Messiah and what it means to be in a new position within the body of the Messiah.

d. Conclusion

The Sermon on the Mount, the Olivet Discourse, and the Upper Room Discourse are three major examples of the teachings of *Yeshua*. In each, the Messiah concentrated on unique issues. In the Sermon on the Mount, He interpreted the kind of righteousness the law demanded. In the Olivet Discourse, He prophesied future events, both near and far. And in the Upper Room Discourse, He began to describe His ideas of the relationship He expected His bride, the church, to have with Him by laying out the foundations of church ethics for this age.

2. The Parables

We could integrate *Yeshua's* usage of parables into the next point, which deals with His different methods of teaching, but because of what is involved, we are going to study them as a separate category.

By definition, a parable is a figure of speech that teaches a moral, an ethical, or a spiritual truth from everyday life and experience. A parable is based on reality, in contrast to an allegory, which is not. The New Testament contains four types of parables: simile, metaphor, similitude, and story-type. In keeping with a Jewish method of teaching, a parable will go from the known to the unknown. Not every detail of a parable necessarily needs to be interpreted, but only those parts that deal with the question or problem. Parables are designed either to answer a question or to solve a problem. In order to interpret a parable, one must investigate the immediate context to determine the question that is being answered or the problem that is being solved. A parable may make one main point or several. In looking at a specific parable, one needs to discover the point or points at issue. Before concluding what the spiritual lesson of a parable is, one must first know the reality behind the parable. One must fully understand the literal sense before determining the spiritual sense.

a. The Timing

Yeshua did not begin His teaching career by use of parables. Rather, He started speaking this way at a certain point in His ministry—after the national rejection of His Messiahship in Matthew 12. When Israel's leaders rejected *Yeshua* as the Messiah, the nation followed their lead and thus committed what is called the unpardonable sin, namely, the national rejection of the Messiahship of *Yeshua* on the grounds of demon possession.

Up until the events of Matthew 12, *Yeshua* taught the masses clearly and distinctly, in terms that they could, and did, understand. After Israel as a nation rejected Him, His teaching method changed. As of Matthew 13, He taught the masses only in parables.

b. The Purpose

The purpose of Messiah's parabolic teaching method is spelled out in several passages. Matthew 13:1-3a states:

> [1] *On that day went Yeshua out of the house, and sat by the sea side.* [2] *And there were gathered unto him great multitudes, so that he entered a boat, and sat; and all the multitude stood on the beach.* [3a] *And he spoke to them many things in parables,*

Yeshua's parabolic method of teaching began the same day that the national rejection of His Messiahship occurred and the unpardonable sin was committed (Mt. 12:22-45).

Matthew 13:11-17 explains exactly the purpose of these parables. After *Yeshua's* first parable, the disciples asked Him a question in verse 10: *And the disciples came, and said unto him, Why speak you unto them in parables?* The fact that they raised this question indicates that He had not been speaking in parables before this point. Until the events of chapters 12 and 13, when *Yeshua* spoke to the masses, He spoke in clear language that all could understand. A good example of this is the Sermon on the Mount in Matthew 5–7. Matthew states that when *Yeshua* finished the Sermon on the Mount, not only did the Jewish people understand what He had said, they also understood clearly where He differed from the scribes and Pharisees. As a result of the rejection of His Messiahship described in Matthew 12, He began teaching the Jewish masses in parables in Matthew 13. This, of course, surprised the disciples, because they knew that *Yeshua* had taught them clearly up to that point. Now, they wanted to know why He had begun speaking to them in parables. Again, the question clearly indicates that this was the beginning of His parabolic method of teaching.

Yeshua responded by stating three main purposes for this change in His method of teaching. In Matthew 13:11a, He gives the first purpose: *And he answered and said unto them, Unto you it is given to know the mysteries of the kingdom of heaven.* The parables would illustrate the truth for His disciples.

The second purpose is stated in verses 11b-13 of Matthew 13:

> [11b] *but to them it is not given.* [12] *For whosoever has, to him shall be given, and he shall have abundance: but whosoever has not, from him shall be taken away even that which he has.* [13] *Therefore speak I to them in parables; because seeing they see not, and hearing they hear not, neither do they understand.*

The parables were to hide the truth from the masses. *Yeshua* said that He would teach them in terms they could not and would not understand. Since the nation had rejected His Messiahship, it had therefore rejected the light they had been given. If one rejects the light he has been given, he will not be given any more light. Since the nation had now rejected the light they had, no more light would be given. Instead of teaching them clearly and distinctly in terms they could understand as He had done heretofore, He began teaching them only in parables so they could no longer understand and would not understand.

The third purpose is given in verses 14-17 of Matthew 13:

> [14] *And unto them is fulfilled the prophecy of Isaiah, which said, By hearing ye shall hear, and shall in no wise understand; And seeing ye shall see, and shall in no wise perceive:* [15] *For this people's heart is waxed gross, And their ears are dull of hearing, And their eyes they have closed; Lest haply they should perceive with their eyes, And hear with their ears, And understand with their heart, And should turn again, And I should heal them.* [16] *But blessed are your eyes, for they see; and your ears, for they hear.* [17] *For verily I say unto you, that many prophets and righteous men desired to see the things which ye see, and saw them not; and to hear the things which ye hear, and heard them not.*

The third purpose of the parabolic teaching was to fulfill prophecy. In this passage, *Yeshua* quoted Isaiah 6:9-10, which prophesied that the Messiah would speak to the Jewish people in such a way that they would not understand. By speaking in parables, He fulfilled Old Testament prophecy, proving His very Messiahship.

Matthew 13:34-35 states:

> [34] *All these things spoke Jesus in parables unto the multitudes; and without a parable spoke he nothing unto them:* [35] *that it might be fulfilled which was spoken through the prophet, saying, I will open my mouth in parables; I will utter things hidden from the foundation of the world.*

Verse 34 re-emphasizes the fact that *Yeshua* spoke to the multitudes only in parables. This was not true before His rejection in Matthew 12. This restates the second purpose of His parabolic method of teaching: to hide the truth from the masses. In verse 35, He again points out that this was a fulfillment of prophecy, and this time He quotes Psalm 78:2. This restates the third purpose of the parabolic method of teaching: to fulfill Old Testament prophecy.

This same point is made in the parallel account in Mark 4:33-34: [33] *And with many such parables spoke he the word unto them, as they were able to hear it;* [34] *and without a parable spoke he not unto them: but privately to his own disciples he expounded all things.* This passage clearly explains that when *Yeshua* was alone with His disciples, He explained to them the meaning of the parables. This restated the first purpose of the parables in that they would illustrate the truth for the disciples. From Matthew 13 onward, this was the method *Yeshua* used consistently.

c. The Parables Listed

Altogether, *Yeshua* told thirty-seven parables. Though each one of them carries unique and important elements of doctrine, it is not the purpose of this study in systematic theology to elaborate on every parable. Rather, insofar as Christology is concerned, we simply want to enumerate the parables and the pertinent passages.

1. The parable of the sower (Mt. 13:3-9, 18-23; Mk 4:2-9, 13-20; Lk 8:5-8, 11-15)
2. The parable of the seed growing of itself (Mk. 4:26-29)
3. The parable of the tares (Mt. 13:24-30, 36-43)
4. The parable of the mustard seed (Mt. 13:31-32; Mk. 4:30-32; Lk. 13:18-19
5. The parable of the leaven (Mt. 13:33-34; Lk. 13:20-21)
6. The parable of the hidden treasure (Mt. 13:44)
7. The parable of the pearl of great price (Mt. 13:45-46)
8. The parable of the net (Mt. 13:47-50)
9. The parable of the householder (Mt. 13:51-53)
10. The parable of defilement (Mt. 15:10-20; Mk. 7:14-23)
11. The parable of the unmerciful servant (Mt. 18:23-35)
12. The parable of the Good Samaritan (Lk. 10:30-37)
13. The parable of the importunate friend (Lk. 11:5-8)
14. The parable of the rich fool (Lk. 12:16-21)
15. The parable of the waiting servants (Lk. 12:35-40)
16. The parable of the wise servant (Lk. 12:42-48)
17. The parable of the barren fig tree (Lk. 13:6-9)

18. The parable of those who are bidden (Lk. 14:7-11)
19. The parable of the rejected invitation (Lk. 14:15-24)
20. The parable of the lost sheep (Lk. 15:3-7)
21. The parable of the lost coin (Lk. 15:8-10)
22. The parable of the prodigal son (Lk. 15:11-32)
23. The parable of the unjust steward (Lk. 16:1-13)
24. The parable of the unprofitable servants (Lk. 17:5-10)
25. The parable of the importunate widow (Lk. 18:1-8)
26. The parable of the Pharisee and the publican (Lk. 18:9-14)
27. The parable of the laborers of the vineyard (Mt. 20:1-16)
28. The parable of the ten minas (Lk. 19:11-27)
29. The parable of the two sons (Mt. 21:28-32)
30. The parable of the householder (Mt. 21:33-46; Mk. 12:1-12; Lk. 20:9-19)
31. The parable of the wedding (Mt. 22:1-14)
32. The parable of the fig tree (Mt. 24:32-35; Mk. 13:28-32; Lk. 21:29-33)
33. The parable of the porter (Mk. 13:33-37)
34. The parable of the master of the house (Mt. 24:43-44)
35. The parable of the faithful servants and the evil servants (Mt. 24:45-51)
36. The parable of the ten virgins (Mt. 25:1-13)
37. The parable of the talents (Mt. 25:14-30)

3. Teaching Methods

When we study the teachings of Messiah, we can examine the contents and concentrate on the prophetic and moral truths found therein. Another way to look at them is to observe and learn from the teaching methods *Yeshua* employed. Altogether, we find Him using five different styles.

The first could be called the "problem method." We see this in Mark 2:9, when *Yeshua* asked the question: *Which is easier, to say to the sick of the palsy, Thy sins are forgiven; or to say, Arise, and take up thy bed, and walk?* We also see this method in Mark 10:17, where *Yeshua* is approached with the question, "What must I do to inherit eternal life?" These are problem-questions which the Messiah used to teach spiritual truth.

The second teaching style could be called the "one-on-one method." *Yeshua* used it in personal conversations with Nicodemus (Jn. 3) and the unnamed Samaritan woman (Jn. 4).

The third teaching style could be called the "leading question method." *Yeshua* used it in Mark 4:30, where He asked, *How shall we liken the kingdom of God? or in what parable shall we set it forth?* Other examples are Mark 10:38, Luke 6:46, and 14:5.

The fourth teaching style could be called the "lecture method." *Yeshua* used it in the Sermon on the Mount, the Upper Room Discourse, and the Olivet Discourse.

The fifth teaching style could be called the "object lessons method." *Yeshua* used it in Mark 12:42-44, where we read:

> [42] *And there came a poor widow, and she cast in two mites, which make a farthing.* [43] *And he called unto him his disciples, and said unto them, Verily I say unto you, This poor widow cast in more than all they that are casting into the treasury:* [44] *for they all did cast in of their superfluity; but she of her want did cast in all that she had, even all her living.*

Other examples are Matthew 9:17, 10:29, and John 12:24.[54]

G. The Miracles

The last theologically relevant area of discussion in the life of Messiah deals with His miracles.

1. The Nature of Miracles

Their nature can be defined by the four words which are used in describing them. These are the words "wonders," "signs," "powers," and "works."

[54] Study Suggestion 3 on page 163.

The word "wonder" refers to the fact that a miracle effects astonishment in the beholder. The miracles of Messiah caused astonishment in those who witnessed them, and in that sense, they were a wonder. We see this in Mark 2:12 where the healing of the leper causes these emotions: *And he arose, and straightway took up the bed, and went forth before them all; insomuch that they were all amazed, and glorified God, saying, We never saw it on this fashion.*

In Mark 4:39- 41, the astonishment is so overwhelming that it leads to fear:

> [39] *And he awoke, and rebuked the wind, and said unto the sea, Peace, be still. And the wind ceased, and there was a great calm.* [40] *And he said unto them, Why are ye fearful? have ye not yet faith?* [41] *And they feared exceedingly, and said one to another, Who then is this, that even the wind and the sea obey him?*

Mark 6:51 gives a similar account. This time, the calming of the wind leads the witnesses of the miracle to be *sore amazed in themselves.*

The second term which is used in Scripture to describe a miracle is the word "sign." The word means "a token" or "an indication of authenticity" of one's claims. The miracles of *Yeshua* were to authenticate His person and His Messianic claims. They were therefore known as signs. This is especially brought out by the Gospel of John, where he speaks about the miracles of *Yeshua* in many places as being signs. A few examples are John 2:18, 4:54, 6:14, 10:41, and 12:18.

The third term used to describe the miracles of *Yeshua* is the word "power." This emphasizes that a miracle is a mighty deed of God. Examples of where *Yeshua's* miracles are referred to as works of power or miraculous powers would be Matthew 11:20, Mark 6:14, and Luke 10:13.

The fourth word is "works," and where it is used, it emphasizes divine accomplishments. The miracles of *Yeshua* were referred to as works in Matthew 11:2, John 5:36, 7:3, and 10:25—to only name a few.

So in dealing with the nature of the miracles of Messiah, they are wonders, signs, powers, and works. They are wonders because they caused astonishment in the beholder. They are signs because they authenticated His message and His person. They are powers because they were mighty deeds of God. They are works because they were divine accomplishments.

2. The Categories

Some of *Yeshua's* miracles showed His power over nature, such as the stilling of the storm. Some were miracles of physical healing. He healed those who were lame, deaf, blind, and so on. Some were miracles over demons. Everywhere He went, He was always casting out demons. Some were miracles over death, and on more than one occasion, He raised people from the dead. Some are known as Messianic miracles. The rabbis in the time of *Yeshua* divided miracles into two categories. The first category contained those that anyone could perform if he was empowered by the Spirit of God. That would include the first four categories we have just noted: over nature, physical healing, demons, and death. But there was a second category of miracles which, according to the rabbis, only the Messiah would be able to perform. In this category, there were three main miracles, and *Yeshua* performed all three of these. They were the healing of a leper, the casting out of a dumb or mute demon, and the healing of a man born blind. For that reason, whenever *Yeshua* performed one of these miracles, the audience always raised the issue of His Messiahship.

3. The Miracles Listed

In the realm of Christology, it is not the purpose to expound on every miracle Messiah performed. Rather, a list of all the miracles and the verses where they are found will be given. Altogether, the Bible mentions thirty-six miracles:

1. Changing the water to wine (Jn. 2:1-11)
2. Healing of the nobleman's son (Jn. 4:46-54)
3. Healing of the man at the Pool of Bethesda (Jn. 5:1-9)
4. First draught of fish (Lk. 5:1-11)
5. Liberating the demoniac (Mk. 1:23-28; Lk. 4:33-37)
6. Healing of Peter's mother-in-law (Mt. 8:14-15; Mk. 1:29-31; Lk. 4:38-39)
7. Healing of a leper—a Messianic miracle (Mt. 8:2-4; Mk. 1:40-45; Lk. 5:12-16)
8. Healing of the paralytic. On this occasion, *Yeshua* declared He had the authority to forgive sins. (Mt. 9:2-8; Mk. 2:3-12; Lk. 5:18-26)
9. Healing of the withered hand (Mt. 12:10-13; Mk. 3:1-5; Lk. 6:6-10)
10. Healing of the centurion's servant (Mt. 8:5-13; Lk. 7:1-10)

11. Raising of the widow's son back to life (Lk. 7:11-15)
12. Casting out a demon which rendered the possessed man blind and dumb—a Messianic miracle (Mt. 12:22)
13. Stilling of the storm (Mt. 8:23-27; Mk. 4:35-41; Lk. 8:22-25)
14. Liberating of the two demoniacs (Mt. 8:28-34; Mk. 5:1-20; Lk. 8:26-39)
15. Healing of the woman with the issue of blood (Mt. 9:20-22; Mk. 5:25-34; Lk. 8:43-48)
16. Raising of Jairus' daughter (Mt. 9:18-19, 23-26; Mk. 5:22-24, 35-43; Lk. 8:41-42, 49-56)
17. Healing of the two blind men (Mt. 9:27-31)
18. Expelling of the dumb demon—another Messianic miracle (Mt. 9:32-33)
19. Feeding of the five thousand (Mt. 14:15-21; Mk. 6:35-44; Lk. 9:12-17; Jn. 6:1-14)
20. Walking on water (Mt. 14:25-33; Mk. 6:45-52; Jn. 6:16-21)
21. Healing of the Gentile girl (Mt. 15:21-28; Mk. 7:24-30)
22. Healing of the deaf and dumb man (Mk. 7:31-37)
23. Feeding of the four thousand (Mt. 15:32-38; Mk. 8:1-9)
24. Healing of the blind man (Mk. 8:22-26)
25. Healing of the epileptic boy by the casting out of a dumb demon—again a Messianic miracle (Mt. 17:14-18; Mk. 9:14-29; Lk. 9:38-43)
26. Finding of the tribute money in the fish (Mt. 17:24-27)
27. Healing of the man born blind—also a Messianic miracle (Jn. 9:1-7)
28. Healing of the dumb demoniac (Lk. 11:14)
29. Healing of the woman's infirmity (Lk. 13:10-17)
30. Curing of the man sick with the dropsy (Lk. 14:1-6)
31. Raising Lazarus from the dead (Jn. 11:17-44)
32. Healing of ten lepers—this Messianic miracle was performed ten times here (Lk. 17:11-19)
33. Healing of the blind men (Mt. 20:29-34; Mk. 10:46-52; Lk. 18:35-43)
34. Cursing of the fig tree (Mt. 21:18-22; Mk. 11:12-14)

35. Healing of the ear of Malchus (Lk. 22:49-51)
36. Second draught of fish (Jn. 21:1-14)[55]

H. Conclusion

This concludes this study of the life of Messiah, one major division of Christology. There are, of course, other facets to the life of Messiah, such as His death, burial, resurrection, and ascension. These are all part of the life of Messiah, but as they all have full theological implications in their own right, they will be studied in their own separate and distinct categories.

[55] Study Suggestion 4 on page 163.

I. Questions and Study Suggestions

Question 1: Luke 1:28 tells us that Miriam, the mother of *Yeshua*, was highly favored by God. In the Greek original, this term is one word, *kecharitomene*, which means "to make graceful" or "to endow with grace." God extended Himself to freely bestow grace on Miriam. What do you know about grace? Who needs it? How does one receive it? How come Miriam needed grace?

Question 2: How does Luke 2:51-52 support the fact that *Yeshua* was fully man?

Question 3: In the context of *Yeshua's* baptism, let's discuss the believer's baptism. Read Ephesians 2:8-9. Is baptism necessary for salvation?

Study Suggestion 1: Taking the Gospel of Luke as your guideline, try to put the events studied up to this point into a chronological order. Try to find out how much time would pass between the transfiguration and the crucifixion?

Study Suggestion 2: Looking at a Bible atlas, find the two mountains that are traditionally believed to have been the place where the transfiguration occurred: Mount Tabor or Mount Hermon.

Study Suggestion 3: Take *Yeshua's* conversation with the Samaritan woman and find out how He taught her (Jn. 4:1-42). Consider the barriers He overcame, the mysterious promise He made her, how He established His prophetic authority, and what the results were.

Study Suggestion 4: Not many people are familiar with the so-called Messianic miracles. Though this idea is supported by rabbinic writings, studying the Scriptures will be enough to see the difference between an "ordinary" miracle and a Messianic miracle. Take Matthew 12:22-37 and compare the account with Luke 7:11-16. Pay special attention to the reaction of the crowd. Notice how, in Matthew 12, the people ask if this could possibly be the Son of David? What title are they giving Him here, and why did this force the religious leaders to explain this miracle?

Chapter XII

The Death of the Messiah

The death of *Yeshua* has led artists, filmmakers, and authors alike to go to great depths when depicting this remarkable historic event. Often, the creative attention is focused on the display of God's love for mankind or on the example this act is to set for man to self-sacrifice for others. Unfortunately, many churches today fail to provide a well-balanced, biblical view on the whole plan of redemption. This has led to a more than mediocre understanding of the true theological implications, significances, and results of the death of the Messiah. We will therefore pay special attention to pointing out the eternal value of this event.

A. The Importance of Messiah's Death

The importance of the death of the Messiah is evident in six ways.

1. The Old Testament Predictions of Messiah's Death

The death of the Messiah is important because it fulfilled Old Testament prophecy. The Old Testament predicted the death in some detail in two key passages. Psalm 22:1-21 described events that could only be true of a crucifixion; but stoning was the Jewish mode of execution, not crucifixion. This prophetic passage emphasized the "how" of Messiah's death: He would die by means of crucifixion. Isaiah 52:13–53:12 gave many additional details concerning the event, emphasizing the "why" of the Messiah's death, particularly the substitutionary nature of His death: that He died in our stead.

2. The Gospels are Devoted to Describing the Messiah's Death

The importance of the death of *Yeshua* can be seen in the fact that one-third of the content of the Gospels is devoted to describing it. The four Gospels give us four biographies. If the material of the four biographies is combined, a total of one-third of the Gospels as a whole deals with the death of the Messiah. Matthew devoted eight chapters of his book to recording the events surrounding the death of the Messiah, which is 33% of his Gospel; Mark devoted six chapters of his book, which is 37% of his Gospel; Luke devoted five and one-half chapters of his book, which is 25% of his Gospel; John devoted nine and one-half chapters of his book, which is 42% of his Gospel.

3. The Purpose of the Incarnation

As regarding the death of the Messiah, the incarnation was paramount. He could not die until He was born. It was by means of the incarnation that the Second Person of the Trinity became a man. Whereas the rest of humanity is born to live, this One was born to die (Mt. 20:28; Mk. 10:45; Heb. 2:9, 14-16).

4. The Content of the Gospel

In I Corinthians 15:1-4, Paul precisely spelled out the content of the gospel and stated three things a person must believe to be saved. First, that *Messiah died for our sins according to the scriptures*. Second, that *he was buried*, which was the evidence of His death. Third, that He rose again *on the third day according to the scriptures*. The death of *Yeshua* is the first of the three key points of the gospel itself. In order to be saved, one must not merely believe that He died, but that He died for our sins.

5. Essential to Salvation

If *Yeshua* had not died, there would have been no salvation (Jn. 3:14-15; 12:24). Some assume that if Israel had accepted Him as the Messiah, He would not have had to die. Quite the contrary, His death was inevitable. Even if Israel had accepted Him as the Messiah, He still would have had to die, though the circumstances of His death would have been different. If the Jewish people had proclaimed *Yeshua* to be the Messiah, the King of the Jews, the Romans would have taken this as an act of rebellion against Rome. They would have arrested Him, tried Him, and crucified Him, and He would have been buried. After He arose on the third day, He would then have destroyed the Roman Empire and set up His Messianic Kingdom rather than departing for a duration of time. The death of *Yeshua* was inevitable and necessary because it is essential to salvation.

6. The Importance to Heaven

The death of *Yeshua* is supremely important to heaven itself (Lk. 9:30-31; Rev. 5:8-12). Not only were things on earth, such as the saints, purified by the death of the Messiah, but things in heaven were also purified.

For example, examine Romans 8:21-23:

> [21] *that the creation itself also shall be delivered from the bondage of corruption into the liberty of the glory of the children of God.* [22] *For we know that the whole creation groans and travails in pain together until now* [23] *And not only so, but ourselves also, who have the first-fruits of the Spirit, even we ourselves groan within ourselves, waiting for our adoption, to wit, the redemption of our body.*

The whole creation was purified by the death of the Messiah. This includes the earth as well as the entire celestial sphere, the heavenly bodies and the first and second heavens.

Hebrews 9:11-12 makes the same point:

> [11] *But Messiah having come a high priest of the good things to come, through the greater and more perfect tabernacle, not made with hands, that is to say, not of this creation,* [12] *nor yet through the blood of goats and calves, but through his own blood, entered in once and for all into the holy place, having obtained eternal redemption.*

Hebrews 9:23 makes the point that *Yeshua* purified *things in the heavens* itself, which leads to the question, "Why did *things in the heavens* need to be purified?" The fall of Satan occurred in heaven. Because of his fall, sin was brought into heaven, and the heavenly sanctuary, of which Satan was once functioning as a priest, was defiled. Therefore, the heavenly sanctuary needed the cleansing of blood just as the earthly sanctuary did. Whereas animal blood was sufficient to cleanse the earthly sanctuary, it was not sufficient to cleanse the heavenly sanctuary. That required better blood, the Messiah's blood. So the blood of *Yeshua* was used to cleanse the heavenly sanctuary.

B. The Prominence of Messiah's Death

The death of *Yeshua* is mentioned a total of 175 times in the New Testament. If the mention of His death were removed from the New Testament, it would simply not hold together, nor would it have any meaning. The prominence of His death can be seen in all of the New Testament books.

There are three specific predictions of His death in the Gospels of Matthew, Mark, and Luke:

- ✡ The first prediction is found in Matthew 16:21, Mark 8:31, and Luke 9:22.
- ✡ The second prediction is found in Matthew 17:22, Mark 9:30-32, and Luke 9:43-45.
- ✡ The third prediction is found in Matthew 20:17-19, Mark 10:32-34, and Luke 18:31-34.

The death of *Yeshua* is mentioned a number of times in the Gospel of John, both prophetically and historically:

- ✡ John 1:29 contains the concept that a lamb would die: *On the morrow he saw Yeshua coming unto him, and said, Behold, the Lamb of God, that takes away the sin of the world!*
- ✡ John 3:14 states that the Son of Man must be *lifted up*.
- ✡ In John 6:51, *Yeshua* explains that *the bread which I will give is my flesh, for the life of the world*.
- ✡ John 11:49-52 states that one man is to give his life for the nation.
- ✡ In John 12:24, He is like the grain that must fall and die.
- ✡ In John 15:13, He lays down His life for His friends.

The prominence of the death of *Yeshua* is also seen in the apostolic preaching of the cross as it is presented in the book of Acts.

The death of *Yeshua* is also mentioned in the majority of Paul's writings (Romans, I and II Corinthians, Galatians, Philippians, Colossians, I Thessalonians, I Timothy, and Titus), in Hebrews, I Peter, and I John, and finally, in the book of Revelation. The fact that this event is part of so many Epistles and books of the New Testament emphasizes its importance.

C. Old Testament Types

The significance of the death of the Messiah can be illustrated through nine Old Testament types that portrayed His death in one way or another.

1. The Melchizedekian Priesthood—Genesis 14:18-20; Psalm 110:4

The concept of the Melchizedekian priesthood emphasizes the idea of offering sacrifice. The book of Hebrews tells us that *Yeshua* became a *priest for ever After the order of Melchizedek* (Heb. 7:17) Indeed, the death of the Messiah was an offering of Messianic blood; it was a sacrifice.

2. The Passover—Exodus 12:1-51

The Passover emphasized salvation through blood. It was comprised of two stages. The first stage was the shedding of the blood of the lamb. If the Jewish people had merely shed the blood of the lamb and had done nothing more, the firstborn son of every Jewish family would have died. There had to be the second stage—the application of the blood. They had to apply the blood on the lintel and the two doorposts of each home. The application of the blood that had been shed brought their physical salvation from the last plague, the plague of the death of the firstborn son.

The death of *Yeshua* is described as the death of the Lamb of God, the paschal lamb. He died as a Passover sacrifice. With His death, there was the shedding of the blood of the Lamb of God, thereby fulfilling the first stage. As with the lamb in Egypt, the mere shedding of the blood is insufficient; there must also be the application of the blood. Only those individual Jews and Gentiles who personally apply the blood will receive spiritual salvation through that blood. The way the blood is applied is by believing that He died for our sins, was buried, and rose again. With this act of faith, the second stage is fulfilled. While the blood of the Lamb of God was shed for the sins of the whole world, that by itself will save no one. There must be the act of faith, the second step—the application of the blood by the believer. So there is a parallelism between the Passover and the death of *Yeshua*; in both instances, shed blood that was, or is, properly applied will obtain, or secure, salvation. This is the significance of the death of *Yeshua* as it relates to the Passover.[56]

3. The Brazen Altar—Exodus 27:1-8; Hebrews 13:9-16

According to the Law of Moses, the sacrifice had to be slaughtered and the blood shed on the brazen altar, which stood on the east side directly in front of the Tabernacle (and later the Temple in Jerusalem). The cross was the anti-type of the brazen altar where the blood of the lamb was shed. Thus, the brazen altar also portrays the death of the Messiah.

4. The Laver—Exodus 30:17-21

The laver, which was also part of the Temple compound, emphasized cleansing. A priest had to cleanse himself before and after the offering of blood. This cleansing was always done at the laver, so blood was always connected in some way to washing at the laver.

The picture here is the believer's continuous cleansing from sins because of the death of the Messiah. At the point one accepts and applies *Yeshua's* blood, he is forgiven of all his sins and given spiritual salvation. He is regenerated and enters into God's family. Although he is now a child of God, he still sins and gets himself dirty as a result of his sin. He then has to be cleansed from the sins he commits as a believer. The means of this cleansing is found in the confession of I John 1:9: *If we confess our sins, he is faithful and righteous to forgive us our sins, and to cleanse us from all unrighteousness.* It was the blood of *Yeshua* that laid

---

[56] Question 1 on page 183.

the basis for the believer's continuous cleansing from his sin. His death not only provides "salvation forgiveness," it is also the basis for "family forgiveness."[57]

5. The Blood-Sacrifices—Leviticus 1:1–6:7

The blood-sacrifices emphasized justification through blood. Justification means "to be declared righteous," not "just as if I never sinned." When one has the blood of *Yeshua* applied to him, he is justified through that blood. He is not "made righteous," he is "declared righteous," because the righteousness of *Yeshua* the Messiah is imputed to the believer.

6. The *Yom Kippur* Goats—Leviticus 16:1-34

The two goats of *Yom Kippur*, the Day of Atonement, emphasized forgiveness through blood. The Leviticus passage teaches that every year on the Day of Atonement, two goats were brought before the high priest. Lots were cast to see which goat would live and which goat would die. The goat that was chosen to die would be slaughtered on the altar of sacrifice. The high priest then took the blood of the first goat into the Holy of Holies of the Tabernacle or the Temple and sprinkled it upon the mercy seat of the Ark of the Covenant. The high priest then came out and laid his hands upon the live goat and confessed the sins of Israel. The second goat was sent into the wilderness, symbolically carrying Israel's sins away. The point was that after the shedding of the blood of the first goat, there was the removal of sins by the second goat.

The two goats of the Day of Atonement emphasized forgiveness through blood. The same thing is true for believers. A believer's sins cannot be forgiven without the shedding of blood, for *apart from the shedding of blood there is no remission* of sin (Heb. 9:22). With the shedding of the blood of *Yeshua* and the application of the blood to the believer's heart, mind, and life, his sins are carried away. Therefore, he receives the forgiveness through the blood.

---

[57] Question 2 on page 183.

7. The Sacrificial Blood—Leviticus 17:11

The sacrificial blood emphasized atonement through blood. There was one kind of atonement in the Old Testament and another in the New Testament. The atonement provided by animal blood in the Old Testament was a temporary atonement that only covered sins, but it did not remove them. With the shedding of the blood of the Lamb of God and the final blood-sacrifice for sin, a permanent atonement came, not a temporary one, because sins are removed, not merely covered.

8. The Kinsman-Redeemer—Leviticus 25:47-49

The kinsman-redeemer emphasized redemption by a substitute. Indeed, since Jesus died as a substitute in the believer's place, He is our Kinsman-Redeemer. The point of Hebrews 2 is that believers have received redemption by virtue of a substitute.[58]

9. The Red Heifer—Numbers 19:1-22

The red heifer is an Old Testament type of the Messiah's death in that it emphasized purification. It was by means of the ashes of the red heifer that purification was made. Hebrews 9-10 emphasizes that the believer is purified by means of the blood of the Messiah.

D. The True Theory of Atonement

The first part of Romans 6:23 makes it abundantly clear that without Messiah, we are going to die and spend an eternity separated from God: *For the wages of sin is death.* The second part of this verse makes it equally clear that eternal life is available through *Yeshua*: *but the free gift of God is eternal life in Messiah Yeshua*

---

[58] Study Suggestion 1 on page 183. For a more thorough analysis of the kinsman-redeemer concept, we recommend Arnold G. Fruchtenbaum, *Ariel's Bible Commentary: Judges & Ruth* (Ariel Ministries, TX, 2015).

our Lord. His death provided a penal, judicial, substitutionary atonement. What do theologians mean by this and why do we call it "the true theory of atonement?"

The Presbyterian theologian and principal of Princeton Theological Seminary, Charles Hodge, summarizes the true theory of the atonement as follows:

> According to this doctrine the work of Christ is a real satisfaction of infinite inherent merit to the vindicatory justice of God; so that He saves His people by doing for them, and in their stead, what they were unable to do for themselves; satisfying the demands of the law in their behalf, and bearing the penalty in their stead; whereby they are reconciled to God, receive the Holy Ghost, and made partakers of the life of Christ to their present sanctification and eternal salvation.[59]

In defining the penal, judicial, substitutionary atonement, we should emphasize five points:

1. Atonement is objective. It had an objective purpose and that was to cause an effect in God.
2. It was vicarious in that it was substitutionary (Mt. 20:28; Mk. 10:45; Jn. 10:11; Rom. 5:8; I Cor. 15:3; II Cor. 5:21, I Pet. 2:24; 3:18).
3. It included Messiah's active and passive obedience. Active obedience means He kept the Law of Moses (Mt. 5:17-19; Jn. 15:10; Gal. 4:4-5; Heb. 10:7-9). Passive obedience means He paid the penalty for sin by the sacrifice of Himself; this indeed was true. It was predicted of the Messiah in Isaiah 53:6 and fulfilled by *Yeshua*, as stated in Romans 4:25, I Peter 2:24, 3:18, and I John 2:2.
4. Atonement means that *Yeshua's* priesthood demanded the offering of innocent blood as a substitution (Eph. 5:2; Heb. 9:11-14).
5. His sacrifice was an offering for sin (Isa. 53:10; Mt. 26:28; Jn. 1:29; I Cor. 5:7; Heb. 9:26; I Pet. 1:18-19).

---

[59] Charles Hodge, *Systematic Theology* (New York: Charles Scribner's Sons, 1895), Vol. II, p. 563.

Through Messiah's death on the cross, the penalty that was due to man according to the law of God was paid. Penal, judicial, satisfactory atonement was accomplished.[60]

E. Accomplishments of Messiah's Death

Altogether, there are fifteen specific accomplishments or results of the death of Messiah. They have great implications for the believer and affect his position before God. It is important to note that the believer does not "experience" these accomplishments. For example, a believer cannot "experience" propitiation. Yet it is an eternal fact of his relationship with God. Also, the position the believer finds himself in because of what *Yeshua* did on his behalf is not progressive. The instant a person enters the position of a believer, he enjoys all that is connected with this position. For example, the moment a person gets saved, he is redeemed. After he has walked with His God for three decades, he is still redeemed. There is no growth of redemption. The position of the believer is eternal. Man may understand more about his position in Messiah the longer he walks with Him, but in reality, it defies human understanding, and full comprehension of what Messiah accomplished by His death will probably only be possible in heaven.

1. Satisfaction

By His death, *Yeshua* accomplished satisfaction. Theologically speaking, satisfaction means "a full, legal equivalent for wrong done." The point is that the law, which was the Law of Moses, has been satisfied for what it demanded concerning the wrong done. *Yeshua's* death answered all the demands of God's law and justice against the sinner. The law no longer condemns the sinner who believes in *Yeshua*; for such there can be *now no condemnation* (Rom. 8:1). The law required satisfaction (Lev. 17:11), and with His death, the justice of God was satisfied, a satisfaction of divine law. It was predicted that the Messiah would satisfy the demands of the law (Is. 53:10-12). This is exactly what *Yeshua* did by

[60] Question 3 on page 183.

His death (Rom. 3:3-4; Gal. 1:4; Eph. 5:2). Therefore, His death is a satisfaction of what the penalty of the law demanded.[61]

2. Redemption

By way of definition, redemption means that *Yeshua's* death paid the price of the penalty of sin. We derive this definition from the way seven Greek words are used in the New Testament. The first word is *agorazo*. Though the meaning of this term is "to buy in the *agora*, or market place," the New Testament also uses it in the salvation sense. The theologian Dr. Charles C. Ryrie describes three basic ideas of this word:

> (1) In His work of redeeming, Christ paid the purchase price for all mankind (2 Pet. 2:1). (2) The price itself is clearly stated to be the blood of Christ (Rev. 5:9-10). (3) Because we have been bought with that purchase price, we are to serve Him (1 Cor. 6:19-20; 7:22-23).[62]

The second Greek word is *exagorazo*, which is compound word. It adds to the root *agorazo* the idea of purchasing out of the forum or buying up. In Galatians 3:13, where it says *Messiah redeemed us from the curse of the law*, Paul uses the word to emphasize the substitutionary nature of Messiah's death. It is also found in Galatians 4:5, where it says, *that he might redeem them that were under the law*. The Messiah's death "bought up" those who were under the law and removed them from the curse of the law.

The third Greek word is *peripoieo* and means "to preserve," or "to get possession of." It is used in the redemptive sense in Luke 17:33, where redemption is correlated to the preservation of life: *Whosoever shall seek to gain his life shall lose it: but whosoever shall lose his life shall preserve it*. In Acts 20:28, Paul uses the word in an admonition to the church, which, he says, Messiah *purchased with his own blood*, emphasizing possession. In I Timothy 3:13, the term is also used in this sense.

---

[61] Question 4 on page 183.

[62] Charles C. Ryrie, *Basic Theology*, Moody Press, Chicago, 1999, p. 334.

The fourth Greek word is *lutron* and means "a ransom." It is found in Matthew 20:28b where it says that Messiah gave *His life a ransom for many*. This word also appears in the parallel verse, Mark 10:45.

The fifth Greek word is *lutrosis* and means "a ransoming," "a redemption." It is used in Luke 1:68: *Blessed be the Lord, the God of Israel; For he has visited and wrought redemption for his people*. It is also found in Luke 2:38 and Hebrews 9:12.

The sixth Greek word is *lutroo* and means "to redeem," "to be liberated because of the payment of a ransom." It is used in Luke 24:21a: *But we hoped that it was he who should redeem Israel.* It is also found in Titus 2:14 and I Peter 1:18.

The seventh Greek word is *apolutrosis* and means "a full or complete redemption that was effected by the payment of a ransom." It is used in Luke 21:28: *But when these things begin to come to pass, look up, and lift up your heads; because your redemption draws nigh.* This compound word is also found in Romans 3:24, 8:23, I Corinthians 1:30, Ephesians 1:7, 14, 4:30, Colossians 1:14, Hebrews 9:15, and 11:35.

Combining the meanings of these seven Greek words, we can say that the New Testament concept of redemption is that believers have been purchased out of the slave market of sin and set free. They have been redeemed in five specific areas:

1. Those who are Jewish believers have been redeemed from the penalty of the law (Gal. 3:13).
2. Jewish believers are also redeemed from the law itself; they are no longer obligated to keep the 613 commandments of the Law of Moses (Rom. 6:14; Gal. 4:4-5).
3. All believers, both Jew and Gentile, have been redeemed from the power of sin (Rom. 5:18-19; 6:6, 14).
4. There has also been a redemption from the power of Satan; a believer is no longer obligated to obey Satan (Col. 1:13; Heb. 2:14-15).

5. Believers are guaranteed a future, final redemption from all evil, which will occur with the resurrection of the body (Lk. 21:28; Rom. 8:23; Eph. 1:14; 4:30).[63]

3. Propitiation

Propitiation means that God is satisfied with what the death of Messiah accomplished (I Jn. 2:2). In its very basic meaning, to propitiate means "to appease." Messiah's sacrifice appeased the wrath of God, which was revealed *against all ungodliness and unrighteousness of men* (Rom. 1:18). God's wrath has now been appeased by the death of *Yeshua*, because now God is satisfied with what His Son's death accomplished. Propitiation does not mean Messiah's death merely satisfied a vengeful God; rather, it satisfied a God who is just, righteous, and holy. The same God who demands satisfaction also shows His mercy in that He sent His Son to be a propitiation.

4. Reconciliation

By way of definition, reconciliation means "to change the relationship of one person to another person," "to change from enmity to friendship." Four different Greek words are translated by the English word "reconciliation," but they all emphasize the same point: The position of the world was changed by the death of *Yeshua* so that all men are now able to be saved. His death rendered the whole world savable. This does not mean that the whole world will be saved, because salvation is only applied to those who believe. While on one hand, God is said to be propitiated, on the other hand, man is said to be reconciled.

Biblical reconciliation can be explained as follows: When God originally created man, man and God were "face to face." But when man sinned, he turned his back on God. As a result, God turned His back on man. Then came the death of *Yeshua* by which God was propitiated and the law satisfied. God has now turned again to face man with outstretched arms. It is now the responsibility of each individual person to turn and face God by accepting the substitution that He has provided.

Some key passages on reconciliation include the following:

---

[63] Question 5 on page 186.

- ✡ Romans 5:10 teaches that men were reconciled back to God while they were His enemies.
- ✡ Colossians 1:20 states that God reconciled *all things unto himself* through the death of *Yeshua*.
- ✡ II Corinthians 5:19 states: *God was in Messiah reconciling the world unto himself.*
- ✡ Romans 11:15 also speaks about the reconciliation of the world.

God's willingness to reconcile the world unto Himself leads to a certain responsibility for believers. They now have *the ministry of reconciliation* because reconciliation has been provided (II Cor. 5:18), and they are to preach *the word of reconciliation* and to admonish people to be reconciled to God, now that He has been propitiated (II Cor. 5:19).

The whole world has been reconciled, thereby rendering all men savable. There still needs to be a personal reconciliation by faith, for only then is salvation applied to the individual.

5. Ransom

Ransom means that the blood of Messiah was the price that had to be paid for the penalty of sin (Mt. 20:28; I Tim. 2:6). In early church history, some misunderstood the concept of ransom in the death of Messiah and taught that the ransom was paid to Satan. While it is very true that the Bible teaches that His death was a ransom, it does not say that the ransom was paid to Satan. On the contrary, God owed Satan nothing! Rather, the ransom was paid to the holy law of God. It was to the law that men were bound. The demands of a righteous law given by God had to be righteously and justly met, and *Yeshua's* death did that. The blood and death of the Messiah is a ransom paid to the holy law of God.

6. The Proof of God's Love for Sinners

Some have taught that God does not love all sinners, only believers who have had their sins forgiven and removed. It is true that God never loves the sin. However, it is clear from Scripture that God loves sinners, even in their unbelieving, sinful state. The evidence of God's love for sinners is the death of *Yeshua* in that He died for the world in its sinful state, not in its redeemed state.

John 3:16 declares: *For God so loved the world, that he gave his only begotten Son, that whosoever believes on him should not perish, but have eternal life.*

This verse teaches that God loved the *cosmos*, the unbelieving world-system that is contrary to Him. Clearly, Romans 5:8 emphasizes that He died for men long before they became believers *in that, while we were yet sinners, Messiah died for us*. That proved God's love for sinners, according to Romans 5:1. This is also affirmed in I John 3:16 and 4:9.

7. The Judgment of the Sin-Nature

The judgment of the sin-nature is found in Romans 6:1-10. The sin-nature is not removed when one believes; it is judged and condemned. It is destined to be obliterated either through the believer's death or at the Rapture, when the believer is perfected. Because the sin-nature has been judged by the death of the Messiah, there is no obligation to obey it whatsoever. If one sins by giving in to his sin-nature, it is because he chose to, not because he had to. And human that we are, we will sin; but the point is that the believer is not obligated to sin.

This fact is developed extensively by Paul in Romans 6:1–8:13. This lengthy passage can be summarized in four points. First, the Messiah died unto sin. Second, the Messiah's substitutionary death included dying for the sin-nature, as well as for personal sins (Rom. 6). Third, the whole merit system, with its appeal to human works and efforts as represented in relation to the law, has passed for the believer. Those who employ this system of working in self-strength will be defeated because of their inability to control the sin-nature (Rom. 7). Paul showed this to be true by his own experiences when, as a young, immature believer, he tried to use the law as a basis for controlling the sin-nature and living the spiritual life. That is when he learned that the spiritual life must be lived by faith, even as salvation is attained by faith. Fourth, there is triumphant victory in which the complete will of God is fulfilled in the believer, but never by the believer; he simply does not have that type of power (Rom. 8).

8. The End of the Law of Moses

Jewish believers are no longer under the Law of Moses, but under a new law, the Law of the Messiah (Rom. 7:4-6; 10:4; Col. 2:14; Heb. 7:11-19; Eph. 2:11–3:6; Gal. 3:17-19). II Corinthians 3:7-11 teaches that even the Ten Commandments have been rendered inoperative. The Law of Moses has come to an end as a result of the death of the Messiah.[64]

9. The Basis for Continuous Cleansing

The grounds for the believer's continuous cleansing from sin were first discussed on page 170 of this book in the context of the laver. In this chapter, it is important to point out that the cleansing is only possible because of *Yeshua's* death. The verses which speak about this are found in I John 1:7-9:

> [7] *but if we walk in the light, as he is in the light, we have fellowship one with another, and the blood of Yeshua his Son cleanses us from all sin.* [8] *If we say that we have no sin, we deceive ourselves, and the truth is not in us.* [9] *If we confess our sins, he is faithful and righteous to forgive us our sins, and to cleanse us from all unrighteousness.*

Not only did His death accomplish a redemption by which the believer has been redeemed from the penalty of sin—salvation forgiveness; it continues to be the basis for the removal of sins committed since one believed—family forgiveness.

10. The Basis for the Removal of Pre-Cross Sins

When the Messiah died, He not only died for the sins that would be committed from that point on, but also for all the sins of the world committed before His death. As Hebrews 10:1-4 emphasizes, animal blood was not sufficient to take away sins; it was only able to cover sin. So the sins of the Old Testament saints were covered by animal blood. When *Yeshua* died, He finally removed these sins. His death was the basis for the removal of pre-cross sins (Acts 17:30; Rom. 3:25; Heb. 9:15).

11. The Judgment of Satan and his Hosts

When the Great White Throne Judgment takes place after *Yeshua's* one-thousand year reign on earth, Satan and every fallen angel or demon will be

---

[64] Study Suggestion 2 on page 186.

judged. The basis for their judgment is the death of the Messiah (Jn. 12:31; Col. 2:15).

12. Righteous Judgment Has Been Deferred

The death of the Messiah is the reason that divine, righteous judgment has been deferred (Rom. 2:4-5). Man's sin is such that God has every right to judge man immediately. However, judgment is being deferred because of the death of the Messiah so that man has an extended opportunity to accept God's free grace. Paul taught this in Romans 9:22 when he wrote: *What if God, willing to show his wrath, and to make his power known, endured with much longsuffering vessels of wrath fitted unto destruction.* Even before the cross, there were examples of times when God deferred judgment, and Peter recalled one incident when he wrote I Peter 3:20; this was *in the days of Noah*. God delayed the Flood by 120 years. The application is that He is still deferring His judgment on the basis of the Messiah's death. Peter repeated this truth in II Peter 3:9 and 15.

13. The Grounds for Peace

The death of *Yeshua* is the grounds for peace in three realms. First, it is the grounds for peace between God and man, according to Romans 5:1: *Being therefore, justified by faith, we have peace with God through our Lord Yeshua Messiah.*

Second, the death of *Yeshua* is also the grounds for peace between Jews and Gentiles. This is the point of Ephesians 2:11-16, as well as Colossians 3:11, which reads: *where there cannot be Greek and Jew, circumcision and uncircumcision, barbarian, Scythian, bondman, freeman; but Messiah is all, and in all.*

Third, the death of *Yeshua* is the grounds for peace in the universe, according to Colossians 1:20: *and through him to reconcile all things unto himself, having made peace through the blood of his cross; through him, I say, whether things upon the earth, or things in the heavens.*

14. Provides for the National Salvation of Israel

Because of the death of the Messiah, one day there will be a national salvation of Israel. This is taught in the Old Testament in Deuteronomy 30:3 and

Jeremiah 31:31-34. Romans 11:25-29 makes this point in the New Testament. Someday, all Israel will believe on Him, and this result of the death of the Messiah is also the precondition to His Second Coming.

15. The Basis for the Establishment of the Millennial Kingdom

Revelation 5:8-14 makes the point that the Millennial Kingdom can not be established apart from the death of the Messiah.[65]

F. Summary

Summarizing what has been said about the death of the Messiah will help us to see the enormous theological implications of this event for the believer. By dying on the cross, *Yeshua* presented Himself as the perfect sacrifice that satisfied the demands of God's justice upon sin. By dying on the cross, He paid the penalty for sin on behalf of man and appeased the wrath of a just God. Thus, He brought forgiveness and reconciled the world to God, making it savable. Through personal faith in this act of Messiah, man accepts His substitution as payment for sin.

[65] Question 6 on page 186.

G. Questions and Study Suggestions

Question 1: An anti-missionary group called Outreach Judaism asks, "Evangelical Christians often draw a comparison between the Paschal Lamb and Jesus, insisting that the former foreshadows the latter. This idea is advanced in the New Testament, particularly in the fourth Gospel, where John portrayed Jesus as the fulfillment of the Passover lamb. Yet how valid a point is this? What is the meaning of this holiday sacrifice? Is there a relationship between this festival offering and atonement for sin?"[66] How would you respond?

Question 2: Dr. Fruchtenbaum makes this point of family forgiveness twice (pp. 170 and 180). Considering your position as a child of God, can you explain what he means by that? Can you think of circumstances and actions that might influence your relationship with God? What role does I John 1:9 play in this relationship?

Study Suggestion 1: The concept of the kinsman-redeemer is first introduced in Genesis 48:16 and Exodus 6:6. It is more clearly defined in Leviticus 25:47-55 and 27:9-25 and further developed in the book of Ruth where Boaz is the kinsman-redeemer. Read this book—it only has four chapters—to get a better understanding of *Yeshua* as our Kinsman-Redeemer.

Question 3: *Yeshua*, the Son of God, bore the sins of mankind. Some believe that a substitutionary atonement makes God unjust since He condemned His Son for sins He never committed. How would you respond to this objection?

Question 4: We just learned that *Yeshua's* death satisfied God's just law. There are many believers today who still want to keep the Law of Moses, especially the Ten Commandments. Does this mean *Yeshua's* death was not enough? If someone is so eager to live a life according to the law, which law would you point him to and how would you encourage him to live in the freedom *Yeshua's* death provided? If the answers to these questions are challenging, we recommend Dr. Fruchtenbaum's book *Faith Alone: The Condition of Our Salvation* for an in-depth study of this topic. To help you understand which law is relevant for the New Testament believer, here is an excerpt from this book:

---

[66] Tovia Singer. "Did the Passover Lamb Foreshadow the Crucifixion of Jesus?" *Outreach Judaism*, accessed 09 Mar. 2015, https://outreachjudaism.org/jesus-passover.

The Law of Moses has been disannulled or rendered inoperative, and believers are now under a new law. This new law is called *the law of Messiah* in Galatians 6:2 and *the law of the Spirit of life* in Romans 8:2. This brand-new law is totally separate from the Law of Moses. The Law of the Messiah contains all the commandments applicable to a New Testament believer.

The reason there is so much confusion over the relationship between the Law of Moses and the Law of the Messiah is that many commandments are the same or similar to those found in the Mosaic Law, and many believers have concluded that certain sections of the law have therefore been retained. But it has already been shown that this cannot be the case, and the explanation for the sameness of the commandments is to be found elsewhere.

This explanation can best be understood if it is realized that there are a number of codes in the Bible such as the Edenic, Adamic, Noahic, Mosaic, and Messianic law codes. A new code will always contain some of the same commandments of the previous code, but this does not mean that the previous code is still in effect. While certain commandments of the Adamic code were also found in the Edenic code, this did not mean that it was still partially in force. The Edenic code ceased to function with the fall of man. The same is true when we compare the Law of the Messiah with the Law of Moses. There are many similar commandments. For example, nine of the Ten Commandments are to be found in the Law of the Messiah, but this does not mean that the Law of Moses is still in force.

Let me illustrate this by using an example many others have experienced. I received my first driver's license in the state of California, and, as long as I drove in California, I was subject to the traffic laws of that state. But after a couple of years, I moved to New York. Once I left California, I ceased to be under California traffic law. The traffic laws of that state were rendered inoperative in my case. Now my driving was subject to a new law—the traffic laws of the state of New York. Both states required me to stop at a red light. But this did not mean that New York borrowed the law from California or California from New York. Both states had their own legislature who passed the same laws. There were many laws that were different. For example, in California I was permitted to make a right turn at a red light after stopping and yielding the right-of-way, but in New York, no right turn was permitted at a red light at that time (the law has changed since then). There were many similar laws between the two states, such as the law demanding that I stop at a red light. When I stopped at a red light, I did not do so in obedience to the state of California as I once had, but in obedience to the state of New York. I proceeded at a green light not because of California law, but because of New York law. If I went through a red light without stopping, I was not guilty of breaking California law, but New York law. Many laws were similar, but they were under two distinctly different systems.

The Law of Moses has been nullified, and believers are now under the Law of the Messiah. There are many different commandments. Under the Law of Moses, one would not be permitted to eat pork, but under the Law of the Messiah, he may. There are many similar commandments, but they are nonetheless in two separate systems. Therefore, if one does not kill or steal, this is not because of the Law of Moses but because of the Law of the Messiah. On the other hand, if one does steal, he is not guilty of breaking the Law of Moses, but of breaking the Law of the Messiah.

> This understanding can solve many problems among fundamental believers, such as the issues of women wearing pants, the Sabbath, and tithing. If the commandments concerning these things are based only on the Law of Moses and not on the Law of the Messiah, then they have no validity for the New Testament believer.[67]

Question 5: Since the Temple in Jerusalem was destroyed by the Romans, the Jewish people do not offer animal sacrifices anymore to achieve redemption for their sins. Today, they believe that forgiveness of sins comes through repentance, prayer, and good deeds, claiming that verses like Hosea 6:6 support this idea. Read Leviticus 17:11 and Hebrews 9:22. Together with our study on redemption, you should be able to develop a solid argument that will help Jewish people—and anyone who is bound to a religious system which promotes these ideas—to see that they need *Yeshua*.

Study Suggestion 2: The Roman Catholic Church, the Lutheran Church, the Eastern Orthodox Church, and even cults like the Mormon Church claim that the Ten Commandments stand eternally. Even among Bible-believing Evangelicals, we find numerous denominations that will teach their eternality. In fact, you might have only now learned that *Yeshua's* death on the cross rendered the Law of Moses inoperative. To be able to help people understand the truth, make a point to read all of the verses Dr. Fruchtenbaum listed and wrap your mind around the consequences of his teaching.

Question 6: After having studied the fifteen results of Messiah's death, do you feel better equipped to explain that this event was more than just a highlight of human history when a man showed to his fellow human beings what self-sacrificial love looks like? Would you be able to use what you have learned to teach others?

---

[67] Arnold G. Fruchtenbaum, *Faith Alone: The Condition of Our Salvation* (San Antonio: Ariel Ministries, 2014), 87-89.

Chapter XIII

The Burial of the Messiah

While the burial of the Messiah is not as important as either His death or His resurrection, it is nevertheless important enough that every Gospel records it (Mt. 27:57-66; Mk. 15:42-47; Lk. 23:50-56; Jn. 19:31-42). In studying Christology, we are not so much concerned with the account of the burial as we are with what theological significance it holds. *Yeshua's* death was the first point of the gospel (I Cor. 15:3-4). The second point was His burial, which was the evidence of His death.

A. The Last Act of Messiah's Humiliation

The burial of *Yeshua* marked the end of His humiliation[68] in two ways. First, it signified the death of the God-Man. Since He was sinless, there was no reason for Him to die; however, He did die, as the burial signified. For the sinless God-Man, death was a humiliation.

Second, none of those who were close to Him were involved in the burial; not His eleven disciples who remained loyal to Him after the betrayal by Judas; not any of the women who had followed Him all the way from Galilee; not Miriam

---

[68] Theologians speak of the humiliation of the Son which began with His incarnation into the likeness of sinful flesh and concluded with His burial.

(Mary) and Martha who lived nearby in Bethany; not even His own mother who was in Jerusalem on this occasion. Instead, *Yeshua* was buried by two Pharisees who, up to that point, had secretly believed in Him. One was Nicodemus, and the other was Joseph of Arimathea. So *Yeshua's* burial marked the end of the period of His humiliation.

B. The Beginning of Messiah's Exaltation

Theologians also speak of the exaltation of the Son. Normally, they say it began with His resurrection and culminated with His ascension and enthronement at the right hand of God the Father. However, it is possible that His exaltation began earlier. The exaltation of *Yeshua* includes the events of the resurrection, by which He became the Firstborn of the dead, as well as the ascension, when He was crowned with glory and honor and received a name above every name.

Just as the burial marked the last stage of *Yeshua's* humiliation, it also marked the first stage of His exaltation in two ways. First, He was buried in a new, unused rich man's tomb, the tomb of Joseph of Arimathea. This was the fulfillment of Isaiah 53:9a: *And they made his grave with the wicked, and with the rich in his death.* Thanks to the intervention of Joseph and Nicodemus, *Yeshua* was not buried in a criminal's grave, but in a new, unused rich man's tomb.

Second, although He was buried in a tomb, that tomb was not in a cemetery, but in a private garden owned by Joseph of Arimathea. The significance of this should not be missed. Centuries earlier, in another garden, the Garden of Eden, the first Adam brought physical and spiritual death. Centuries later, in this garden, the last Adam brought physical and spiritual life.

C. The Burial is a Part of the Gospel

First Corinthians 15:1-4 states the three points of the gospel:

> [1] *Now I make known unto you brethren, the gospel which I preached unto you, which also ye received, wherein also ye stand,* [2] *by which also ye are saved, if ye hold fast the word which I preached unto you, except ye believed in vain.* [3] *For I delivered unto you first of all that which also I received: that*

> *Messiah died for our sins according to the scriptures; [4] and that he was buried; and that he has been raised on the third day according to the scriptures;*

According to these verses, the gospel includes three events in the life of Messiah: His death, burial, and resurrection. He died *for our sins according to the scriptures*. He then *was buried*. Finally, He rose *on the third day according to the scriptures*. This is the full gospel message; there is no more to it than that. Any addition is false. The burial of *Yeshua* is very much part of the gospel, for it is the evidence of His death. True, the burial is not as important as the death and resurrection, but it marks the transition from one to the other. Out of His burial came the resurrection.[69]

[69] Study Suggestion on page 190.

D. Questions and Study Suggestions

Study Suggestion: Read Isaiah 53:9. Now consider the words of Dr. Jodi Magness, who tried to defend the accuracy of the burial accounts in the Gospels:

> Today many scholars believe that since Crucifixion was a sadistic and humiliating form of corporal punishment reserved by the Romans for the lower classes (including slaves), Jesus "died a criminal's death on the tree of shame." John Dominic Crossan, for example, argues that Jesus would not have been buried at all, but would have been eaten by dogs. In my opinion, the notion that Jesus was unburied or buried in disgrace is based on a misunderstanding of the archaeological evidence and of Jewish law . . . I believe that the Gospel accounts of Jesus' burial are largely consistent with the archeological evidence . . . the Gospel accounts describing Jesus' removal from the cross and burial are consistent with archaeological evidence and with Jewish law.[70]

Do you think Dr. Magness's defense could have been more effective if she had included the Old Testament references? How would you defend the accuracy and importance of *Yeshua's* burial?

---

[70] Jodi Magness is Professor for Teaching Excellence in Early Judaism at the University of North Carolina at Chapel Hill. The text quoted here is an excerpt from an article titled "Jesus' Tomb–What Did It Look Like?" in *Where Christianity Was Born* (H. Shanks ed., Washington, D.C.: BAS, 2006), 220-21, 24.

Chapter XIV

The State of Exaltation

In the last chapter, we briefly touched on two states theologians have determined as carrying important theological implications. They named these states "the State of Humiliation" and "the State of Exaltation." We saw that Messiah's burial marked a pivotal point in the transition from one state to the next. It ended the period of *Yeshua's* humiliation and began His exaltation.

Philippians 2:9 speaks of the second state when it says, *Wherefore also God highly exalted him, and gave unto him the name which is above every name.* The Messiah's exaltation consists of seven points.

First, the state of exaltation includes the resurrection, because *Yeshua* is the firstborn of the dead, according to I Corinthians 15:20 and Colossians 1:18. Since the next chapter of this book deals with the resurrection in greater detail, this is all that will be mentioned at this point.

Second, Messiah's ascension relates to His exaltation insofar as *Yeshua* was crowned with glory and honor when He ascended into heaven (Heb. 2:9; Rev. 1:12-18). Furthermore, He received a name at the ascension which was above every name (Phil. 2:9; Rev. 5:12-13; 19:12, 13, and 16).

Third, His present session relates to His state of exaltation insofar as He is now seated at the right hand of God the Father (Mk. 16:19). He is seated on His Father's throne (Rev. 3:21). It also means the resumption of the independent use of His divine attributes. In His state of humiliation, *Yeshua* had given this up—a fact we looked at in chapter nine when we discussed the kenosis. But now, with the exaltation, during His present session, Messiah has resumed the independent use of His divine attributes. All limitations of His humanity have now been removed. He no longer suffers the limitations of hunger, thirst, fatigue, etc.

Fourth, His exaltation will also be evident at the Second Coming because when He comes, He will come with power and great glory. This is brought out in Revelation 1:7 which states: *Behold, he comes with the clouds; and every eye shall see him, and they that pierced him; and all the tribes of the earth shall mourn over him. Even so, Amen.*

Fifth, the occupation of the throne of David in the Millennial Kingdom will also be part of His exaltation. Luke 1:32-33 tells us that this is what He was destined to do when it says: [32] *He shall be great, and shall be called the Son of the Highest: and the Lord God shall give unto him the throne of his father David:* [33] *And he shall reign over the house of Jacob for ever; and of his kingdom there shall be no end.*

Sixth, Messiah will judge all unbelievers in His state of exaltation. This is brought out by John 5:22, 27, Acts 10:42, 17:31, and II Timothy 4:1.

Seventh, *Yeshua* will receive eternal exaltation in the new heavens, the new earth, and the New Jerusalem (Rev. 21:1-22:5).

These are the basic elements of Messiah's state of exaltation. We covered it at this point, in the chapter between His burial and His resurrection, because His burial marks the end of His humiliation and the start of His exaltation.[71]

---

[71] Study Suggestions 1 and 2 on page 193.

Questions and Study Suggestions

Study Suggestion 1: Now that you have a better understanding of the Messiah's exaltation, read Ephesians 2:1-10. How do you feel about what you read in verse 6 regarding your status in the Messiah?

Study Suggestion 2: Read Romans 6:1-14. How does this passage compare to Ephesians 2:1-10? How does it affect your thinking about your walk with the Messiah?

Chapter XV

The Resurrection of the Messiah

The resurrection of *Yeshua* is a central element of Christology with enormous theological significance, and the Scriptures provide conclusive evidence as to the accuracy and historicity of the event. Matthew 28:1-20 reports it, and so do Mark 16:1-20, Luke 24:1-53, and John 20:21-25. The resurrected Messiah also appears in Acts 1:1-11. Before discussing the proofs contained within these verses, it is important to study which Old Testament passages predicted the resurrection.

A. The Old Testament Foreview

That the resurrection of *Yeshua* was predicted in the Old Testament is clear in two ways: in typology and in prophecy.

1. In Typology

There are three types in the Old Testament that teach the concept of Messianic resurrection. The first type is Melchizedek. The account of Melchizedek is recorded in Genesis 14:18-20. Melchizedek suddenly appeared in history and just as suddenly disappeared. There is no record of his genealogy, birth, or early life, and no record of his death. As far as recorded history is concerned, he lives forever. That Melchizedek was a type of the Messiah is taught in

Hebrews 7:15-25—Messiah is a priest forever after the order of Melchizedek, and He lives forever because of the resurrection.

The second type is that of the two birds of Leviticus 14:4-7: one was killed, and one was let go, free and alive. This, too, pictures death and resurrection.

The third type is the Feast of the Firstfruits of Leviticus 23:9-14. Paul teaches in I Corinthians 15:20-24 that the Feast of Firstfruits was fulfilled by the resurrection of the Messiah.

2. In Prophecy

Prophecies concerning the resurrection are found in four passages. The first passage is Psalm 16:9-10 which states: [9] *Therefore my heart is glad, and my glory rejoices: My flesh also shall dwell in safety.* [10] *For you will not leave my soul to Sheol; Neither will you suffer your holy one to see corruption.*

Twice in the New Testament, this Psalm is declared as having been fulfilled by the resurrection of the Messiah: Acts 2:24-30 and 13:32-37.

The second passage is Psalm 22:22-31. Verses 1-21 prophesied the death of the Messiah; but in verses 22-31, the same One who died in verses 1-21 is very much alive. Thus, this, too, predicts the resurrection.

A third passage is Psalm 118:22 which speaks about *the stone which the builders rejected*. In Acts 4:10-11, Peter explains that this verse predicted the resurrection of the Messiah.

The fourth prophecy is Isaiah 53:10-12. Verses 1-9 prophesied the death of the Messiah, but He is very much alive again in verses 10-12, because *he shall see his seed, he shall prolong his days*. This was also fulfilled by the resurrection.

B. The Fact of the Resurrection

That the Bible clearly teaches *Yeshua's* physical resurrection from the dead can be seen in three ways. First, the Messiah predicted His resurrection several times as in Matthew 16:21, Mark 8:31, Luke 18:33, and John 10:17-18.

Second, the resurrection is emphasized in the fact that none of the Gospels concludes with the death of the Messiah; all of them conclude with accounts of

His resurrection and post-resurrection appearances (Mt. 28:1-20; Mk. 16:1-18; Lk. 24:1-49; Jn. 20:1-21:3).

Third, there is a major emphasis on the resurrection in the historical book of Acts and in the Epistles (Acts 2:24, 32; 3:15, 26; 4:2, 10; 5:30; 10:40; 13:30-37; 17:3; Rom. 4:24-25; 6:4, 9; 7:4; 8:11; I Cor. 6:14; II Cor. 4:14; Gal. 1:1; Eph. 1:20; Col. 2:12; I Thess. 1:10; II Tim. 2:8).[72]

C. The Theories of the Resurrection

There are various theories about *Yeshua's* resurrection. Because people choose not to believe in the resurrection, they must somehow explain the empty tomb. Unbelievers have come up with seven different explanations.

1. The Conspiracy to Lie Theory

The first common explanation is that the resurrection was a fabrication, that the apostles conspired to lie, that it was a conspiracy to deceive the public. However, there are two things that militate against this theory. First, why did the Jewish authors give prominence to the women who witnessed the resurrection, knowing very well that this would not be acceptable to the Jewish community? The testimony of women was not acceptable in a Jewish court of law. Therefore, if the accounts in the four Gospels were fabrications, they would not have reported that women were the first ones to see the resurrected Messiah. Second, why would the apostles be willing to die terrible martyrs' deaths if they knew it was all a lie?

2. The Stolen Body or the Fraud Theory

This is the oldest theory (Mt. 28:13). Only two groups would have been interested in stealing the body. The first group is the disciples, but why would each be willing to die a terrible martyr's death for what they knew to be a lie? The second group is His enemies, yet they could not produce the body in order to

[72] Study Suggestion 1 on page 207.

disprove the apostolic preaching of the resurrection. Furthermore, the presence of the Roman guard would have made stealing the body impossible.

3. The Swoon Theory

This theory states that *Yeshua* fainted on the cross and only appeared to be dead, but was revived in the coldness of the tomb. However, the Gospels make it quite clear that He was dead, and His death was clearly evident by the pouring out of the blood and water from His pierced side (Jn. 19:33-34). Furthermore, to faint on the cross would automatically mean death, because an unconscious person would not be able to raise himself up in order to breathe. When a person was crucified, he eventually died by suffocation because, over the course of time, he no longer had the strength to raise up his body.

This theory requires a lot of faith. It requires believing that after three days without food, water, or medical attention, and after being scourged and crucified, *Yeshua* was able to free Himself from the tightly wrapped burial cloths, roll away the stone, terrify the Roman guards, and proceed to escape on His nail-pierced feet. It takes a great deal more faith to believe this than to believe the simple fact of the resurrection.

4. The Wrong Tomb Theory

This theory claims that the women who were looking to embalm *Yeshua's* body went to the wrong tomb. However, the Gospels make it clear that the women took careful note of where He was laid and sat by the tomb for some time. Some came again to the tomb on Saturday evening. The right tomb was marked by the Roman guard and with a Roman seal, and there was an angel present. There was no way to mistake the tomb. Furthermore, *Yeshua* was not buried in a public cemetery where there were many other tombs; He was buried in a privately-owned garden.

5. The Spirit Theory

This theory states that only the spirit returned, not the body; hence, *Yeshua's* was only a spiritual resurrection. However, all four Gospels teach that His resurrected body was of flesh and bone, a body that could be touched and felt.

6. The Vision or Hallucination Theory

This theory claims that the disciples hallucinated. However, hallucinations happen to individuals, not to groups, and they are not contagious. They usually concern events that are expected, but the disciples did not expect a resurrection. Furthermore, there were too many appearances and too many differences in these appearances for all of it to be one big hallucination.

7. The Wild Animal Theory

This theory states that a wild animal devoured the body. However, even a wild animal would have left some remains, such as the bones. A wild animal could not have rolled away the stone. A wild animal would have greatly disturbed the grave cloths, and yet *Yeshua's* grave cloths remained undisturbed. Furthermore, the presence of the Roman guard would have kept a wild animal away.[73]

D. The Proofs of the Resurrection

There are six evidences that the resurrection really occurred.

1. The Empty Tomb

The very emptiness of the tomb is evidence of the resurrection. As previously noted, unbelievers have developed seven different theories to try to explain away the empty tomb. Believing any of these theories takes a lot more faith than just believing the truth: *Yeshua* was resurrected from the dead.

2. The Varied Eyewitness Accounts

There are eleven eyewitness accounts from those to *whom he also showed himself alive after his passion by many proofs* (Acts 1:3). These accounts are quite varied and distinct:

[73] Study Suggestion 2 on page 207.

1. Mary Magdalene spoke to the resurrected Messiah after His resurrection (Mk. 16:9-11; Jn. 20:11-18).
2. A group of women reported seeing Him (Mt. 28:9-10).
3. There were the two disciples on the Emmaus Road (Mk. 16:12-13; Lk. 24:13-32).
4. There was the special eyewitness resurrection experience by Peter (Lk. 24:34; I Cor. 15:5).
5. The resurrected Messiah appeared to the ten apostles (Mk. 16:14; Lk. 24:36-43; Jn. 20:19-25).
6. Eleven apostles saw Him a week later while they were still in Jerusalem (Jn. 20:26-31; I Cor. 15:5).
7. Seven of the eleven disciples met Him by the Sea of Galilee (Jn. 21:1-23).
8. He appeared to the eleven apostles while they were in Galilee (Mt. 28:16-20; Mk. 16:15-18).
9. He appeared to five hundred believers at once, many of whom were still living at the time Paul wrote about it in I Corinthians 15:6.
10. The resurrected Messiah appeared to James (I Cor. 15:7).
11. He appeared to the eleven on the Mount of Olives on the day of His ascension (Lk. 24:44-49; Acts 1:3-8).

These eyewitnesses saw *Yeshua* over a period of forty days. Their accounts evidence the accuracy and historicity of His resurrection.

3. The Post-Resurrection Appearances

The resurrected Messiah appeared to at least three people after His ascension. He appeared to Stephen on the day of his martyrdom (Acts 7:55-56).

He appeared to Paul at least four times. The first appearance was the day that Paul became a believer on the Damascus Road (Acts 9:3-6; 22:6-11; 26:13-18). Paul himself reaffirmed this in I Corinthians 15:8. *Yeshua* also appeared to Paul while he was in Arabia (Gal. 1:12, 17) and when he was praying in the Temple (Acts 22:17-21). He appeared to Paul at least one more time in Jerusalem (Acts 23:11).

Third, He appeared to the Apostle John. The details of this appearance are given in Revelation 1:9–3:22.

4. The Transformation of People Who Knew Him

Before *Yeshua's* resurrection, the disciples were characterized as fearful, paranoid men who had to lock themselves in a house because they feared the leadership of Israel. Suddenly, after the resurrection and the Day of Pentecost, they became bold proclaimers of the resurrection (Acts 4). They were no longer intimidated by the threats of the leadership of Israel, and their boldness even led to martyrdom. They faced death in full faith.

A second example is the transformation of *Yeshua's* half-brothers. Even until His death, His four half-brothers did not believe in His Messianic claims. Suddenly, after His resurrection, at least one of His half-brothers, James, saw the resurrected Messiah (I Cor. 15:7), became a believer, and the first head of the Jerusalem Church (Acts 15). Another half-brother, Jude, became a believer and wrote the Epistle of Jude (Mt. 13:55; Mk. 6:3).

5. The New Testament

The existence of the New Testament is evidence of the resurrection. It was the resurrection that caused the disciples to write the Gospels. The New Testament has survived in spite of many, many attempts to suppress it. Even today, there are attempts to suppress it in various parts of the world, and yet the very existence of the New Testament is evidence that it is the word of God and that the testimony of the resurrection is true.

6. The Existence of the Church

The existence of the church is evidence of the resurrection. The fact that this entity came into existence because of the resurrection and has continued to exist in spite of countless attempts to annihilate it or pervert it, is also evidence of the resurrection.

E. The Agent of the Resurrection

All three members of the Trinity played a role in the resurrection of *Yeshua*. That God the Father played the major role is evidenced by a number of Scriptures:

Acts 2:24, 32, 3:26, 5:30, 13:30, Romans 6:4, I Corinthians 6:14, Galatians 1:1, Ephesians 1:20, and I Peter 1:3. The Son also had a role in the resurrection, for He had the power to bring His life up again as He Himself proclaimed in John 2:19 and 10:17-18. The Holy Spirit also played a role in the resurrection of the Messiah, which is mentioned in Romans 8:11.

F. The Reasons for the Resurrection

The resurrection was necessary for four reasons. First, the Messiah was resurrected because of who He is. This is found in John 1:4 and 5:26. Because He is the Son of God, the God-Man, the Messiah of Israel, God the Father could not leave Him dead.

Second, *Yeshua* was resurrected to fulfill the Davidic Covenant. The Davidic Covenant promised four eternal elements: an eternal house, an eternal throne, an eternal kingdom, and an eternal descendant. If He had died and never been resurrected, the fourth eternal element would have remained unfulfilled. Because the Davidic Covenant promised an eternal person, it was necessary for *Yeshua* to be resurrected so that He could indeed be the fulfillment of that fourth eternal promise. Prophetically, this promise is given in I Chronicles 17:14 and reaffirmed by Psalm 89:29 and 36-37. In Isaiah 9:6-7, the prophet expounded on this aspect. The New Testament reaffirms this truth in Luke 1:31-33 and Acts 2:24-31.

Third, the resurrection occurred so that He could become the source of resurrection life. This is found in John 10:10, 11:25-26, Colossians 3:1-4, and I John 5:11-12. The reason believers will someday also have resurrection life is because He was resurrected.

Fourth, *Yeshua* was resurrected so He could become the source of resurrection power. Because He is the source of resurrection power by virtue of His own resurrection, believers can fulfill their commission. This is found in Matthew 28:18 and Ephesians 1:19-20.[74]

---

[74] Question 1 on page 207.

G. The Nature of the Resurrection Body

There are nine specific things to consider concerning the nature of *Yeshua's* resurrected body. First, as noted earlier, He was not always recognized immediately. Enough changes had occurred in His body that recognition was not always instantaneous, yet there were enough similarities that eventually those who knew Him recognized Him to be exactly the One they had known before. This is found in Luke 24:16, 31, John 20:15, and 21:7.

Second, *Yeshua* had the ability to appear and disappear (Lk. 24:31-36; Jn. 20:19).

Third, His new body had no problem with physical barriers. He was able to pass right through walls and closed doors (Jn. 20:19).

Fourth, His resurrected body was a material body. Although He had the ability to appear and disappear and was not subject to any physical barriers, it was a material body of *flesh and bones*, according to Luke 24:39-40.

Fifth, *Yeshua's* resurrected body still had the nail-prints and spear-wound. According to John 20:24-27, the marks of the crucifixion were still very visible on His body.

Sixth, His resurrected body was not merely spirit. Luke 24:41-43 says that *Yeshua* ate fish and bread to show that He was not merely spirit, an apparition, or a ghost.

Seventh, His resurrected body could be felt. Although He had the ability to appear and disappear and go through walls, there was enough *flesh and bone* material that His body could be felt (Mt. 28:9; Lk. 24:39; Jn. 20:17).

Eighth, *Yeshua's* resurrected body was visible. It was not merely a vision or a dream, but it was a normal, everyday sight (Jn. 20:20).

Ninth, the resurrected body of the Messiah could and did breathe (Jn. 20:22).

In light of these nine things, we can conclude that the resurrected body was the same as the one that died. This was not a newly created body, but the very same body that had been placed into the tomb. That same body underwent a change—not an absolute, total change, but a major change in many areas. There were enough changes so that He was not recognized immediately; nevertheless, enough elements remained so that He was recognized as being the same person. The Messiah's resurrection body was not yet glorified during the forty days of His post-resurrection ministry. Therefore, when He appeared, He looked just like a normal man, as was the case with the women in the garden and with the two disciples on the Emmaus Road. He still had the scars of the crucifixion. Only with His ascension was He glorified (Phil. 3:21; Rev. 1:12-18).

These are the facts concerning the nature of the resurrection body of *Yeshua*. It is not clear whether some things are true because it was a resurrected body or because He is God. Some of these things will be true of our resurrected bodies, but some may not.

H. The Importance of the Resurrection

The preaching of the resurrection is important for two reasons. First, it is very much a part of the gospel (I Cor. 15:4; II Tim. 2:8). As previously noted, the gospel contains three points: the Messiah died for our sins, according to the Scriptures; He was buried; and He rose again on the third day, according to the Scriptures. Because the resurrection is part of the gospel, it is something that must be believed, proclaimed, and preached.

The second reason the resurrection is important is because it is the basis of the believer's future resurrection. In I Corinthians 15:12-19, Paul explains that if *Yeshua* was not raised from the dead, *then is our preaching vain*. If the Messiah remained dead, then salvation would go no further than the grave itself, leaving no hope.

If He was not raised from the dead, our faith is vain (I Cor. 15:14 and 17). That is, it would be an empty faith, a faith that produces no eternal results. It would produce temporary results in this life, but with death, it all would end. Therefore, faith is vain if the Messiah did not rise from the dead.

Paul makes the point in I Corinthians 15:15 that the apostles witnessed not only His death, but also His resurrection. If their testimony is not true, then they are false witnesses.

If He did not rise from the dead, believers are still in their sins (I Cor. 15:17). While *Yeshua's* death provided the atonement for sin, His resurrection provided the power over sin. Believers would still be in their sins if He had not been raised from the dead. To receive forgiveness for our sins, it is necessary to believe the gospel, and the resurrection is part of the gospel.

If He had not risen from the dead, there would be no hope for those who have already died (I Cor. 15:18). If *Yeshua* did not rise from the dead, then neither will the saints who have already died rise from the dead.

Finally, I Corinthians 15:19 points out that believers would be the *most pitiable* of all people for having conformed their lives to that which is unreal. Indeed, they would be living a false lifestyle by changing their lives in accordance with the resurrected Messiah if the resurrection had not really occurred.

I. The Significance of the Resurrection

The significance of the resurrection lies in four specific areas.

1. The Significance to the Messiah

The resurrection is significant to the Messiah in that it proved Him to be the Son of God (Rom. 1:4). It confirmed the truth of all that He said (Mt. 28:6). His resurrection means that He is the "Firstfruits of the First Resurrection" (I Cor. 15:20-23). Furthermore, it was a declaration of the Father that the Messiah met all the requirements of the Law of Moses (Phil. 2:9).

2. The Significance to All Men

The resurrection is significant to all people in general, especially to the unbelieving world insofar as it makes certain the resurrection of all human beings, both believers and unbelievers (I Cor. 15:20-22). Furthermore, His resurrection guarantees judgment. The Messiah is the One who will judge the unbeliever, which He would not be able to do had He not been raised. Thus, His resurrection guarantees the judgment of all men (Acts 10:40-42; 17:30-31).

3. The Significance to Old Testament Saints

The resurrection is significant to the Old Testament saints in that it includes the fulfillment of the Old Testament promise concerning their salvation: the removal of their sin and the guarantee of their future resurrection (Acts 13:32-33). So *Yeshua's* resurrection is significant to saints who died even before His own death.

4. The Significance to Believers

The resurrection is significant to believers for six reasons. First, it proves the believer's justification, as we can see in Romans 4:24-25: [24] *but for our sake also, unto whom it shall be reckoned, who believe on him that raised Yeshua our Lord from the dead,* [25] *who was delivered up for our trespasses, and was raised for our justification.* The Greek preposition that Paul used to express that *Yeshua* died *for* our transgressions and was raised *for* our justification is *dia*, which means "on account of." The basis of justification is the death of the Messiah. This passage states that He was raised "because of" or "on account of" our justification having been accomplished. Because justification has been accomplished by His death, on the basis of that accomplishment, He was raised from the dead to prove that we have been justified by our faith.

Second, the resurrection guarantees power for service (Eph. 1:17-20). Believers can partake of resurrection power to fulfill their calling.

Third, the resurrection guarantees the believer's individual resurrection (Rom. 8:11; I Cor. 6:14; II Cor. 4:14).

Fourth, the resurrection of the Messiah means the forgiveness of the believer's sins (I Cor. 15:3).

Fifth, it designates the Messiah as the head of the church (Eph. 1:20-22).

Sixth, the resurrection means that the Messiah now has the keys of death as far as believers are concerned (Heb. 2:9-18). Satan no longer has the authority to put a believer to death. The Messiah has the keys of death because He entered Satan's domain, the realm of death, took the keys away from him, and "passed through" that death by means of His resurrection. He still has the keys of death, according to Revelation 1:18.[75]

[75] Question 2 and Study Suggestion 3 on page 207.

J. Questions and Study Suggestions

Study Suggestion 1: Dr. Fruchtenbaum lists numerous verses here. It is recommended to take some time to look them all up and study them in the context of the resurrection accounts in the Gospels.

Study Suggestion 2: Looking at the different theories refuting the resurrection, we realize to what lengths people are willing to go to explain away the fact that *Yeshua* is alive. Read I Corinthians 15:17. Meditate on this verse and try to develop a good understanding as to why this is such an important point of our faith.

Question 1: Of the reasons given for the resurrection, which one means the most to you? Explain your choice.

Question 2: Looking at the Bible as a whole, one cannot help but recognize that *Yeshua's* resurrection was not the only time that a dead person came back to life. The prophets Elijah and Elisha raised two young men from the dead. The Messiah Himself raised at least three people back to life. Upon His death, tombs opened up and many dead came back to life. What makes *Yeshua's* resurrection unique?

Study Suggestion 3: Take the online test for this section of the study of the Messiah found on http://ariel.org/come-and-see.htm under "The Resurrection of the Messiah (075)."

Chapter XVI

The Ascension of the Messiah

There are five specific aspects to be noted concerning the theological implications, significances, and results of the ascension.

A. The Old Testament Prophecies

The ascension was foretold in at least two different verses of the Old Testament: Psalm 68:18 and Proverbs 30:4. To the question—*Who has ascended up into heaven, and descended?*—the answer is none other than the Son of Man.

B. The Historical Fact of the Ascension

The Messiah Himself predicted that He would ascend into heaven and return to God the Father (Jn. 3:13; 6:62; 14:2, 12; 16:5, 10, 17, and 28).

The event itself is described historically in three places: Mark 16:19-20, Luke 24:50-53, and Acts 1:9-11. It is reaffirmed in Ephesians 4:8-9.

The Acts 1:9-11 passage, in particular, gives the most detail:

> [9] *And when he had said these things, as they were looking, he was taken up; and a cloud received him out of their sight.* [10] *And while they were looking steadfastly into heaven as he went, behold, two men stood by them in white*

apparel; [11] who also said, Ye men of Galilee, why stand ye looking into heaven? this Yeshua, who was received up from you into heaven shall so come in like manner as ye beheld him going into heaven.

Luke uses four key Greek words or terms to give the details of the ascension. The first word is *epairo* and means "to lift up," showing that the ascension was upward (v. 9). Furthermore, the verb is in the passive voice, showing that the Son was taken up into heaven by God the Father.

The second word is *hupolambano*, which has the concept of "being under something else" (v. 9). The Messiah was in the atmospheric heaven and was received by the clouds. The point is that the cloud was under Him; He was being supported in the ascension by the cloud. Of course, the cloud also hid the ascension from the apostles' view.

The third word is *poreuomai*, which literally means "as he went" (v. 10). It means "to pursue a journey." *Yeshua* simply went on a trip. The word conveys both the aspects of departure and journey. The aspect of departure means that there was a departure from the earth; the aspect of journey means that it was a journey to heaven.

The fourth word is *analambano*, meaning "to be received up" (v. 11). It means that the ascension ended when *Yeshua* was received up into heaven. Every journey has its destination. While the third term emphasizes the aspects of departure and journey, the fourth term emphasizes the destination of this journey: heaven itself. Like many journeys, this journey was not permanent, but temporary. Someday, He will return to this earth to set up His kingdom.

C. The Characteristics of the Ascension

There are six characteristics of the ascension. First, it was the ascension of the whole God-Man. It was not just the humanity of *Yeshua*, nor was it only the deity of the Messiah; it was the Theanthropic Person that ascended.

Second, the ascension was visible. The disciples could see *Yeshua* going up into the atmospheric heaven until a cloud hid Him from their view.

Third, it was bodily. The resurrected body that He received was the body that ascended.

Fourth, it was gradual. He was not instantaneously caught up with the speed of light, or in a wink of an eye, to disappear suddenly. It was gradual and in four stages, as illustrated by the four Greek terms.

Fifth, the ascending Messiah was received by clouds. *Yeshua* went up in the clouds of heaven, the very clouds that hid the rest of the ascension from the view of the apostles.

Sixth, the ascension meant a transfer from one location to another location: from earth to heaven. [76]

D. The Arrival in Heaven

The termination and the goal of the ascension was the bodily arrival of the Messiah into heaven. This fact is so important that fifteen specific passages speak of it: Acts 3:20-21, 9:3-6, 22:6-10, 26:13-18, Philippians 3:20, I Thessalonians 1:10, 4:16, I Timothy 3:16, Hebrews 4:14, 6:20, 7:26, 9:24, I John 2:1, and Revelation 5:5-12.

At this point, His divine glory was unveiled, His body was glorified, and His crucifixion scars disappeared. When John saw Him again on the Isle of Patmos in Revelation 1:12-16, he saw Him with unveiled glory and without the scars.

E. The Significances of the Ascension

The ascension is significant for twelve reasons. First, it proved the truth of what *Yeshua* had said. He prophesied that He would go to the Father in John 14:28 and the ascension fulfilled His claim.

Second, the ascension means that He is preparing a place. In John 14:2, He said He was going to heaven, to the Father, to prepare a place for believers. The ascension and arrival of *Yeshua* into heaven mean that He is preparing a place for us.

---

[76] Question 1 on page 214.

Third, the ascension marks the culmination of His exaltation. This is found in Ephesians 1:20-23. Upon His arrival into heaven, the exaltation, which began with His burial in a new, rich man's tomb, was complete.

Fourth, the ascension marks His headship over the church. This is seen in Colossians 1:18. This means that He is head of the church by virtue of His ascension into heaven.

Fifth, the ascension means there is a man seated at the right hand of God the Father (Acts 2:32-35).

Sixth, the ascension marks the beginning of the high priestly ministry of *Yeshua* (Heb. 4:14-16). Upon His ascension, He took on His function as a priest, ever making intercession for us. By means of His ascension, He can function in His priestly office in heaven. Because there is a man seated at the right hand of God the Father who is performing a high priestly ministry, the writer of the book of Hebrews encourages believers to make use of this high priest. As our high priest, He can intercede. As a man who was tempted in all points but without sin, He is a sympathetic high priest.

Seventh, the ascension marks the coming of the Holy Spirit. The new type of ministry that the Holy Spirit began in Acts 2 could not have occurred before the ascension of *Yeshua*. Only after His ascension could the Holy Spirit come and indwell believers forever and begin His work of Spirit-baptism. This is brought out prophetically in John 7:39 and 16:7 and in fulfillment in Acts 2:33.

Eighth, in Hebrews 6:20 the ascension makes the Messiah *a forerunner* into heaven. Being *a forerunner* means "the first of more to come later." The believers are "the more to come later."

Ninth, the ascension marks the believer's new position as being seated *in the heavenlies*. This is found in Ephesians 1:20-21 and 2:6. Because believers are *in Messiah*, they are in a new position. Because the Messiah is seated in the heavenlies at the right hand of God the Father and because believers are in the Messiah, God views believers as being seated in the heavenlies, not yet physically, but positionally.

Tenth, by means of the ascension, the gifts of the Holy Spirit could be given. This is found in Ephesians 4:7-11. This passage points out that the gifts of the Holy Spirit were available only after the Messiah ascended into heaven. So the Son ascended into heaven and then gave the spiritual gifts to men.

Eleventh, the ascension provides the manner, not the place, of His return (Acts 1:9-11). He ascended in the clouds of heaven, and someday, He will come in like manner: in the clouds of heaven (Mt. 24:30).

Twelfth, the ascension means that the Old Testament saints are now also in heaven. This is seen in Ephesians 4:8. Before His ascension, the souls of the Old Testament saints were still kept in the center of the earth in *Sheol* or *Hades*. When *Yeshua* ascended, He took the souls of the Old Testament saints with Him.[77]

[77] Question 2 and Study Suggestion on page 214.

F. Questions and Study Suggestions

Question 1: The ascension contradicts the laws of nature. How do you explain that it was possible for the Messiah to ascend into heaven?

Question 2: Read John 20:17 and Colossians 1:20. As Dr. Fruchtenbaum explained on page 167, *Yeshua* went to heaven to cleanse the heavenly tabernacle. How would you explain to another believer the two different events, or the two ascensions?

Study Suggestion: Take the online test for this section of the study of the Messiah found on http://ariel.org/come-and-see.htm under "The Ascension of the Messiah (076)."

Chapter XVII

The Present Session

Bible teachers often speak about the work of the Messiah in the past, during His lifetime. They also speak about what He will do in the future, such as at the Rapture, the Second Coming, the Messianic Kingdom, and the eternal state. It is rare to hear someone teach on what *Yeshua* is doing today. This will be a discussion on the present session, as theologians call it, or the present work of the Messiah. It will be about what *Yeshua* is doing today.

A. The Present Position of the Messiah

Positionally, *Yeshua* is seated at the right hand of God the Father. After He took on human form at the incarnation, after He fulfilled in His life the purpose of the incarnation, and after His death, resurrection, and ascension, He was seated at the right hand of God the Father. He left heaven in the form of God, but He returned to heaven having two natures: divine and human. He is now the God-Man and, as the God-Man, He fulfills the prophecy that He would be seated at the right hand of God the Father.

The first of these prophecies is found in Psalm 80:17: *Let your hand be upon the man of your right hand, Upon the son of man whom you made strong for yourself.* The second prophecy is found in Psalm 110:1, where God the Father is viewed as speaking to the Messianic Son, saying to Him: *Sit you at my right hand, Until I make your enemies your footstool.*

The New Testament verifies that Psalm 110:1 speaks of the Messiah (Mt. 22:43-45; Mk. 12:35-37; Lk. 20:41-44). In fact, *Yeshua* quoted this very verse to the Pharisees with the question, "Whose son was the Messiah to be?" They correctly answered, "David's." Then *Yeshua* answered, "If the Messiah is David's son, why does David call Him his Lord?" It was a question that the Pharisees could not answer. But the answer lies in the God-Man concept: as to His humanity, *Yeshua* is David's son, but as to His deity, He is David's Lord.

In addition to the Old Testament predictions, there are the Messiah's own predictions. While still on earth, *Yeshua* Himself prophesied that He would be seated at the right hand of God the Father (Mt. 26:64; Lk. 22:69).

Finally, the New Testament contains the record of the fulfillment of these prophecies. *Yeshua* is now seated at the right hand of God the Father, in fulfillment of the Old Testament passages. This fulfillment is verified by Mark 16:19, Acts 2:33-36, 5:31, 7:55-56, Romans 8:34, Ephesians 1:20-22, Colossians 3:1, Hebrews 1:3, 8:1, 10:12-13, 12:2, and I Peter 3:22. Insofar as His present position is concerned, *Yeshua* is seated today at the right hand of God the Father.[78]

B. The Messiah's Present Work in Heaven

The Messiah is in heaven seated at the right hand of God the Father, but what is He doing there?

1. Exercising Universal Authority

To begin with, the Messiah is exercising universal authority: *All authority has been given unto me in heaven and on earth* (Mt. 28:18). He controls the universe in general, and He also controls the affairs which come into a believer's life (Eph. 1:20-22; Col. 1:16-17; Heb. 1:3-13; I Pet. 3:22).

[78] Questions 1 and 2 on page 224.

2. Preparing a Place in Heaven

At the present time, *Yeshua* is also preparing a place in heaven. This is what He promised His disciples He would be doing after He left them (Jn. 14:1-3). He is preparing a place right now for believers so that when they go to join Him in heaven, He will have a place all ready for them.

3. Mediating

Furthermore, *Yeshua* is mediating. He is the one mediator between God the Father and men (I Tim. 2:5). It was necessary for the mediator to be human, and that is why *Yeshua* became a man. Israel had the Levitical high priest as their mediator, but believers today have the *Yeshua*, the lion of the tribe of Judah.

4. Acting as an Advocate and Comforter

Another work that the Messiah is doing in heaven is that of an advocate (I Jn. 2:1). The Greek word translated "advocate" is *parakletos*, which literally means "comforter." It speaks of one who is called upon for aid, one who pleads the cause of another, one who gives wise counsel. Indeed, *Yeshua* is the One upon whom we can call for aid. He is the One who is pleading our cause before the throne of God, especially in those cases when Satan has grounds for accusing us. *Yeshua* is the One who gives us wise counsel and wisdom. Thus, He is the *parakletos*; He is the Comforter and the Advocate.

This can be seen from three key passages. The first is John 14:16, which reads: *And I will pray the Father, and he shall give you another Comforter, that he may be with you for ever*. The term *Comforter* in that passage is speaking of the Holy Spirit and not of the Messiah. But notice the word *another*. The Holy Spirit is ***another*** *Comforter*. Of the two Greek words which mean "another," the one that *Yeshua* uses here is the one that means "another of the same kind." The Holy Spirit is *another Comforter* of the same kind. Of the same kind as what? The same kind as *Yeshua*! Just as He is a comforter, so is the Holy Spirit. The Holy Spirit is a divine comforter and, therefore, so is *Yeshua*. The second passage is Hebrews 9:24, which teaches that being an advocate is part of His present priestly ministry: *now to appear before the face of God for us*. The third passage is the aforementioned I John 2:1, which spells out our need for an advocate. We need *Yeshua* to be our Advocate because of actual sins committed by us. When a believer sins, he offends a righteous God, and that is why we still need the Messiah as our Advocate: in order to plead our cause.

The last thing to note is that the basic necessity of having an advocate is to counteract the accusations of Satan. According to Revelation 12:10, Satan has the right to appear before the throne of God to accuse the brethren. Whenever a believer falls into a state of unconfessed sin, sooner or later, Satan will appear before the throne to accuse that believer before God the Father. That is why believers need the ministry of *Yeshua* as an advocate: Whenever Satan has any grounds for accusation, *Yeshua* can then say, "Lay that sin upon my account; I have already paid for that sin when I died for that person on the cross."

5. Interceding on Our Behalf

Yeshua is presently interceding on our behalf. His work of intercession is necessary because of our weakness and our helplessness.

The two main passages of Scripture that talk about the intercessory work of the Messiah are Romans 8:34 and Hebrews 7:25. These passages, taken together with Hebrews 9:24, picture vividly the Messiah as our Intercessor. Because He is seated *at the right hand of God*, He has the continuous, unending ability to appear before the face of God the Father and *makes intercession for us* (Rom. 8:34). The Greek word translated *for us* means "on our behalf" or "for the benefit of." Hebrew 7:25 tells us that He draws near to God. The Greek word translated *draw near* means "to meet with." In other words, the picture of the Messiah as our Intercessor is that He appears before God the Father, meeting with Him on a face-to-face basis on our behalf and for our benefit as He pleads our cause.

The nature of His intercession is priestly. *Yeshua* is now functioning in the second of His three offices, the office of high priest. One of the functions of a priest is to do the work of intercession. So the nature of the intercessory work of the Messiah is that of a priest in his priestly office. The objects or beneficiaries of His intercession are believers only, as He promised in John 17:9 and 20. He never intercedes on behalf of unbelievers.

As to the content of His intercession, we can note that He intercedes when believers are tempted (Heb. 4:14-16). His concern is the purity of believers, to keep them from sinning (Heb. 10:21-22).[79]

C. Messiah's Present Work on Earth

While *Yeshua* is in heaven seated at the right hand of God the Father, He is accomplishing eleven things here on earth:

1. *Yeshua* is the head of the church on earth (Eph. 1:22-23; Col. 1:18).
2. He is building His church (Mt. 16:18) and will continue to do so until the church is complete, at which point He will remove it from the earth and take it to heaven where He is.
3. He is present in the church (Mt. 28:20; Jn. 17:23, 26). The Messiah is divine as well as human. In His humanity, He is in heaven only. However, in His deity, He is omnipresent, so He is also in the church.
4. He imparts eternal life. It is *Yeshua* who imparts eternal life to those who believe. Every person who is saved receives eternal life. This impartation of eternal life is a work of Jesus here on earth (Jn. 1:4; 10:10; 11:25; 14:6; I Jn. 5:12; Col. 3:4).
5. He indwells believers (Jn. 14:20, 23; 15:4-5; Gal. 2:20; Col. 1:26-27; I Jn. 3:24). Again, in His humanity, He is seated at the right hand of God the Father; but in deity, He is omnipresent, and He indwells every believer.
6. He is the source of strength for believers here on earth (Phil. 4:13).
7. He is the source of power for believers here on earth (Mt. 28:18-20).
8. He answers prayers that believers are praying here on earth; every answer to prayer is a work of the Messiah (Jn. 14:14).
9. He helps believers who have particular needs. When a particular need is met, that is a work of the Messiah here on earth (Heb. 2:18; 4:16).

---

[79] Question 3 on page 224.

10. He is the ground of the believer's hope. Although believers on earth may suffer physical limitations and struggle in spiritual battles, they have *the hope of glory*, the hope of *adoption* and *the redemption of our body*. *Yeshua* is the basis, the foundation, and the ground of that hope (Col. 1:27; Rom. 8:23).
11. He sends the Spirit. He is responsible for the various works and ministries which the Holy Spirit performs (Lk. 24:29; Jn. 14:16, 17, 26; 15:26; 16:7-15).

D. The Seven Figures

In seven different ways, the Scriptures portray, symbolize, or illustrate the relationship of the Messiah to the church. This relationship is unique in that He is seated in heaven, while His church is here on earth. Each figure emphasizes one or more key points of this relationship.

1. The Last Adam and the New Creation

The last Adam is *Yeshua*, who is now in heaven; the new creation is "the body of the Messiah," the church. This relationship is given in I Corinthians 15:45 and II Corinthians 5:17. The basic meaning of this relationship is to give new life. For as in Adam all die, in the Messiah, the last Adam, all shall be made alive. The basic thrust of this first relationship is that of giving new life, the impartation of eternal life.

2. The Head and the Body

The Messiah is the head of the church, and the church itself is His body. The main passages for this relationship are Colossians 1:18 and 24. This relationship emphasizes four things. First, it has the meaning of giving direction. Just as a physical head or brain gives direction to a physical body, even so, the Messiah as the head gives direction to the church. Second, it means control. Just as the head controls the actions of the body, even so, the Messiah controls the church. Third, it means nurturing. The head with its controlling power of the brain nurtures the rest of the body. Even so, the Messiah nurtures His church. Fourth, it means the giving of spiritual gifts. The greatest passage on spiritual gifts, I Corinthians 12, bases its teaching on this relationship of the head to the body.

3. The Shepherd and the Sheep

The main passage that describes this relationship is John 10:1-30. The meaning of this relationship is threefold. First, it means leading. A shepherd leads a flock of sheep, and so it is the Messiah, the Good Shepherd, who leads the church. Second, it means caring. Just as a good shepherd cares for his sheep, even so, the Messiah cares for the church. Third, it also has the meaning of provision. It is not the responsibility of the sheep to find the pasture; it is the responsibility of the shepherd to bring the sheep to a place where they can be fed. Thus, the Messiah takes the responsibility of providing for the basic physical and spiritual needs of the church.

4. The Vine and the Branches

The key Scripture for this relationship is John 15:1-7. This relationship has two meanings. The first meaning is that of fruitfulness. A branch cannot bear fruit unless it remains on the vine, where it can partake of the life-giving sap of the vine. When it partakes of the life-giving sap of the vine, then the branch becomes fruitful. The believer is to abide in the Messiah; if he abides in the Messiah, he will be bearing fruit. A second meaning of this relationship is that of reproduction. Not only does the vine produce fruit, it also produces seeds to produce more vines that will, in turn, produce more fruit. The believer has the responsibility of reproduction, to produce saints by witnessing and sharing the gospel, and when they are born again, they, too, can produce fruit.

5. The Chief Cornerstone and the Stones of the Building

The key Scriptures for this relationship are I Corinthians 3:10-11 and I Peter 2:4-8. This relationship has two key meanings. The first is that of life and stability. If the believer rests upon a sure foundation, which is the Messiah, then he is building a stable building. If he does not, he is building on a foundation of sand, and the result is instability. The second meaning of this relationship is that of a foundation for the spiritual life. The Lord *Yeshua* is the foundation, and *other foundation can no man lay than that which is laid, which is Yeshua the Messiah* (I

Cor. 3:11) The Messiah and His work on the cross are the foundation for the spiritual life.

6. The High Priest and the Royal Priesthood

The major passages for this relationship are Hebrews 7:1–10:18 and I Peter 2:5 and 9. This relationship has four meanings. First, it has the meaning of sacrifice, because it is the duty of a priest to offer up sacrifices. The sacrifice that *Yeshua* offered was the sacrifice of His own blood. The sacrifices that believers are to offer are praise, thanksgiving, hospitality, and monetary support for the Lord's work (Heb. 13).

Second, it means intercession. Just as *Yeshua* is interceding for believers, even so, believers are to be interceding for other believers.

Third, it means cleansing, because the function of a high priest was to cleanse the people he represented, the people of Israel. Today, *Yeshua* is cleansing believers by means of the sanctifying work of the Holy Spirit. Believers are to do the work of cleansing as well, to co-participate in this work by means of our confession, as stated in I John 1:9.

The fourth meaning of this relationship is prayer. The function of a priest was to represent the people to God, and that is why *Yeshua* prayed on the behalf of believers (Jn. 17). By the same token, believers should be praying on behalf of one another.

7. The Bridegroom and the Bride

The main Scripture for this relationship is Ephesians 5:25-32. This relationship has three basic meanings. First is the meaning of preparedness. Just as the bride prepares herself for the husband, even so, believers must live in constant preparation. *Yeshua* has not yet come for the church, but believers should always be prepared and ready for the moment that He does come. Second, it means union. The church is united in a very unique way with the Messiah; all believers are now *in Messiah*. Third, it means communion. A husband and wife share a level of communion that is not shared by others, and believers are to share a unique communion with the Messiah.

These are the seven figures that illustrate the present work of the Messiah. *Yeshua* is active, and because He is active, believers are the recipients of many blessings.[80]

---

[80] Study Suggestion on page 224.

E. Questions and Study Suggestions

Question 1: To some people it seems wrong that God the Son would sit at the right hand of His Father. After all, this implies that God the Father sits at the left hand of His Son. How would you respond to this objection?

Question 2: Read Acts 7:55. Does the account of Stephen seeing the risen Messiah standing at the right hand of God contradict the verses where *Yeshua* is depicted as being in a seated position?

Question 3: Which one of the five works of Messiah seems most important or dear to you? Explain your choice.

Study Suggestion: Take the online test for this section of the study of the Messiah found on http://ariel.org/come-and-see.htm under "The Present Work of the Messiah (078)."

Chapter XVIII

The Return of the Messiah

The return of the Messiah is the final division of Christology. The topic is dealt with in a summary fashion, because all of the details rightfully belong to another main division of systematic theology, which is eschatology.[81] We will therefore briefly discuss the subject in four categories.

A. The Rapture

The Rapture concerns Messiah's coming for the church. It is described in I Corinthians 15:50-58 and I Thessalonians 4:13-18. The body of the Messiah, the church, is composed of both Jewish and Gentile believers, and entrance into this body is by Spirit-baptism only. Since Spirit-baptism did not begin until Pentecost, described in Acts 2, the church could not have existed prior to that time. When *Yeshua* spoke of building His church in Matthew 16:18, He used the future tense, showing that the church had not yet begun. A major reason was that both His resurrection (Eph. 1:19-20) and His ascension, with the subsequent giving of spiritual gifts (Eph. 4:7-12), were necessary prerequisites for the building of the

[81] The volume of Come and See which will deal with the topic of eschatology will be published in due course. For a complete eschatology, see the author's work, *The Footsteps of the Messiah: A Study of the Sequence of Prophetic Events* (San Antonio, TX: Ariel Ministries, 2004).

church. The church is composed of all true believers from Pentecost in Acts 2 until the Rapture of the church. The Rapture excludes Old Testament saints and post-Rapture, or Tribulation saints. Therefore, the only saints who will be Raptured are church saints. The Rapture passages clearly state that only those *in Messiah* will partake of the Rapture. Throughout his writings, Paul uses terms such as *in Messiah, in Yeshua, in Yeshua Messiah, in Messiah Yeshua, in him, in whom, in the Lord,* in a very technical way, referring to those who were baptized by the Spirit into the body of the Messiah, the church. That church will be removed from the earth. As I Thessalonians 4:17 puts it: *then we that are alive, that are left, shall together with them be caught up in the clouds, to meet the Lord in the air: and so shall we ever be with the Lord.*

B. The Second Coming

Whereas the Rapture is concerned with Messiah's return for the church, the Second Coming is His return for Israel.

There are three Greek terms describing the Second Coming. The first word is *parousia* and means "presence." It refers to a coming preceding a presence. Scriptures that use this word for Messiah's return are Matthew 24:3, 27, 37 and 39, I Corinthians 15:23, I Thessalonians 2:19, 3:13, 4:15, 5:23, II Thessalonians 2:1, James 5:7-8, and II Peter 3:4.

The second word is *apokalupsis* and means "revelation." In fact, it is the title for the book of Revelation in Greek. It means "the unveiling of something that was previously hidden from view"—in this case, the visible glory of the Messiah. Scriptures that use this word in conjunction with the Second Coming are II Thessalonians 1:7, I Peter 1:7, 13, and 4:13.

The third word is *epiphaneia* and means "glorious appearing." It refers to something which is uncovered and found to be glorious. Scriptures that use this particular word in connection with the Second Coming include II Thessalonians 2:8, I Timothy 6:14, II Timothy 4:1, 8, and Titus 2:13.

There are a number of Scriptures that deal specifically with the Second Coming and the work the Messiah will accomplish at that time:

- ✡ Deuteronomy 30:1-10 points out that He is coming for the purpose of regathering Israel.

- ✡ Isaiah 63:1-6 shows that when He comes back, He will come first to Bozrah, also known as Petra.
- ✡ Daniel 2:34-35, 44-45, and 7:13-14 state that He is coming to bring an end to "the times of the Gentiles."[82]
- ✡ Zechariah 14:1-4 and 11 explains that He is coming to save Jerusalem.
- ✡ Matthew 24:26-31 states that He is coming to be seen by all.
- ✡ Acts 1:9-11 describes that He is coming in the clouds of heaven.
- ✡ Acts 15:16-18 gives a reason: He is coming to establish the Davidic throne.
- ✡ Romans 11:25-27 states that He is coming in response to Israel's salvation.
- ✡ First Thessalonians 3:13 adds that He is coming with His saints.
- ✡ Second Thessalonians 1:7-10 gives more detail: He is coming back with vengeance.
- ✡ Second Thessalonians 2:8 gives another reason: He is coming to destroy the Antichrist.
- ✡ Jude 14-15 repeats that He is coming with His saints.
- ✡ Revelation 1:7 reiterates that He will be seen by all.
- ✡ Revelation 19:11-16 finally states that He is coming to destroy all enemies.[83]

C. The Messianic Kingdom

The Messianic Kingdom will be inaugurated with the return of *Yeshua*. This is clearly stated at least five different times in the Scriptures. When Messiah returns, He will sit upon David's throne (Isa. 9:6-7; Jer. 23:5-6; Lk. 1:31-33; Acts 2:30). He will come to rule over Israel (Ez. 37:21-28). In fact, He will exercise universal rule (Dan. 7:13-14).

---

[82] See p. 47-48.

[83] Study Suggestion on page 230.

Concerning the nature of the Messianic Kingdom, we can make four summarizing statements:

1. The kingdom will be theocratic, because the ruling king is going to be Immanuel (Isa. 7:14), which means "With us, God." This king will be the heir to the Davidic throne (Isa. 9:6-7; Jer. 23:5-6).
2. The kingdom is to be heavenly in character (Isa. 2:4; 11:4-5; Jer. 33:14-17).
3. The kingdom is going to be an earthly kingdom (Ps. 2:8; Isa. 42:4; Zech. 14:9). It is going to be centered in Jerusalem (Isa. 2:2-4; 62:1-12; Zech. 8:20-23). It will be a kingdom over Israel (Isa. 11:11-12; 14:1-2; 60:1-22; Jer. 23:5-6; Ez. 37:21-28; Micah 4:6-8). While its rule will be over Israel, it will extend over all nations (Ps. 72:11, 17; 86:9; Isa. 55:5; Dan. 7:13-14; Mic. 4:2; Zech. 8:22).
4. The nature of this kingdom is going to be established by the returning King (Ps. 9:6-11; Zech. 2:10-12; Mal. 3:1-4).[84]

D. The Eternal Order

After the earth is fully subjugated during the Messianic Kingdom, the eternal order will be established. This is taught in I Corinthians 15:24-28:

> [24] *Then comes the end, when he shall deliver up the kingdom to God, even the Father; when he shall have abolished all rule and all authority and power.* [25] *For he must reign, till he has put all his enemies under his feet.* [26] *The last enemy that shall be abolished is death.* [27] *For, He put all things in subjection under his feet. But when he says, All things are put in subjection, it is evident that he is excepted who did subject all things unto him.* [28] *And when all things have been subjected unto him, then shall the Son also himself be subjected to him that did subject all things unto him, that God may be all in all.*

The eternal order is the high point of New Testament prophecy. Whereas most of the information in the first twenty chapters of the book of Revelation can also be

[84] Question 1 on page 230.

found in the Old Testament, chapters 21 and 22 contain brand-new material not revealed to the prophets of the Old Testament.

The Millennium itself is only one thousand years long, as the name indicates. However, according to the promises of the Davidic Covenant, there was to be an eternal dynasty, an eternal kingdom, and an eternal throne. The eternal existence of the dynasty is assured because it culminates in the eternal person: *Yeshua* the Messiah. But the eternal existence of the throne and kingdom must also be assured. The millennial form of the kingdom of God will end after one thousand years. But the kingdom of God in the sense of Messiah's rule, His position of authority on the throne of David, will continue into the eternal order. All that is known about the eternal order is to be found in Revelation 21:1–22:5.[85]

[85] Question 2 on page 230.

E. Questions and Study Suggestions

Study Suggestion: We often hear our brothers and sisters in *Yeshua* pray for the return of our Lord, and looking at modern-day worship songs, the topic is a favorite of Christian composers and song writers. The lines between the Rapture and the Second Coming occasionally get blurred, though. Try to develop a solid definition of the two events so that you will be able to explain the difference to others.

Question 1: One objection to *Yeshua* being the promised Messiah goes something like this: "God said that His Messiah would bring peace to the world. He would be a political leader who would rebuild the Temple and reunite the Jews. Looking at what has happened in the world over the past two thousand years, it is hard to see any of these things. Christians like to explain this away by saying that it would all happen at Jesus' return, or what they call the Second Coming. This argument implies that I won't be able to recognize the Messiah until one comes who has accomplished all these things. How then can I accept Jesus to be this Messiah, considering that He has not fulfilled these prophecies?" How would you help this person understand what's happening?

Question 2: Just as there is a certain misconception of the difference between the Rapture and *Yeshua's* Second Coming, there is also confusion about the Messianic (or Millennial) Kingdom and the eternal order. This confusion has led many to believe that these terms or the descriptions of these events, if you will, have to be looked at through an allegorical lens. What makes you want to take these things literally? How would you defend your stand on the literal interpretation of all Scriptures?

Chapter XIX

Conclusion

The study of Messiah, or Christology, analyzes the person and work of *Yeshua* the divine Redeemer. There are numerous important questions we answered in this book: Who is this man? Did He ever declare Himself to be God? How can someone be both God and man? Why are His birth, His life, and His death so important? Do we have proof of His resurrection and ascension?

The answer to these and other questions is vitally important for a healthy, biblical understanding of who *Yeshua* is and what He has to do with our salvation. The Scriptures clearly teach that Satan and his demons believe that He is the Son of God, and many cults and world religions claim to believe in Him. The problem is that they do not believe in the God-Man as He is presented by the Scriptures. This is what makes a proper understanding of Christology so important.

As you might have experienced while reading this book, the study of this field of systematic theology can have an enormous impact on the believer's life. As one begins to understand the kenosis, this mind-boggling concept of the God-Man, he will also receive a deeper knowledge of God's unfathomable love, which led Him to provide a way of salvation. The various names and titles of the Messiah will offer comfort for the daily trials and tribulations the believer experiences. The analysis of what *Yeshua* is working on today and will do in the future has the power to provide hope for the days to come. All this, and so much more, can be accomplished by a thorough study of the Messiah. Paul, in his epistle to the Ephesians, calls it the *unsearchable riches of Messiah* (Eph. 3:8). This book, then, will close with his words of prayer for the believers of Ephesus, which is a model for what was supposed to be accomplished through this work:

*[14] For this cause I bow my knees unto the Father, [15] from whom every family
in heaven and on earth is named, [16] that he would grant you, according to
the riches of his glory, that ye may be strengthened with power through his
Spirit in the inward man; [17] that Messiah may dwell in your hearts through
faith; to the end that ye, being rooted and grounded in love, [18] may be strong
to apprehend with all the saints what is the breadth and length and height
and depth, [19] and to know the love of Messiah which passes knowledge, that
ye may be filled unto all the fulness of God. [20] Now unto him that is able to do
exceeding abundantly above all that we ask or think, according to the power
that works in us, [21] unto him be the glory in the church and in Messiah
Yeshua unto all generations for ever and ever. Amen.*

CPSIA information can be obtained
at www.ICGtesting.com
Printed in the USA
FSOW02n1009050615
7672FS